THE RITE OF RETURN

COMING BACK FROM DUTY-INDUCED PTSD

KAREN LANSING, LMFT, BCETS
&
SOME UNNAMED HEROES

To My Band of Brothers

and

To Alex

TABLE OF CONTENTS

PART IV: TRAUMA RESOLVED, LIFE REDEEMED

PREFACE

On an autumn evening, as the sun shone golden, low on the horizon, guests arrived at an idyllic hotel just outside of Belfast. An unusual sight, given Ireland's tendency for rain. Even so, this was not nearly as unusual as the Leaving Do (send-off) being hosted by the Police Federation of Northern Ireland. It was the first time that such an honour ever had been extended to a civilian and a Yankee. We were there to celebrate the service rendered to the Police Service of Northern Ireland (PSNI) by a most unusual American woman who came to live and work among us for nearly seven years.

As with all things Irish, the night was filled with toasts, good food, great Guinness, and the *craic* (humour and good cheer) was mighty. The evening commenced with a speech thanking Karen Lansing for her work with the officers on the front lines. The speaker stressed that without her services, many would not have survived much less have returned with new strength to provide again admirable policing service to our communities.

Then, the evening was punctuated with hard-bitten Northern Irish police, quite out of character, standing up to extol Karen's broad reaching impact upon their lives, their families and their futures.

And this is where I come in. A few years ago my best friend, also an officer, was shot by a terrorist. He survived and recovered physically, but the mental trauma that he went through was horrific. This is a man who had justifiably prided himself on his shooting abilities. We competed internationally (he was way better than I). He believed, as most of us do, that if the day came for him to face down a gunman, he would be as ready as any officer could be. He practiced, and he competed against the best in the world to be ready. Yet when that night came, the terrorist didn't play by the rules. He shot this officer in the back from a concealed spot out in the darkness.

This coward didn't kill this good man, but he broke him. He broke a father, a son, a brother, and a friend. We all watched this proud and wonderful man descend into his own personal hell; there was nothing any of us could do to save him.

And then came Karen. She might as well have ridden in on a white steed carrying a sword and shield, because for all who love and admire this man, she was a knight in shining armour. She picked up the broken pieces and skillfully put him back together again. Today we have that wonderful man back.

Karen came to us with an extensive CV and range of experience, having worked across a diverse array of uniformed services. Arriving in January, 2005, after having consulted the PSNI from 2003-2004, she tirelessly treated officers affected by traumas encountered while policing in Northern Ireland. From 30 years of the "troubles" to current terrorist attacks, Karen attended to trauma cases that included RPGs and mortar attacks, car bombs (still being planted under the family cars of officers), sniper attacks and violent riots. She was always there in the aftermath of such events, always there for even the toughest cases.

With her expertise in lethal-contact/combat trauma and her training in tactics and weapons, Karen's skills go far beyond the clinical confines into strategic, tactical and command performance levels. She's become a renowned keynote speaker and trainer on effective leadership for UK Police Services and LE organizations around the world. She added a unique and significant aspect to trainings found nowhere else within the UK or the EU. These she brought with her in the 'Tactical Psych Training' delivered to the Public Order Commander and the Specialist Firearms Team courses.

Karen's determination to improve the adherence to the human rights of police officers, the ethical and scientific practices in critical-incident-investigation techniques, and the duty-of-care manifested fully when she directed a groundbreaking Memorandum of Understanding (MoU) while with the PSNI. This agreement-in-principal brings to bear critical considerations to post-incident investigations that hadn't been recognized as vital or relevant up to that time. In that MoU, Karen saw to it that findings of research studies regarding memory, perception distortion and human dynamics during critical incidents be foundational.

This MoU has been woven into the fabric of the PSNI and is now a living document. It provides evidence-based applications for more fully and accurately understanding the complexities that can occur during rapidly unfolding events officers may find themselves in. It set up a system so that ongoing lessons from tactical failures or errors can be captured and learned from. This was done in order to take a preventive posture against PTSD out-on-the-ground.

Karen would not have accomplished such things without one trait she possesses in great supply: courage. I'm referring to the original Latin word *coraticum*, meaning from the heart. Her courage is not driven by fear for herself or any motivation for personal gain. Karen's courage is driven by a desire to assist officers by seeing that they are granted basic human rights along with the best and most advanced care possible as they serve and protect. This serves to effect positive changes in their lives, which helps to strengthen the police organizations and, in turn, the communities they serve. Officers have never been numbers to her.

There is a forensic theory called Locard's Principle, which states, "Every contact leaves a trace." Karen showed us that this not only applies to the physical world but also to our interactions with each other, within our hearts. Having been with us through some incredibly challenging times, Karen Lansing didn't just leave a trace in Northern Ireland, but rather a shining and indelible mark across the terrain of countless brave and recovered hearts.

It is often said that in Policing, particularly at a command level, one of the key responsibilities is to find the people you need to know *before* you need to know them. If you are going to be at a critical incident, or command those who are, or help with the post-incident fallout, you need to know about Karen Lansing and her work.

The Rite of Return will help you to do this.

Allan Jones, QPM
Head of Public Order Training (Retired)

ACKNOWLEDGMENTS

In pages to come, you will discover the phrase, "Without a herd we perish." We need each other and this book exemplifies that truth. It is the result of the contributions and sacrifices of an amazing herd—my herd.

This book is part of an adventure that began over 17 years ago with the entry of the first officer into my office. Since then, I've been working with some of the most courageous, and honorable individuals I could ever be blessed to know. Writing this now, I see faces and recall stories that occurred in the coastal regions of California and in points far outside my home state and even my own country. I only wish I could thank each of you by name in this small space for such a huge debt of gratitude. Please know that you all have helped me write this book. I thank you for everything you have given to me.

To Dr. Francine Shapiro, thank you for this magnificent model of therapy, EMDR, and for your unceasing supportive encouragement for the six PTSD-officers EMDR study. What an amazing thing a simple walk, skilled observation and incredible innovation have done to improve the fate of so many in this world. Seeing the progression from broken to victorious in the culmination of one EMDR session never fails to take my breath away.

Dr. Daniel Amen, you were so open to initial idea to conduct the first single case study with "Aaron." It was a wonderful process of discovery. You provided a window into incredible and important information, and you cared for those who came into this research, not just as subjects but as human beings. It was a joy to have worked with you.

Dr. Andrew Leeds, without you that study on EMDR with PTSD officers involved in shootings would never have occurred. When I showed you Aaron's SPECT scans you moved heaven and earth to open doors so we could to repeat that study with six officers. Thank you for having the eyes to see.

To my first generation of cops, who brought me into this grand adventure and who gave me a new name (that I can answer to without blushing). I'm so proud of how you finished your tours of duty. Thanks for putting me on this wild ride before I ever knew what hit me.

To the courageous paramedic and six officers who entrusted me with the images of their brains as they healed, you have done an amazing service to your brothers and sisters in uniform. I have witnessed walls of silence come down all over the world because of you. Warriors and Rescuers with PTSD have gained the courage to get treatment and your brain images and your stories have shown them the way. May this book make that kind of courage go viral.

To the Peelers on the northern side of that invisible border, you took me in and made me "family." Thank you for your trust, which doesn't come easily in such a place, and for your loyalty. Especially in the hard times, I've seen that run so deep. To all of you, I give my deepest gratitude and respect for the dangers you face and for the jobs you do.

To Dr. Gary Quinn, your clinical EMDR brilliance, compassion and humor have inspired me since we first crossed paths at that Congress in Rome. You've helped find words to describe what it is that my officers and I designed. Thank you for the tenacity to stay with me in this quest until the protocol found words. You are a most brilliant EMDR trainer, and I'm blessed to have you on my speed dial.

Dr. Sandra Foster, the EMDR Performance Enhancement protocol that you and Dr. Jennifer Lendl designed has made the difference between a return to duty or unwanted early retirement for countless athletes in "the deadly game." Thank you for your sincere interest in the work that is described in the chapters to follow.

Dr. Bill Lewinski, Dr. Anthony Pinizzotto, Sgt. Betsy Bratner Smith (Ret.), Lt. Col. Dave Grossman (Ret.), and Dr. Alexis Artwhol, you all have been beacons to me in my work. Thank you for your contributions to this book in both quotes, research and photos so graciously shared. These have helped convey such important facts and concepts throughout the pages to come.

My dear Warrior and author/colleague Theo Knell, I deeply appreciate your kindness in allowing me to include a collection of your incredible work in chapters that cried out for them. Thank you for your gracious and your generous heart. I am so proud to call you "friend."

To Dr. Alexis Artwhol and Randy Sederquist: Randy, you were the first to lay eyes on these chapters. I gained so much from your feedback. Alexis, you were on the far side of many edits and you found the last hidden vestiges of rewrites that were still needed. Thank you both for being the alpha and omega to the desperate need for eyes-on-the-ground that could catch any frailties of thought or inaccuracies.

To my editor Cindy Barrilleaux, your place in this project was nothing short of a miracle. The fact that we've done an 18-month edit in 3 months is incredible enough. Yet we did that while you were in New Mexico and I was in Kosovo. We faced down horrifying computer crashes and hours of lost work, rumors of wars, sudden death of Internet connections and a 9-hour time difference. Despite all of those distractions, no rock was big enough to conceal from you poor thought content, mushy phrases or just plain bad sentence structure. You are a gritty, tenacious, exquisite and delightful editor. Throughout the process you gave wings and roots to thoughts and words. You have been simply remarkable! And don't your *dare* edit anything out of this!

My sincere thanks also to Jeny Lyn Ruelo for the design and formatting of this book. Hats off to you for your creativity with a true eye for space where it appears there is none and for beauty!

To Tricia, I was in awe of you as I toddled behind trying to keep up in our early years and I still am. You taught me the first important lessons in life—how to laugh, and that it hurts less to pull the Band-Aid off really fast. That grew out of your logic of *why let the pain linger?* I'm sure this is why I took so well to EMDR. Thank you for being my sister and longest held friendship.

To Sally Cahill, LMFT, you are a true friend and a highly skilled colleague. I can't repay you for your constant support and ability to see out there beyond the present. Without your insistence that there was a desperate need for this book "NOW!" it would still be awaiting my attention. Thank you for your faith in what I'm doing and for your friendship.

Donelyn Miller, LMFT you are the best clinical supervisor an MFT intern could have ever landed. You have been a piece of solid ground beneath me for 20 years. If I can be even half the healing presence you are by the end of this run, I'll be overjoyed. You're a true gift in my life. Thank you for your wit and wisdom.

To Chief Inspector Ken Pennington and Alan Jones, QPM (Ret), you two are the best I've ever trained with in "the deadly game." I admire and respect your passion for excellence; thank you for being there with me shoulder-to-shoulder and at times, with our backs against the wall, taking stands for things that were right. This book reflects our mutual goal to improve the welfare of officers on the front lines as they serve and protect.

Finally, to my Kosovo branch of the herd: Jola, Ine, An, Ylva and Fraser. You all cheered me on toward the finish line and were such wonderful colleagues, friends and dinner buddies. Thank you for always asking right off, "How's the book coming?" and really wanting to know. I'll remember those times in Kosovo with you with great fondness.

To all whose gracious, creative and instructive DNA is found within these pages, I humbly offer you my deep appreciation. Everybody needs a herd and I thank you all for running in mine.

Godspeed.

GLOSSARY

5150: Suicide

AD: Accidental discharge (also called **ND** in EU ~ negligent discharge)

AIP: Adaptive Information Processing

ASD: Acute Stress Disorder

ASR: Acute Stress Reaction

Back to the land of the living: My term for being fully recovered from PTSD and able to come back into a good and normal life, bringing whatever the journey enroute to healing from this injury has taught, only without the symptoms. In clinical terms this is referred to as a *"return to a pre-morbid level of functioning."* I prefer my term.

Caught in irons: A sailing term used when a sailboat can't change course due to the strength of the wind. Every time it tries to tack on to a new course, the wind pushes it back. This is the ultimate nautical example of being "stuck in the mud" and in life being just plain stuck.

CBT: Cognitive Behavioral Therapy

CI: Critical Incident

CID: Criminal Investigation Division

Close to the sunrise: The Middle East

Cotton on: To catch on to something

Dead ground: Aspects of terrain that render good concealment for instigators of ambush

DSM: Diagnostic Statistical Manual *The Diagnostic and Statistical Manual of Mental Disorders,* 4th ed. *(DSM-IV-TR).*

Duty-induced PTSD: My term for PTSD contracted directly from and while on-duty or operational

Dance Card: The list of traumatizing critical incidents (CIs) that have become "hauntings" and will require EMDR

Down Range: The combat zone in a war

EMDR: Eye Movement Desensitization and Reprocessing

Endogenous depression: Caused by a chemical imbalance not related initially to life events.

Familius Humanus: My gender neutral term for Mankind

First generation officer clients: The very first group of officers I treated for PTSD

FTO: Field Training Officer, who does the practical training of probationary officers and (ideally) officers returning from extended leave/deployments in military reserves.

Hauntings: My term for anything stemming from a traumatic event that haunts a person.

ICD: International Classification of Diseases
(go to: http://www.who.int/classifications/icd/en/)

IPS: Information Processing System

Kit: Gear. A term used in WWII (i.e. Kit Bag). Still commonly used in the UK.

LE: Law Enforcement

Logging: An EMDR Containment technique that identifies reactions and things that may trigger them, and rates their strength

Log worthy: Observational info that's worthy of putting into the Log for future reference

MRI: Magnetic Resonance Imaging. A means to view hard tissue in the brain and the body.

Negative belief: The overriding belief that comes out of a traumatic incident and falsely defines the one who's lived through that event. It focuses on unrealistic and errant attributes of responsibility (self-blame), helplessness, or helplessness. These often replay through a person's life until the trauma has been resolved and more accurate beliefs are taken in. The replacement positive beliefs can then allow for adaptive learning and growth at a deep and lasting level. Then the negative belief will loose it's influence over a person's life.

OSM: An oh-shit-moment

Positive Affect Tolerance: The ability to take in positive emotions (affect); also a pattern of avoidance or defensiveness in taking in positive emotional states (including around self-identity or self-worth). Impediments to positive affect tolerance are typically to due to PTSD and/or depression.

Positive belief (aka Positive cognition): One or a number of new realizations that occur in an EMDR session as the reprocessing of a traumatic incident is coming to completion. The new insight can take shape and significance once a traumatic incident has been neutralized of its highly disturbing, "it's still happening now" characteristics. That shift in the nature of the traumatic memory allows the brain to move from fight/flight/freeze and into a reality-based perspective beyond the fray. The three attributes of a positive belief are that it must be (1) accurate, (2) positive (regarding what was done, what was factual, what was survived, intended or attempted) and (3) true. If a positive belief doesn't not include all of those attributes, the brain cannot take it "on board" and it will not take the place of a pre-existing negative belief. That shift from negative to positive belief allows the newly adapted learning to take the wheel. Setting a positive course that can redirect a person's life away from a vicious cycle of negative or destructive life patterns.

PTSD: Posttraumatic Stress Disorder is a condition that meets the criteria in the DSM IV-TR

PTS: Posttraumatic Stress is a condition made up of a partial grouping of symptoms for PTSD that will not be enough to qualify for a full case of PTSD but should non-the-less be treated if it's encumbering a person's life, relationships, work, health and general wellbeing.

PTSD Affiliates: My term for PTS, ADS and ADR

Put off your feed: can range from just feeling sick to "loosing your cookies"

RP: Reporting party or person ~ someone reporting a crime or a complaint to police

Saccadic eye movements: Rapid lateral eye movements often observed in REM sleep or replicated during EMDR sessions.

Secondary gain: Any advantage, such as increased attention, disability benefits, or release from unpleasant responsibilities, obtained as a result of having an illness. See "Wanting to stay alive."

Sheepdogs: A metaphor originated by Lt. Col. Dave Grossman that depicts police officers as the protectors of the sheep; not perhaps always loved or appreciated until at least a wolf shows up.

Somatic: Comes from the Greek word σωματικός which means "of the body." "Psychosomatic" refers to real physical manifestations that originate from psychological causes. Somatic memories are believed to be memories of historical events in a person's life stored in the body. These can later reoccur (i.e. re-experiencing the pain of being shot in a session dealing with that traumatic incident, even if it occurred years ago and the bullet wound has fully healed and pain free up to that session).

Source handlers: Those who recruit and manage intelligence informants

SWAT: Special Weapons and Tactics team; these are specialist; weapons officers also at times referred to as "elite" officers.

The Job: Term used by cops for policing

The Man Cave: The practice of men to isolate and withdraw from others when enduring difficult emotional times...i.e. women talk, men walk (away).

Things going sideways (aka When the wheels come off): When things go terribly wrong in an incident.

Tradecraft: The term I've heard mostly in Intelligence and UC divisions to describe the skills, training and well-honed instincts that make someone a master of the trade.

Trauma-Based Memory: My term for the hotspots (i.e. the most highly traumatizing segments) of a memory of a critical incident. It's as though the person were still in the traumatic incident and having to relive it in a present tense verses past tense. These memory segments typically monopolize flashbacks, nightmares, intrusive images, etc.

Wanting to stay alive: A more accurate term than "Secondary Gain" for those on the pointy end of the arrow.

Waypoint: One or more points to steer to on a course set by a global positioning device (via satellite navigation) in order to get to a final destination.

INTRODUCTION:
THIS GREAT AND TERRIBLE STORM
(ESSENTIAL READING)

As I sit to write this book, the view in the harbour just outside my window is that of a foreboding, winter morning just beginning to dawn. At first light, I can just make out boats pitching violently in their berths from the gale-force winds that pummel them. Churning waters are tossing them in all directions. Over the course of this day and into the coming night, this is to become a great (as in massive) and terrible (as in destructive) storm.

The two forces of wind and water are working in concert together, attempting to dislodge these boats that I know by name. Each of them is straining at dock lines that are attempting to hold them in place...to keep them safe...to keep them from going adrift...to keep them from being lost to this storm.

There is no better imagery of what *duty-induced* trauma and posttraumatic stress disorder (PTSD) can cause. The trauma is an uninvited storm that crashes into the lives of my highly specialized clients. I work with men and women who risk their lives to protect and save others, men and women whom I'll refer to throughout this book as Warriors and Rescuers,

The high winds on this storm's leading edge have arrived first, blasting across land and sea. In PTSD, the critical incident (CI) comes first. In a storm, what follows are the churning

9

waters and then the rain. What comes after a widely covered or controversial CI (such as a shooting) are the media, the Monday-morning quarterbacks and investigations. Added to these external factors, and just as brutal, can be the internal judge of the Warrior/Rescuers, second-guessing every decision, rendering harsh self-judgements.

The combined forces of the CI and post-incident reactions can generate a globally destabilizing effect on the life of the person caught in the storm of trauma. In that storm, those in closest proximity (the loved ones and close friends) are the dock lines that strain and fight to hold the one caught in the turmoil that is PTSD. They struggle as best they can to hold on, to keep their dear one safe, to keep this one from being lost to the storm.

Just like dock lines in foul weather, significant others are overtaxed and overstretched. They suffer the ravages right along with the one they're trying to help hold. Trauma travels through families and friendships, just like an unrelenting storm. No one in its path is untouched. No one.

The pressing question in the throws of this storm that is PTSD is how will things end up? Will the dock lines (those friends and family members) fray and loose their hold? Will the vessel—the officer/emergency responder/soldier/veteran—make it through or be lost?

In every case, it depends on the force of the storm as well as the strength and endurance of those who are caught up in it.

There's one more critical element to be factored into this metaphor: How good is the one keeping storm watch over the harbor? This is the psychotherapist who's tending to the PTSD client. How skilled an observer is she? How experienced is he with this specific type of PTSD and with this client population? Most importantly of all, how wise and how teachable is this professional?

So then, this book is borne of winds and waters having changed from sun-drenched and gentle, to menacing and seemingly intent upon destruction. It adds to an already rich array of work on the topic of trauma and healing. It's not my desire to replicate those masterpieces I hold dear, some of which I will be referring to along the way. Rather, I want to offer what I have learned from a very specific population: those Warriors and Rescuers who have known the terrors of this great and terrible storm.

In these pages, I'll share what they have taught me. Their voices are once again strong and clear; the din of rain, waves and wind failed to take them under. Their stories hold substantive hope for others still out there; their stories matter and this book will describe why. In these pages, you will find information about the effects of PTSD on the brain and a course to chart to healing, which can serve both those now in the midst of the storm and any who may be battered by the winds of trauma in the future.

I have been asked, no—ordered to write this book by those who have given me their trust, their knowledge and their stories. Seven courageous heroes (a paramedic and six police officers) allowed me to take images of their brains in order to show that this condition is real and altogether treatable. You will see a number of these in chapters to come.

One thing these unnamed heroes and I now know for sure is that no storm needs to last forever. Not everything is lost in a wake of devastation. Lives can be redeemed. We can heal. What I have witnessed in my own life and in the lives of my amazing clients comes down to one simple fact: PTSD will leave you stronger or weaker but never the same—so choose strength. This book and all who have contributed to its writing are calling the reader to set a course for the other side of the storm. There is reason for good hope—again I say, choose strength.

THE MAKING OF A COP WHISPERER

This job is an adventurous and at times a wild ride. I didn't choose it; it chose me, back in the mid 1990s. As a licensed marriage and family therapist and board-certified expert in traumatic stress, I was brought into this work (at first kicking and screaming) by a group of hard-bitten cops. When I later asked these officers, who were a group of close friends, why they'd chosen to work with me, the answer was a surprise. They stated that they saw in me a healer with a warrior's heart, albeit desperately in need of training in *the job,* which they knew could be remedied.

It was the cops who first dragged me out on patrol, onto the weapons ranges, into tactical trainings and even into situations such as armed bank robbery pursuits and riots in exotic places. They made me a better therapist, they dubbed me their Cop Whisperer (a name that's stuck) and I in turn helped them to heal.

Stateside, I've been trained in hostage negotiation, done numerous 48-hour tours of duty with firefighters, ridden into tense situations with police officers and into dangerously isolated places with state park rangers.

Offshore, I've ridden with military police and have "hung on for grim death" with ARVs (UK special weapons teams trained to drive 110 mph as though it was 40) as they've flown at top speed through hectic city streets of England on wet roads. I've been billeted in military bases where I was trained on the weapons and tactics with police specialist teams or attended to soldiers returning from war. These firearms and tactics instructors, officers, military and emergency responders have taught me well.

At the heart of all this cross-training, I've developed tactical psychological (aka tactical psych) trainings. Some that I've delivered from places like the amazing NPIA International Police Training facility, housed at the 17th century Bramshill Estate in England, to the spectacular Asilomar State Park's William Pen Mott Jr. Training Center in Monterey, California.

I've trained public-order commanders, special weapons teams and commanders, close protection, intelligence and those on the front lines. Integrated into these are the most well-designed research studies on weapons and tactics being done today by the likes of Force Science Research Institute and others. This tactical psych integration also enabled my first-generation officers and me to design the foundations for a highly effective protocol that integrates treatment, along with weapons and tactics sessions in partnership with certified police firearms instructors (hand picked).

Paying the Dues … Learning the Game

PTSD—NOT FOR DUMMIES OR THE FAINT OF HEART

Despite the variety of law enforcement, emergency response and military I've served in the U.S. and overseas, and the diversity of mission objectives, tactics and rules of engagement, one thing is extremely consistent: the nature of duty-induced trauma and the course that it runs. PTSD is a "constant object."

Inside all those different uniforms, for all of those dedicated to their calling to serve, protect and assist, is a Warrior's heart (even if you're a Rescuer). Whether you're battling a mountain avalanche that has trapped skiers, a fire that's trying to consume the floor beneath your feet, live rounds out on the ground or massive injuries that could cause a patient to bleed out before you get her to the hospital, you're all engaged in a tactical/strategic conflict of some kind when you step into your uniform and go out on to duty.

You're going to need that heart. PTSD is not for the faint of heart and, more than likely, none of you came by PTSD by being that way. Duty-induced PTSD is given birth and life on duty. "Duty" means you were standing in the gap, serving your country, community or one of your own-like-kind in a potentially lethal or fatal pinch.

PTSD is also not for dummies, so I won't treat you, dear readers, as though you were. When I'm out with you guys, I see your brilliance, your medical skill and your resolve to save others from a hungry sea. I see your local intell, your savvy and your instincts that are finely honed by your training and experience. Even so, PTSD will drop you into a war the likes of which you've never fought before. I hope this book will make you smarter and more savvy about the nature of this condition, of this war that's come inside.

PTSD is my sector, and I want to make it yours as well. You need to understand it intimately— as intimately as a firefighter understands how the forest fire breathes, or as the lifeguard understands the way the current and riptides will play out. You need to know it as the soldier or the SWAT team knows the *dead ground* within their "patch" where the enemy/ suspect is most likely to set up for an ambush. Knowing PTSD that intimately is no different. It is an entity to be reckoned with, which requires that you know it—and know it really, really well. This you must do with the same intention that all of the above hold going in to do a job. You must approach it as an operative coming in as a visitor and not as a permanent resident.

THE PLAYERS IN THE "DEADLY GAME"

Because I specialize in bringing those I work with fully back and at a higher level of competency and performance than before the trauma, their specific roles play a critical part in how we work.

Integrated into many of our treatment plans, especially for OIS incidents, are weapons and *FATs* range sessions, along with tactics refining or retraining. I believe it's healthy for each of us to remain mindful of our roles in the work we do in session (both in the clinical office and out on the weapons range). That is why, in this book, I use the designation "officer" interchangeably with "client." I see those who come in to work with me by their role. That doesn't cease to exist once they bring me into the mix.

The Warrior/Rescuer roles affect the way I work with each person. For example, when I treat officers for PTSD, it's more like an advanced-level training course with elements of sports psychology than conventional therapy. I'm always very proud to witness what players of the deadly game can accomplish after they have completed the "course" and moved beyond PTSD. They qualify for specialist weapons teams; they promote and are exceptional leaders: lifeguards accomplish impossible rescues at sea; in the field, paramedics skilfully deliver babies who should have died but didn't. In other words, after our work together, Warriors and Rescuers become vital assets rather than damaged goods.

WHAT'S THIS THING CALLED EMDR?

I'll be referring to a model of therapy I use for the treatment of PTSD called EMDR (Eye Movement Desensitzation and Reprocessing)[1] well ahead of the chapter that deals with it in detail. The logic of that choice is that first you need (and probably want) a good understanding of PTSD and how it behaves in the brain.

You need to know the lay of the land, how to better control symptoms, possible ways to improve your sleep, the importance of the "herd" and a bunch of other things first. I figured that a description of EMDR could wait. However, if you want to learn about it from the gitgo, by all means skip ahead to the EMDR chapter, where I describe the treatment and how my officers and I customized the protocol slightly to work even better for the tactical/ operational brain.

Warriors and Rescuers are not wired like civilians; they are "hunters in a farmer's world."[2] They are mentally put together differently, which is what makes them run toward the things that go "bang." Rescuers run into the carnage to render aid. This is why both are so good to be with in the trenches. That's also why they can't be treated like civilians in therapy—it just doesn't work.

A CAUTIONARY NOTE ABOUT READING THE STORIES

In writing this book, my goal has been to avoid creating triggers to your distress or causing any vicarious trauma by presenting horrifying incidents. And yet stories of traumatic incidents to show the effects on the brain of trauma are central to the book. That being the case, I chose each story either because 1) it relates to one of my research client's brain images (that show his PTSD before, during and after treatment with no more PTSD); or 2) it illustrates critical learning points important to the goals of this book.

It is possible that when reading some of the incidents, similarities will tap into your own experiences. Because the element of surprise increases the likelihood of heightened distress or relived trauma (the same is true of any book on duty-induced trauma), I have taken measures to help you avoid surprises. In the Table of Contents, beneath a number of the chapter titles, I have included short descriptions of the incidents that might have potential to trigger your trauma.

If you're mentally prepared for an incident's description of, for example, the death of an infant (as in Chapter 2), then you're fortified for it. If you don't feel up to reading that incident, you can opt to bypass it (or any other potentially triggering incident) and pick up with the section at the end of the story. All illustrative stories/accounts are formatted in italics to make it easier to see where they begin and end.

Making it a point to review the Table of Contents for your own self-care is exercising responsible maintenance on the hardware of your soul. Choose your battles wisely.

TERMINOLOGY, PRONOUNS AND SOME BACKING & FILLING

As for terminology used in this book, I want to explain myself up front and well ahead of possibly irritating some readers.

First item: When I use the term "guys," please be aware that, in the U.S., this is considered a gender-neutral term.

Second item: Names of clients are completely fabricated. I like the way they use one name for every police officer in the UK ("Bobbie") or in Northern Ireland where they use "Peeler" or "Robert." Bobbies, Robert and the term Peelers are all "handles" taken from references to Sir Robert Peel (the first Chief Constable)…kind of handy. It simplifies things. But I do make up names. So, if Robert seems to be involved in almost every critical incident, it may just be that I ran short on imagination and made use of tradition instead.

Third item: The use of pronouns referring to gender. My Warrior/Rescuer client population for the past 17 years has been comprised of 99.9% males. To date I've worked with a total of 10 females, ranging from police, medics, soldiers (one was female), but not one female firefighter.

Since I specialize in lethal contact (officer-involved shootings, aka OIS/s), I've worked clinically with a disproportionately higher number of male than female officers who were "shooters."

I have made every effort to write an all-inclusive book for both genders, but I ask that you not judge me too harshly if the breakdown between "he's" and "she's" doesn't end up being an even 50–50 split. While that statistical breakdown may closely reflect our planet's human population, it's not quite represented in the world of my office just yet.

Fourth item: This book will be of practical use to a wide range of disciplines: the Warriors, which include police officers, state park rangers, fish and game wardens, military assets, boarder enforcement officers, prison officers, FBI, private security forces, et al; and the Rescuers, who include firefighters, paramedics, lifeguards, ski patrols and mountain search and rescues. All to say, this book can relate across the lines of duty, despite differences in uniform or duties. I will be using the term "officer" most often for convenience. I hope that this won't make any feel disrespected.

IN THE INTEREST OF SECURITY AND CONFIDENTIALITY

For security and confidentially, I often alter nonessential details and descriptions in cases and incidents. I also combine some aspects of separate clinical stories in order to consolidate and simplify the presentation of the material.

YOUR PRE-OPERATIONAL BRIEFING

If you or someone you love has PTSD or PTS (Posttraumatic Stress, which just misses fitting a full diagnosis of PTSD but can be equally as difficult to live with), then you're going to want to get to the relevant stuff pretty quickly. On the other hand, some officers may be happier getting the context and the story behind the story first.

Keeping both types of readers in mind, I've put what I believe to be vital stuff in each chapter so that those who desperately need to get through as much information as quickly as possible, can. For readers who have the insatiable curiosity for the story behind the story on certain topics, I've included some chapter notes at the end that hopefully will satisfy even the most curious of minds out there. Indulge yourselves.

THE GLOSSARY

I have added to this book an item I wish would be given to me whenever I am called to work in a mission/agency/organization of law enforcement (including the FBI, medics, firefighters and soldiers): a glossary of terms and acronyms. It is located strategically in the front of this book so it's easy to find when—not if—the need arises. With the exception of stories and some quotes, most *italicized words* in this book can be found in the glossary.

May it expand your vocabulary and perhaps even rub off as a great idea for an incredibly handy bit of *kit* ("kit"...look it up, it's in the glossary) to hand to me whenever I show up to go to work in your PD, on your Base, at your Station, or in your country. One can always hope…

FINALLY—THIS BOOK IS NOT THERAPY

While this book may help you alleviate some PTSD symptoms temporarily, it will not be able to serve as a substitute for psychotherapy or as a comprehensive course of treatment for duty-induced PTSD. What it can do is give you some added "intelligence" and useful tools as resources as you make your way out of this PTSD terrain with your own highly trained professional/s.

So now I encourage you to read on. May this Rite of Return help you to realize a "safe home."

INTRODUCTION NOTES:

1. To learn about the 8 phases of EMDR (without our adjustments) visit http://www.emdr.com/briefdes.htm

PHOTO CREDITS:

1. A Storm Coming In © Karen Lansing 2012
2. On the Other Side of the Storm © Karen Lansing 2012
3. Range Time © Karen Lansing 2012
4. The Tanks Are Home © Karen Lansing 2012
5. Is It Me Or Is It Hot in Here? © Karen Lansing 2012
6. My "WE NEED A BIGGER BOAT!" Face © Karen Lansing 2012
7. Safe Home © Karen Lansing 2012

ENDNOTES:

1. F. Shapiro. *Eye Movement and Reprocessing: Basic Principles, Protocols and Procedures.* Guilford Press, New York: 2001. http://www.emdr.com/briefdes.htm
2. T. Hartmann. *Attention Deficit Disorder: A Different Perspective.* Underwood Books, Grass Valley CA, 1993 & 1997.

CHAPTER 1
WHEN THE WAR COMES INSIDE

"The war came inside…and we felt it deeply."
Ernie Pyle,
Returning Bomber Series 1943

REFLECTIONS OF A FATAL CAR COLLISION (9/22/01)

The last thing I heard over the radio just as we closed in on the accident scene was a captain from Engine 3110 reporting two fatalities. I silently prayed, "Dear Lord, please don't let them be children."

I was out of the aerial ladder truck 3170 and heading into the middle of the intersection as the A-Team began to unpack the extraction equipment from the deep recesses of the unit. I saw the patrol sergeant marking off the parameter with crime tape. Restraining officers then dropped their invisible hold on the bystanders to move onto other jobs inside the scene. The onlookers pushed right up to the yellow tape, like flies to flypaper.

Standing with my back to the growing crowd, I started to count heads. Ten, thirteen, maybe as many as sixteen cops; four, five—I lost count of the firefighters. Near the vehicles, three firefighters who'd been cutting the front passenger door grabbed hold of the mangled metal and pulled hard in unison. After several tries, it begrudgingly tore away with a metallic groan.

Paramedics reached inside the vehicle to stabilize and place neck braces on the middle-aged driver and his wife. One firefighter and four ambulance paramedics moved in to begin the delicate job of hoisting the injured out of the tangled metal cavern, which had once been a family van, and onto the backboards, then onto the ground; clothing was cut away, IV's were inserted into limp arms.

I looked back at the van and saw an officer I knew make his way around to the van's far side. He shone his flashlight into the back of the van behind the driver's seat. In the dim light, I was able to make out a look of unabridged pain on his face. He closed his eyes, turned his head slightly in my direction and took a step back. I knew then that the dead were children.

I saw officers between tasks stop and momentarily get that glazed, 1000-miles stare. One walked through the scene towards the van with a camera, for a second or two looking like these were the last images he wanted to focus a camera's eye on. Another officer, between interviews of witnesses, would stop to look over, yet again, at the metal carnage. It was as if he was reminding himself that this wasn't just a story spun out of thin air by total strangers out on a street.

If you didn't know what to look for, these flashes of humanity would go all together unnoticed. As they went to work and focused on their jobs, my job was to focus on them. I began to estimate how many would need time in my office to work this tragedy through. I wondered how many would have a hard time sleeping tonight, or the next or the next. How many would dodge trauma's bullet this night, only to have their emotional number come up in the next call, or on the next shift?

After the discovery of the dead children, a captain hung a yellow tarp across the rear passenger windows of the van. He did this so his men wouldn't have to stare into the now-vacant faces of the two young sisters—faces that might remind them of their own children—as the men worked to save the parents. Much later, an engine captain told me that before the tarp went up, he kept imagining that he'd seen movement in the back seat. "I'd turn and look, thinking— just hoping—that maybe they were alive, maybe we'd missed a pulse earlier.... But we hadn't. They were gone, but I still hoped..."

Tragically, they were gone. Yet these two young beauties will remain as sad hauntings for any that attended that call. The officer who'd unexpectedly discovered their lifeless bodies reported to me later that it was an image that kept coming to him at night as he closes his eyes to try to sleep. He said, "They looked so broken, so fragile...like birds. They looked younger than they really were. More like 10 or 11 than 14 and 16...I have a daughter who is 10."

That night on scene, officers would come to stand with me for brief moments and tell me the ages of the girls. One officer said 12 or 13; another said 9 or 10, while an investigator had reported, "14 to 16, one of them is wearing braces." The girls began to take on the ages of daughters whose fathers were now hoping that their own girls, their own children, were home safe. Safe with their mothers, who were hoping their husbands were having an easy tour of duty out on the streets that night.

That wasn't to be.

A sergeant, who was usually one of the funniest people I know, summed up that call-out. On that night he was short on humor, but long on a heavy heart. We stood together in the intersection, as my team was packing up. His parting comment as I turned to leave with A-Team was, "Some days, Karen, this job just really sucks." In the language of those I serve, translated it meant, "This call, what I'm seeing here tonight, is going to leave a deep, painful tear ripped into my soul."

In the fire truck heading back to quarters, three firefighters and I were quiet. Some bits of conversation, but not much. Sometimes the wisest thing a therapist can do is to hold her own counsel. Sometimes silence is the most profound thing we can render. Talk will come later, when sorrow finds words. When it does, I will return to this scene time and time again, with a cop, or a firefighter, or a paramedic who's trying desperately to finally lay these two girls to rest and go in peace. Then I will once again take up my post at the scene. That is when I will go to work.

Even so, my job is different than theirs in this sad place. While they were called to try to save young lives taken too far beyond their reach, I am called to help them save their own humanity, which may be in the process of slipping away. But there's still hope. There's still time. So I will return to that place with those who discover that they must go back...those who are brave enough to go back. I'll work along side them so that this can be done...so that this call can be finished...so that their souls can mend.

THE INVISIBLE INJURY MADE VISIBLE

The condition of posttraumatic stress disorder (PTSD) is often called the "invisible injury." Paraphrasing what Lawrence Blum, Ph.D., points out in the introduction of his book, *Force Under Pressure,1* when an officer is asked to explain how he got placed on the disabled list (DL), it's far easier to point to the physical wounds, the breaks, dislocations or the soft tissue damage. It is more complicated, and, tragically, often shameful, for an officer to be sidelined because of PTSD.

The fact that there are officers and administrators on just about every force in the world who still don't believe that PTSD exists doesn't help, of course. An officer struggling with PTSD can internalize the mistaken idea that this condition is "all in your head." This doubt about the reality of PTSD can happen despite the horrid nightmares or the night sweats in those early morning hours. It can exist no matter how rapidly the startle reaction sends an officer through the roof, or a soldier returning from the Middle East, under the table. For most, that lie that says, "I must be making this up," hides behind all the symptoms, no matter how dark the moods or how unstoppable the trauma-based memories.

I use the word "lie" intentionally here because that false belief is nothing more, or less, than a lie for those who suffer from the diagnosis. If only PTSD were a lie, then those who are tormented by it could simply come clean and return to a normal, productive and relatively enjoyable existence. No one wants that more than those with posttraumatic stress disorder.

I'll state the obvious here: no one would sign up for this kind of a misery. PTSD is a real condition; it's not made up. That said, the fact is that it *is* in your head. At least that's where PTSD starts; given enough time, trauma will manifest in your body, too.

PTSD is like a war that comes inside to live within your own skin, but doesn't politely remain there. It ricochets around like a loose bullet, hitting all aspects of your life. Job performance, memory, energy levels, health, attitude—it's a long list. Suffice it to say, that with PTSD in the mix, everything that makes you who you are is significantly impacted.

PTSD also impacts others, as well. Loved ones, including the children (sometimes especially the children), suffer right along with the adult who has PTSD. In fact, they can develop anxiety disorders or even PTSD themselves, no matter how hard you may try to protect them from the "war inside." Many of my clients truly believe that they're keeping their torment to themselves and that no one else in their lives knows about their injury. That is, until it becomes obvious to them that the PTSD is not staying neatly tucked within a secured perimeter.

It's often the children who show them this: the toddler has magnified startle responses, or the 8-year-old suddenly is bedwetting at night, or the kids are fighting with each other far more frequently. Let's face it, most want to "soldier on" and deal privately with whatever PTSD throws at them. The ethos of very skilled, very professional Warriors and Rescuers is to consider injury and even death the cost of doing business. But when it impacts the children, *then* it becomes personal.

Besides impacting you and the family, PTSD affects how you engage (or don't) with others in your life. Your relationships with those you love can be the hardest hit, but your fellow officers, soldiers, first responders are affected as well. Friends on the force, on your team, on your crew may see you shutting down or isolating. They may see you popping off over things that don't warrant any frustration or anger. They may notice your lack of humor, or that you're physically just wearing down. Eventually, they may communicate their worry or frustration directly to you (or worse yet, to your commander). The truth is if you're not feeling like your old self because of PTSD, you're not the only one who's noticed.

Not until the latter half of the 20th century was the connection commonly made between having PTSD and the dramatic and dark changes to personality it could cause. When PTSD was out-of-sight, its life-altering effects on those struggling with it were also out-of-mind. Thankfully, due to the technology now available, we can see PTSD's effects on the brain. Brain imaging has forced this condition out of the shadows and is now forcing others out of denial. It's no longer an invisible injury.

My colleague, Dr. Daniel Amen, refers to the brain as the "Hardware of the Soul."[2] In later chapters you will see brain images we took at his clinic of that "hardware." Those will show areas where PTSD impacts brain functioning and how that impacts your life in such a global way.

Through SPECT imaging technology, you or someone you love who has PTSD, can see in other first responders' brain images, the changes in activation in specific sectors of the brain caused by PTSD. Those changes cause the symptoms of this condition. The beauty of this technology is that with it we've also seen that when properly treated, PTSD no longer wreaks havoc in your brain, body and life. The imaging shows that there is such a thing as healing from trauma and from PTSD.

That means that all is not lost with PTSD—not by a long shot. In fact, my clients commonly share with me at the end of treatment that going through the journey that PTSD caused them to embark on has proven to be one of the most significant and defining events in their lives. They arrive at this after making it through a full course of treatment and are finally, fully back home from that inside war. Of course, no one feels that way at the beginning of this journey.

DIAGNOSING PTSD

In the U.S., mental health professionals use the guidelines of the *Diagnostic Statistical Manual of Mental Disorders* (DSM),[3] put out by the American Psychological Association (APA), to set all mental health diagnoses, including posttraumatic stress disorder. The DSM is routinely updated as the profession gains greater understanding of mental health problems. Currently it's the DSM IV-TR.

For example, PTSD was not recognized as a diagnostic term before 1980. Of course, people had the condition, but it was given a number of different names: war neurosis, battle fatigue, shell shock, even cowardice, (we've come a long way from those dark days). It was because of the huge population of young soldiers returning from Vietnam that finally a pattern of symptoms and physical reactions was identified, and the criteria for PTSD was decided on by the APA. The diagnostic criteria have continued to be updated since it was first introduced in 1980.

In the EU, the diagnostic manual is the *International Classification of Diseases* (ICD). If you're reading this book in the EU *(*along with being highly distracted by my American spelling), your current rendition is the ICD-10[4]. This was accepted in 1994, but the very first ICD came into existence in 1893.

THE PTSD "AFFILIATES"

While this book is primarily about issues related to PTSD, two other diagnoses, which I refer to as PTSD "affiliates," are relevant, as well. A brief summary of each will clarify how they are different from and similar to PTSD, and how, in some case, they are closely related. A list of websites that have the full descriptions of these conditions can be found in the References Page at the end of this chapter, under Additional Resources.

ACUTE STRESS REACTION

The DSM-IV-TR doesn't include acute stress reaction (ASR) as a diagnosis, but the ICD-10 describes it as a relatively short-lived (1 hour to 3 days), immediate response to a traceable traumatic event. The individual may have transient symptoms of a dazed state, depression, anxiety, anger, despair, overactivity and/or withdrawal. No one symptom dominates for long; rather symptoms shift from one to another. ASR resolves rapidly in most cases when the danger has passed or the person is no longer in the stressful environment. Even when that's not possible, the symptoms diminish within 24-72 hours. (Both the DSM-IV and ICD-10 are listed on the reference page at the end of this chapter).

ACUTE STRESS DISORDER

Both the DSM IV-TR and the ICD include the diagnosis acute stress disorder (ASD). This disorder occurs if a person doesn't move out of the acute stress reactive condition. ASD stems from a traceable traumatic event and lasts from two days to four weeks. The onset may be delayed, but by no more than four weeks after the traumatic event.

During the actual trauma, the person experiences three or more of the following symptoms: (1) a subjective sense of numbing, detachment or lack of emotional responsiveness; (2) a reduction of awareness of his/her surroundings (i.e. a sense of being dazed); (3) derealization—the feeling that things occurring are surreal; (4) depersonalization—the feeling outside of one's body; (5) no memory of important aspects of the trauma).

ASD can cause symptoms such as avoidance of places/things/activities that bring back upsetting memories of the incident. A person may experience flashbacks, nightmares or increased arousal that cause difficulties with sleep, irritability, or poor concentration. Social functioning and work functionality are significantly impacted.

HOW ASR & ASD RELATE TO PTSD

As you can see, there is a progression of severity of symptoms in ASR and ASD. That is, if an individual is unable to fully recover from ASR within the 72 hours following a CI, symptoms will progress into acute stress disorder (ASD). If the same or heightened symptoms continue after four weeks, the person may well meet the criteria of PTS (a condition less severe than PTSD), or the person may end up in a full case of PTSD.

However, it is possible to get PTSD without ever having ASR or ASD. Even if a person has handled a traumatic event exceptionally well operationally or medically, PTSD can have a delayed onset, developing even years later.

Research has found that a staggering 60-70% of those who meet the criteria for ASD will have PTSD within 24 months of the traumatic incident (Brier & Scott, 2006).[5] According to the National Center for PTSD of the U.S. Department of Veterans Affairs, 80% of ASD cases end up with PTSD six months later (see ptsd.va.gov website, listed in Additional Resources at the end of this chapter).

No matter what the actual percentage of such cases, there is a very strong argument for getting treatment sooner than later if you've begun to experience symptoms related to trauma. In fact, symptoms, such as the feeling of surrealism and the sensation of watching yourself from above, are considered warning signs that PTSD may develop, because they indicate a high level of trauma.

Now let's take a very brief overview of the diagnosis for PTSD.

POSTTRAUMATIC STRESS DISORDER (PTSD)

As you can see from the progression from ASR and ASD, the symptoms of PTSD have similarities to ASD. For a diagnosis of PTSD, symptoms must have been present for four weeks or more. They may have delayed onset that can come years, rather than days or weeks, after the traumatic event. The first criterion that must be met is that a person experienced or witnessed a traumatic event.

There are three subsections within the diagnostic criteria: (1) Re-experiencing (2) Avoidance/numbing, and (3) Hyperarousal.

Re-experiencing includes symptoms such as flashbacks, intrusive memories, nightmares and becoming upset when reminded of the event. Re-experiencing can also include physical reactions, such as sweating or shaking, to reminders of the trauma.

Avoidance/numbing involves conscious efforts to avoid thoughts, feelings, discussions or exposure to places, people, situations or events that might remind the person of the trauma. Loss of interest in activities or events that were important or enjoyable prior to the trauma can occur, as well as a feeling of being distant or cut off from others. Numbing can cause an inability to experience positive feelings such as happiness or love.

Hyperarousal is related to the increased level of anxiety. According to the DSM-IV-TR, this includes sleep difficulties, irritability, outbursts of anger, difficulty concentrating, increased startle response and a feeling of constantly having to be on guard.

Setting a diagnosis with a client involves more than just running down a checklist. There also must be a comprehensive history and assessment done along with going over the more specific lists of symptoms within the PTSD diagnostic criteria.

PTSD may be caused by "single-incident trauma" or "cumulative trauma." Single-incident cases typically progress fairly quickly in treatment when the client is ready to do the "trauma work." You can see from this how important it is to get treatment quickly if your symptoms are the result of a single traumatic event.

Cumulative trauma stems from a number of CIs or events. These cases take longer to heal simply due to the amount of work involved in attending to the traumatic events in order to resolve things for the brain. However, you are not doomed to endless treatment if you've had multiple CIs. I once worked with an officer who listed over 50 traumatic incidents (he served in a county that was at war). Using EMDR, we only needed to go through six of those incidents to deliver him from a case of PTSD that had tortured him for over 15 years.

THROWING DARTS IN THE DARK ISN'T GOOD ENOUGH

In 1995, I was treating officers for duty induced PTSD using EMDR[6]. The dramatic results I'd seen using EMDR with my civilian clients showed up in these hardened cops throughout the course of their treatment. All of these first-generation officer clients were Vietnam veterans. This meant that they came in with over 25-years worth of trauma from both war in Vietnam and the conflicts with the criminal element on the city streets. Despite what I was witnessing first hand (over the course of the four years from 1995 to 1999), a nagging question had formed in the back of my mind.

Were these outcomes from EMDR therapy a phenomenon of nurture versus nature? Or maybe, a combination of the two? In other words, were these officers and my other emergency response clients' lives being pulled back together and made stronger, happier and safer because of the working therapeutic alliance between client and clinician (nurture)? Or, was it because EMDR was actually changing something within their brains (nature)? And if that was the case, could we see it by using the brain imaging technology available to us?

SPECT BRAIN IMAGERY—NIGHT VISION GOGGLES IN THE BRAIN

It is almost unthinkable in this day and age to go into a war zone, or even into dangerous sectors of a major city in pursuit of an armed and deadly suspect, without night vision. There's a good reason that night vision technology is commonly provided to military and law enforcement. It saves lives and makes a significant difference between success and failure.

The same can be said for X-ray and imaging technology in the medical world. They play critical roles in the assessment and treatment of conditions that can't be seen by the human eye. In the 1990s, Dr. Daniel Amen began to speak out about a counterintuitive attitude in the mental health profession. As a neuropsychiatrist, he was one of the first to use SPECT brain imagery to see what was going on in his patients' brains. Amen was viewed as quite the controversial maverick back in those days, but then innovators typically are.

His issue with the mental health field was that professionals were treating clients without looking at the very thing they were working on—their brains. Being a "show-me" kind of person, that way of thinking appealed to me then, and continues to now. While SPECT imaging is not appropriate as a routine procedure in psychotherapy, it has its place in both the clinical and research realms of the mental health world. It has given us eyes to see.

SPECT stands for Single Photon Emission Computed Tomography (now you know why they call it SPECT). It's a type of brain imagery that measures brain activity vicariously through blood in the brain. SPECT scans give a 3-D view of the brain's activity, focusing on three areas: (1) those that are working well, (2) those that are low in activity, (2) those that are overactive.

I'd learned about SPECT imaging back in the mid 1990s. I was impressed with what could be seen and measured with the technology. While magnetic resonance imaging (MRI) shows the grey and white matter of the brain to assess for physical injuries/abnormalities, SPECT imaging shows brain activity. That activation (either normal, underactive or overactive) has a powerful effect on how we behave, relate to others, process information, feel and interpret things occurring around us.

By 2000, I had been working with police and other emergency responders for five years. I had refined a treatment protocol that was proving to be consistently successful. I began to wonder what SPECT imagery could show, if we were to do pre- and post- EMDR brain images.

A tipping point for answering that question came about in the spring of 2000. Working in conjunction with Dr. Amen (CEO of the Amen Clinics) and my first willing client (a paramedic with eight years on that job and previous experience in the military), we rendered the first brain SPECT images of a first responder's PTSD brain before, during and after EMDR.

Chapters 2 and 3 offer a unique perspective of what trauma can do to the brain, and life, of a first responder with a severe case of PTSD. You'll see how EMDR can allow the brain's natural capacity to heal to be reactivated if it gets *"caught in irons."*

CHAPTER NOTES:

1. On Acute Stress Reaction:
   http://anxietytoday.info/diagnostics/acute-stress-reaction.html
2. On Acute Stress Disorder:
   http://www.ptsd.va.gov/public/pages/acute-stress-disorder.asp
3. On PTSD:
   http://helpguide.org/mental/post_traumatic_stress_disorder_symptoms_
   treatment.htm
4. National Center for PTSD of the U.S. Department of Veterans Affairs:
   http://ptsd.va.gov
5. http://www.emdr.com/shapiro.htm
6. To view the DSM IV-TR diagnostic criteria for PTSD Go to:
   http://www.psych.org/MainMenu/Research/DSMIV/FAQs/
   WhatisthemostrecentversionoftheDSM.aspx)

PHOTO CREDITS:

1. "Santa Cruz FD Out on a Call" – Taken by an unknown Firefighter out of St 1 (circa 2001)
2. & 3. "Sadness at Cayuga & Windsor" – Shmuel Thaler Santa Cruz Sentinel Photographer*
3. "The Light Shining in the Darkness" – © Karen Lansing 2012

* My sincere thanks to Shmuel Thaler for his permission to use these photos for this book.

ENDNOTES:

1. L. Blum. *Force Under Pressure: How Cops Live and Why They Die.* Lantern Books, New York: 2000.
2. D. Amen. *Healing the Hardware of the Soul: How Making the Brain–Soul Connection Can Maximize Your Life.* The Free Press, New York: 2002.
3. *The Diagnostic and Statistical Manual of Mental Disorders* (4th edition) American Psychiatric Association, Washington DC: 2000.
4. *The ICD-10 Classification of Mental and Behavioural Disorders.* World Health Organisation, 1992.
5. J. N. Brier and C. Scott. *Principals of Trauma Therapy: A Guide to Symptoms, Evaluation, and Treatment.* Sage Publications, 2006.
6. F. Shapiro and M. Silk Forrest. *EMDR; Eye Movement Desensitization and Reprocessing: The Breakthrough Eye Movement Therapy for Overcoming Anxiety, Stress, and Trauma,* Basic Books, 1997, http://www.emdr.com/shapiro.htm.

CHAPTER 2
INVISIBLE NO MORE

AARON'S STORY

Aaron focused on the infant he had just ushered into the world...feet first. He could see that the newborn was small, which had significantly aided his delivery; but his color was not good and he wasn't breathing. The paramedic handed the baby up to the outstretched hands of the firefighters. These big guys, squeezed into a tiny room of that house trailer, were ready to start the work to get this little guy to breathe. He had to survive. After all it had taken to bring him into this world; he had to live.

"Please let him breathe," Aaron silently prayed as he turned his attention back to the baby's mother. Keenly aware of the silence and that her baby wasn't breathing, she desperately looked Aaron in the eyes and pleaded with him to save her baby. To not let him die. He'd heard and seen that desperation before.

As he worked hard to reassure her—to quiet her increasing panic—inside, he was amazed at what he was doing and more significantly, how he was doing in the midst of the crisis. He felt solid, skilled and focused. He wasn't coming undone, despite the deja vu aspects of this emergency-delivery he'd just accomplished. He couldn't help but compare it to another baby-in-distress call he'd taken just a year ago to the day. So many similarities between the two different calls: the lives of two male infants in the balance, with him attending. That first one, 12 months ago, had nearly undone him.

ONE YEAR EARLIER

It was lunchtime on an unseasonably warm February afternoon. Aaron and his ambulance partner had just pulled into Burger King when a call was sent out describing a mother with a sick 3-month-old male infant who wasn't breathing. The address was only three minutes from their location, so they headed the ambulance out of the parking lot and went Code 3 to the call.

On arrival, they pulled into the driveway. Once out of the ambulance, Aaron could hear a woman's screams coming from inside the house. The first in, he was immediately faced with the hysterical mother standing in the middle of the living room, clutching a small baby to her. Aaron reached out with both hands and almost had to pry the infant out of her arms. He could feel warmth from the baby's body and his first thought was, "It's not too late. I can bring him back."

Between sobs, the mother was pleading to him, "Save my baby! Please don't let him die!"

Aaron started CPR as his partner tried to get the mother to quiet down and give him some details. Looking past Aaron's partner and looking directly at Aaron, all she could do was sob and plead for her baby's life....over and over again.

By the time the firefighters arrived, it was necessary to move the mother to the back of the house because she'd begun to fight the men to grab her baby back. The police officers arrived as Aaron and his partner were heading out the door to run the infant, Code 3, to the local ER.

The hospital was 25 minutes from the home, if nothing went wrong en route. They never stopped CPR during that time, but the baby remained unresponsive. Once at the ER, they ran the baby in. A doctor took the infant and started working on him in a room to the left. Aaron, outside the room, listened intently for the sound of a baby's cough, or gagging, and then tiny cries. But they never came

A short while later, two nurses and the same doctor filed out of the room. Aaron could see one nurse still inside with the baby. The silence from the room and their faces told him that they'd declared the baby's time of death.

The nurse in the room noticed him standing there and went to him in the doorway. Gently, she assured him that he'd done his best but that sometimes these cases just can't be saved.

All Aaron could do was silently nod his head and look at the tiny figure lying on the table inside, wrapped in a small, fluffy yellow hospital blanket. The nurse had cleaned him up for his mother, who would be told any second now. The nurse told Aaron that he could go in the room and quietly left him alone with the infant.

Aaron walked up to the little baby. His fine, dark hair had been slightly wet, parted to one side and neatly combed. The infant looked as though he were sleeping. Aaron reached down and gently touched the little blanketed figure and whispered, "I'm so sorry...I wanted so much to bring you back."

Overwhelmed with sadness, he turned and walked out the door. Just as he was making his way down the corridor, he looked up to see the baby's mother. She had just been told. That moment was burned into his memory.

"She looked at me and cried out again, blaming me for letting her baby die. She didn't say the words, but I knew what she was thinking. I could see it in her face...in her eyes. I killed her son."

IN THE WAKE OF THAT CALL

"I killed her son." Aaron's brain fused together those four words, along with the trauma from that tragic sudden infant death syndrome (SIDS) call out. Together they formed the *negative belief* that attached itself to the memory of that fateful call. While Aaron knew in his logical mind that he'd done everything in his power to save that infant's life, in his heart he didn't believe it. The 18 inches between the head and the heart is a long and deep divide to bridge. Especially if *trauma-based memory* is blocking the way. That was the case for Aaron.

Aaron was married to a delightful woman named Kelsey. They had an 18-month-old son named Justin, who was the pride and joy of his parents. Kelsey worked outside of the home part time, so Aaron had an active role in parenting his son. He loved spending time with Justin. The CI almost immediately impacted Aaron and his family.

Aaron understood that toddlers get bumped and banged up and usually just need to be hugged, cuddled and given a kiss on the "owie." With a bit of reassurance that life will go on, the average toddler is ready to be set loose to "crash and bruise" another day.

Now, after the incident, Aaron began to question his ability to take care of Justin if anything happened to him that needed attending to. Aaron had seen that despite the best training and efforts, life doesn't always go on for small children. He began to panic whenever his son was hurt in the natural course of his adventurous life. When Justin cried, Aaron would panic and become extremely anxious. He began to withdraw from his son and shut down and isolate from his family.

Other symptoms began to affect his life. His startle response increased sharply, causing him to jump at the slightest things. And the incident was intruding in on his life in upsetting ways. He couldn't keep himself from recalling the incident in horribly vivid detail numerous times every day. Along with those disturbing images, Aaron began to have auditory flashbacks of the mother's screams and her pleading for her son to be saved. When driving alone in the car, he'd suddenly relive that last image of the mother in the hospital, looking right at him and screaming. When he held Justin, the warmth of his little body took him back to the moment when he'd first taken the baby from the mother's arms. This would bring up the thought of what sheer folly he'd had in ever believing that he could save that child...or any child's life.

Aaron was having nightmares about the event with his own son's face superimposed on the baby's face. Sleep became almost impossible, which soon led to memory and concentration problems. He'd forget things; he couldn't keep track of what he'd read just one sentence before, or what people were saying to him in conversations. He was losing things on a regular basis (keys, bills, etc.). In short order, Aaron's life began to unravel.

Kelsey became increasingly concerned about her husband. She could see in the weeks following the incident, that he was getting worse. She also was clear that Justin, who'd been so happy and easy-going, was becoming clingy and easily distressed. He obviously sensed that his dad was not the same. Justin, too, stopped sleeping through the nights and often woke up screaming.

These changes worried Aaron, as well. He knew that for everyone's sake, he needed to take back his life and re-establish his relationship with his family. It was with Kelsey's solid support that he and I started working together. Thankfully, we began sessions just several weeks after the critical incident had occurred, so not too much time had passed. That kept the wear and tear rendered upon the family to a minimum.

THE CI IS ABNORMAL, NOT YOU

Most people who have PTSD, or even its affiliates, say that they feel like they are crazy—or, as described in one part of the world where I've worked, "as mad as a bag of frogs." When your brain doesn't function as it used to, that's a natural assumption. Suddenly your coping skills, normally far higher than the average civilian's, disappear. These are replaced with anxiety, rage, sleeplessness and inability to recall things....This just isn't *you.*

So it may be hard to believe that professionals who facilitate Critical Incident Stress Debriefings (*CISDs*), as well as trained therapists like yours truly, stress repeatedly that the symptoms that often follow a CI are, in fact, *normal* reactions to a very abnormal event. This bears repeating: symptoms of PTSD, PTS, Acute Stress Reaction (ASR) or Acute Stress Disorder (ASD) are considered normal reactions to a deeply horrifying, terrifying, and/or highly distressing experience. In other words, normal healthy people end up with these conditions and this should not cause them to be stigmatized or viewed as crazy.

The relief a therapist sees wash over the faces and even the body posture of clients who have heard that crucial information in their first session is a wonderful thing to behold. The relief on learning that truth ("you mean I'm *not* crazy?!") replaces anguish, and the new expression of gratitude reflect the first of many "liberations" that clients will experience in that rite of return *back to the land of the living*.

That in no way denies the fact that the hard-to-miss symptoms that accompany the diagnoses are not fun. For this reason, sound, competent professional help is imperative. Books, including this one, are not a replacement for excellent clinical treatment.

I can say confidently that unless you have a pre-existing mental health condition (i.e. Depression, Manic Depression, Borderline Personality Disorder, etc.) and all you have is PTSD or one of its affiliates, then with skilled clinical treatment, you have a good chance of fully recovering from this condition. In the wake of PTSD, you can, in fact, become more resilient, more tactically competent, and more able to take care of the most important weapon/piece of kit you've got going for you...your brain. I can't guarantee this for all of you, because there are numbers of variables, which may factor into the matrix and create exceptions to the rule. It can also be that EMDR is not suited for 100 per cent of us. Thankfully, those cases are extremely rare.

All of that aside: the question remains as to why some of us, when traumatized significantly enough, develop PTSD. My best answer is that *PTSD comes about when the normal healing process within the brain following a traumatic event has seized up.* In other words, the brain's incredible ability to recover from a highly disturbing event has become stuck. That "stuckness" disables the natural healing abilities of the brain so it can get beyond a CI and move on

In following chapters, you will see the images of the brains of a number of my research clients who had severe cases of PTSD and then recovered. These images and the clients' stories describe the journeys they courageously made to come back to the land of the living in the wake of PTSD. For now however, before I get ahead of myself, I present to you two proposals.

TAKING ON A NEW TACTIC

Besides getting excellent clinical treatment, you can aid your own healing. You'll need to take on a tactical and strategic mindset by adopting attitudes based on the truth of PTSD as my clients and I have found over and over. Take on these two new tactical beliefs to set up for your recovery:

1). PTSD is an injury, not a mental illness.

Yes, the diagnosis includes the word "disorder," but that's inaccurate. Nowadays, with latest brain imaging technologies, we can see PTSD's effects on the brain. We can see when it's injured, just like with broken bones. And after having endured both PTSD and a significant traumatic head injury, I myself can attest to the fact that the two behave amazingly alike.

You may have recognized Aaron's symptoms when you read them. You also might be struggling other difficulties related to a CI. It may be hard to concentrate, to recall things, to filter out distracting noises, to read, to recall what you've read. You may catch yourself having sat on the couch for a long time just staring into space. PTSD can feel like you've sustained a traumatic brain injury without, hopefully, the slam to the head.

As long as you have no other psychological diagnosis, I encourage you to stop considering yourself "mentally ill" and accept that PTSD (or an affiliate) is like an injury to the brain—an injury that can heal. Getting through to the other side of this condition is hard going, so the last thing you need to believe is that you're damaged goods and destined to remain that way. It doesn't even matter how long you've had PTSD.

My first generation of officers all came to treatment with about two decades of PTSD under their helmets (they were all Vietnam vets prior to becoming cops). They *all* recovered fully and retired out on schedule rather than early. In fact, the majority of my clients had lived with PTSD for a decade or more before coming in to get it resolved.

2). Your brain is not out to get you when it has PTSD.

Although you may feel like you've lost your mind, it's still there with you. It's struggling to heal and to access information in order to learn and put things into a proper perspective. It's trying to put things into a context that makes sense. But that's not easy when it is injured.

Consider for a moment that a large part of all the brain does on an average day is aimed at helping us to learn and to survive. The simple act of blinking just before something (or someone) hits your eye is a neurological accomplishment of perception and speed that should impress us to no end. As one officer remarked to me at the end of a training on PTSD and recovery, "The brain is an amazing bit of kit." He was right.

However, when the brain is traumatized, it hyperfocuses on the most disturbing aspects of the CI to the near exclusion of nearly everything else. It can't get past the most disturbing points of the CI. It's trying to remind you, "Don't forget this…it could happen to us again!"

In the sailing world, this is akin to being "*caught in irons.*" This means that every time the boat tries to tack on to a new course in heavy winds, it gets pushed back on to the old course. This is the ultimate nautical equivalent to being stuck in the mud. In either case, you're not going to be able to head home until something unsticks you.

If you think back to Aaron's case, his brain hyperfocused on his flashbacks about (1) the mother's screams and pleading for her baby to be saved, along with that final upsetting scene of her in the hospital, and (2) the physical memory of the baby's warmth and resulting belief that there was a good chance to "make the baby viable" again. As you'll later see, both of those elements of his trauma were fully neutralized once he was completely done with PTSD.

A BRIEFING ON SPECT IMAGING

Unlike *MRIs,* which look at the grey and white matter of the brain, SPECT images measure brain activity by viewing the blood supply to various regions. An undersupply of blood to an area of the brain reflects a drop in activity in that sector. The degree of brain activation has a significant impact on our behavior, thoughts, perceptions, concentration and moods. For instance, when you're in a dangerous situation, the brain redirects blood supply to the survival center—the limbic system. In that maneuver it's borrowing from Peter to pay Paul. The end result can be a temporary drop in functioning of regions of the brain not essential for survival. So, for instance, you may have difficulty understanding radio traffic in the midst of making life and death decisions.

Overactivity in a region of the brain requires more blood to feed the demand for energy. This is the same as when muscles are being used to lift or to sprint or to jump. Blood flow increases to those muscles being activated to allow them to increase performance. Even

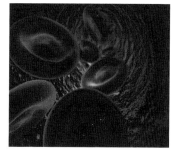

so, too much of a good thing can be as much of a problem as too little. Increased blood flow to one area often means decreased flow—and underactivity--in another.

SPECT images are taken by first injecting an isotope ink (low radiation with a half-life of 15 hours) into the patient's arm. The ink molecules bond to blood cells, which are reflected in the SPECT image. This will make more sense when you look at Aaron's brain both with and without PTSD.

Blood Cells

WHAT YOU'LL SEE

All the SPECT images of our research clients[1] are taken from the same perspective, though comparative images may show different perspectives.

The top of the SPECT images shows the front/top of the brain (what's behind the forehead). The bottom of the images shows the back and the base of the brain.

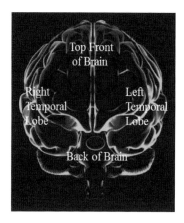

Because we're viewing the brain from the underside rather than the top, the right side of the brain in in the images shows the left temporal lobe; the left side of the brain images shows the right temporal lobe. This makes it easier to view the sectors of the brain that are of greatest interest to us.

Unlike this first brain graphic, you'll notice in Aaron's SPECT images to follow the blue, red and white areas. The red and white areas indicate increased activation caused by an overabundance of blood supply. These areas of the brain with PTSD are larger than those in the no-longer-PTSD brain, in which activation has returned to a normal level.

The pre- and post-EMDR images of Aaron's brain clearly show the difference between his brain when he had PTSD and when he no longer had it. In Chapter 3, I describe what each of those sectors enable us to do with no PTSD and the symptoms those sectors generate when one is suffering with PTSD.

AARON'S CASE

Below are Aaron's SPECT images. The top image was taken in Stage 1, before he had received EMDR treatment. I had fully assessed his condition, had taken a complete history, and had trained him in how to manage his symptoms effectively so that he was in control of them more often than they were in control of him. In fact, he felt measurably better by the end of Stage 1 and even wondered if he really needed EMDR. I explained that containment of symptoms isn't a cure, as he came to understand.

The graphs to the right of the SPECT images show Aaron's scores on a standardized assessment tool called the Posttraumatic Stress Diagnostic Scale (PDS)[2] that measures the PTSD symptoms he reported and the degree of their severity (mild, moderate or severe).

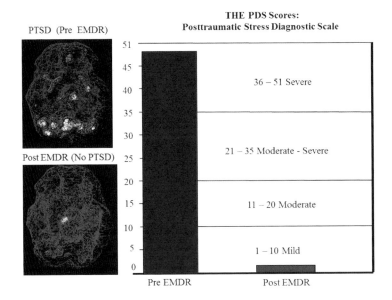

PTSD (Pre EMDR)

Post EMDR (No PTSD)

THE PDS Scores:
Posttraumatic Stress Diagnostic Scale

36 – 51 Severe

21 – 35 Moderate - Severe

11 – 20 Moderate

1 – 10 Mild

Pre EMDR   Post EMDR

HISTORY AND SYMPTOMS BEFORE SPECT

Aaron's history revealed two other fatal calls that needed resolution in addition to the one that brought him in. This meant that Aaron's PTSD was cumulative, due to a combination of three incidents rather than from just a single trauma. The infant's death was the one that finally sent Aaron over the falls. In fact, he realized as he gained understanding of PTSD in the training segment of Phase 1 that he'd actually started to experience difficulties prior to the failed attempt to resuscitate the infant. More than likely, before that incident he would not have met the full criteria for PTSD, but would have had a good number of the PTSD symptoms.

Even so, it's fair to ask what would have happened had Aaron gotten treatment earlier to deal with the previous incidents that were "hauntings" prior to the SIDS callout? Would he have ended up with PTSD if he had done EMDR on those two earlier CIs? If he had developed PTSD, would it have been as severe as it later became? We'll never know. However, I have seen PTSD averted when I've been able to attend to officers who do not fully meet the diagnostic criteria. I believe in early intervention. I long to see First Response agencies/ employers aggressively pursue proactive treatment to resolve ASD, PTS and mild PTSD. It could mean not having to contend with moderate or severe PTSD and all the collateral damage that can upend one's life and career.

The first SPECT image was taken one week prior to Aaron's first EMDR session, which dealt with the SIDS callout. At that time his PDS assessment score was 49 out of 51. This put his PTSD into the severe range. The lower, post-EMDR brain image was taken after we'd done three EMDR sessions over the course of six weeks. In his PDS assessment after the EMDR sessions, he had a score of 2, reporting normal life stressors for a first responder (not sleeping well due to shift work; feeling distant from family due to excessive overtime). He no longer had chronic or enduring PTSD symptoms. He just needed more sleep and more time with his family.

POST PTSD TREATMENT: INTO THE LAND OF THE LIVING WITH A JOYOUS BEGINNING

On that February morning—nine months after Aaron had finished treatment for the SIDS and the two other fatal incidents—he gave me a call. In that discussion he recounted with unabashed joy the incident that opened this chapter. It's also described in a newspaper article excerpted below. I've taken editorial license to protect Aaron's identity, but the actual incident occurred as recounted here.

FIREFIGHTERS PARAMEDICS HELP BABY ENTER THE WORLD FEET FIRST[3]

The ___ Times, Sunday, February 11

A tiny boy came into the world at his mother's mobile home Friday night, with paramedics and firefighters acting as midwives. Weighing less than 5 pounds, arriving a month and a half early, in a near breach, feet first position.

At birth he did not breathe or have a pulse, but tender loving care—including CPR—brought the boy back to life. He is reported doing well at the ___ Medical Center, firefighters said.

Paramedic ___, along with an EMT, arrived first, followed closely by the Firefighter Team from Station 21. Upon arrival, the paramedic realized the boy's tiny feet were presenting out of his mother's body and the rest of his body was still in the birth canal. There was no way they could transport the mother, already in the process of giving birth, to a hospital. Instead, the paramedic carefully guided the mother in her delivery. He then handed the baby off to firefighters in order to continue attending to the mother. The firefighters wrapped the child in sheets contained in the "baby delivery kit" on the fire truck.

An ____ administrator estimates that the company delivers a handful of babies each year, but usually it does not occur in the field in such a difficult situation. He voiced pleasure that everything had worked out so well.

THE SIMILARITIES

What's not described in this article are the following details that Aaron told me about in our phone conversation.

1. Aaron was the first one to the door of the mobile home; he could **hear a woman screaming** inside.
2. Finding his way to the back bedroom, he saw the labouring mother lying on the bed. When he took up his position, he saw one of the baby's feet presenting.
3. On delivery of the baby, **also a little boy**, he could **feel the baby's warmth**; there was no sound and the baby's color was not good.
4. At that point, the mother began to *look directly at him and plead, "**Please save my baby! Don't let my baby die!**"*
5. Aaron still had to attend to the mother or he'd have commenced CPR on the baby. A firefighter now standing behind Aaron, reached down as he passed the baby up and took the baby to begin CPR.
6. All this time **the mother is still crying out to Aaron to please save her baby.** Finally, the baby was resuscitated fully and the room was filled with his very first cries.

From start to finish Aaron was able to focus on his job, without any flashbacks, acute stress reactions or fear of failure. He never had any residual difficulties with this call later on—that is, no delayed onset of ASD or PTSD—and the baby boy survived to start his life because of the skill and competency of this paramedic, the EMT and the firefighters who all answered the calls.

If you re-read the account of the original SIDS incident at the start of this chapter, you can see that this second incident was almost an exact re-enactment of all of the sensory "trip wires." Any of them could have initiated a flashback, or, at the very least, an acute stress response for Aaron had he not been fully free of the traumas he'd been severely impacted by prior to this later incident.

This is what a finished work on behalf of a client and his/her therapist should look like. The second callout was an *in vivo* clinical crosscheck I couldn't have designed better to confirm that Aaron was done with the case of PTSD he'd suffered from just one year earlier.

In a conversation with Aaron's wife in the summer of 2011, by then a little more than 10 years after Aaron had accomplished that delivery, she made mention to me that this little baby is now a delightful little boy who's been in their own second-born son's class in school.

Life…you've got to love it.

PHOTO CREDITS:

1. Normal: ©Karen Lansing 2012
2. Blood: ©iStockphoto.com/tose
3. Brain: ©iStockphoto.com/angelhell
4. All SPECT images ©Karen Lansing & Daniel Amen, taken at the Amen Clinic, Fairfield, California.

ENDNOTES:

1. K. Lansing; D. G. Amen; C. Hanks; L. Rudy. "High resolution brain SPECT imaging and EMDR in officers with PTSD." *Journal of Neuropsychiatry and Clinical Neurosciences*, 17, 2005.
2. E. B. Foa. *Posttraumatic Stress Diagnostic Scale Manual*. National Computer Systems, 1995.
3. The publication and date of the article recounting the successful delivery and resuscitation of the baby is being withheld with permission to protect the confidentiality of "Aaron's" identity

CHAPTER 3
THOSE THINGS THAT HAVE CHANGED US
THE SYMPTOMS

"After surviving the ambush, I remember waking up the next morning. I found myself sitting on the edge of my bunk, just staring at the wall. I realized right then that I felt different...in my head...in my brain...a brain that felt pressure inside...a brain that hadn't worked as well as my own had, just before that ambush."

Police officer
Name withheld

As the officer's comment above describes, when you're living with PTSD, you can feel as if you have someone else's brain residing inside your head. That can be disorienting, even frightening, and can make the terrain of PTSD all the more foreign as you struggle to find your way through.

The last chapter closed with an overview of the SPECT images of Aaron's brain as he progressed through treatment for his PTSD. That overview brought into the light of day that the brain can recover from this trauma-inflicted injury. That's important, but it isn't enough. You need to know more.

The pages to follow serve two objectives: The first is to give you a more complete vision on how one can be redeemed from PTSD. The second objective is to help you get your bearings.

Then you can begin to chart a course for home. The more you know about PTSD and the brain, the more you'll understand about this rite of return.

Gaining a good understanding of both the brain and PTSD takes much of the fear, mystery, shame and blame out of the condition. That's crucial, because those things do nothing to help the healing process. In fact, they generate more collateral damage.

In this chapter, we'll go over the sectors of the brain overactivated by PTSD. First, we'll look at images of the brain when it's working just fine (in this case, when Aaron no longer had PTSD). Then we'll look at the brain images showing us where "the wheels come off," when Aaron's brain was contending with PTSD.

These brain SPECT images have brought down that seemingly impervious "blue wall of silence," regarding duty-induced PTSD, everywhere I've worked on this planet. Warriors and Rescuers with PTSD want to heal—it's a universal human drive. So strap in and hold on. Knowledge is empowerment and this chapter is a crucial part of the journey.

Working jointly with Dr. Daniel Amen on the study of PTSD with officers involved in shootings (OIS), I have drawn heavily from his extensive research. At the time of our study, Dr. Amen had studied over 10,000 SPECT images of brains. At this point, the Amen Clinics have conducted over 72,000 SPECT images, and they continue to excel in study of the brain. Daniel and his clinical teams are able to see what specifically occurs pre and post treatment, and this is what you will see with Aaron below.

ON COMPASSES, MAPS & HOPE

No one should ever go into a new, unfamiliar place without a map and compass. The SPECT images of the paramedic and police officer later in this book serve as reference points if you have PTSD. More than likely, not all of the symptoms listed will match what's going on for you. However, in some of them, you may see yourself. If that happens, don't panic. Aaron's story and his SPECT images prove that all is not lost.

If your life is connected to someone who has PTSD, I hope that this information will keep you from feeling so lost in their presence. He may not seem like the same one you promised your life to. Or she may not seem like the little one you raised from birth to adulthood. Or he may not seem like the guy you grew up with as a lifelong friend or sibling. I hope that by the end of this book, you too will feel less isolated and confused.

NEUROSCIENCE & COMMUNICATIONS IN THE BRAIN

The areas of the brain you will learn about have been observed through SPECT imaging, which is able to show normal and irregular brain activation. That allows us to compare and contrast degrees of brain activation in specific regions of an individual's brain pre- and post treatment.

The brain is able to think, feel, sense, and communicate in a seamless fashion when it's working as it should. That said, however, the brain's actions do not occur in neurological isolation. It cross-communicates freely between different sectors; it forms alliances to accomplish amazing things. The brain understands and carries off teamwork exquisitely well. With its many different regions, the brain is still very much a land without borders.

With the remarkable advances we're seeing in brain research, the understanding of its landscape is ever changing and expanding. This creates, for any intrepid soul putting words to paper on this topic, a high potential, given enough time, of being humbled. Things will not remain in one place for too terribly long as the wonder of the human brain pushes us forward to broaden our understanding of its amazing ability and intricacy. So be it.

Suffice it to say, what follows is a layman's tour of the brain, given by a psychotherapist, not a neurologist. If you want long, multisyllabic terms that resemble really tough words to be landed with in a spelling bee, such as *"habenulointerpeduncular tract"* (oh, please!), you'll have to go elsewhere. Terminology here will be kept down to five syllables or less whenever humanly possible. In return, I ask that you soldier on through this chapter. Trust me, the material coming up is really important to you. So make it your friend.

Before we, "go in, " however, it would be good to do some pre-emptive recon.

THE LIMBIC SYSTEM & RELATED AREAS

The limbic system, introduced in the last chapter, is the "Survival Command Center." This goes for survival of both our species and ourselves. Lt. Col. Dave Grossman, U.S. Army (Ret)[1], eloquently depicts this sector's responsibilities as "the 4 F's": (1) Feeding (2) Fleeing (3) Fighting and (4) *F– finding a delightful little bistro in Paris to pop into and then perhaps strolling along the Seine under a full moon...* Okay, Lt. Col. Grossman's forth "F" is a far more abbreviated 4-letter descriptor, but you get the general idea. The first three "F's" are involved in facilitating an individual's more immediate survival. The forth "F" involves a more long-term survival strategy for the species in general.

The limbic system is made up of five structures: (1) the amygdala (2) the cingulate gyrus (3) the formix, (4) the hippocampus and (5) the hypothalamus.

A number of related areas in the brain also interface with the limbic system. While all are important, this chapter examines the first four sectors, which relate to PTSD and its symptoms: (1) the cingulate gyrus; (2) the basal ganglia; (3) the amygdala; (4) the cerebellum. The symptoms that come with PTSD occur when these areas become overactivated due to trauma. (For more information on them, check out the endnotes at the end of the chapter or the bibliography.)[2]

The hippocampus, which doesn't show up in the SPECT scans, is another area relevant to PTSD. Like the amygdala, this sector is also important to memory. It receives processed memory from the amygdala and helps to allocate the storage and retrieval of those memories throughout the brain. It also plays a role in our ability to overcome fear reactions, such as to parachuting out of planes, when it's working in partnership with the amygdala.

PTSD can severely impair this "fearless" function. For instance, it's not uncommon for officers with PTSD to develop a primal fear of the dark. This can occur in other first responders, but in my practice, I've only seen it in officers.

One of my clients put words to this phenomenon that defined his struggle eloquently. He sadly told me one day in session, "I'm too scared at night to get out of bed to even go to the bathroom. I used to love working nights, because of the dark, but now it just terrifies me."

That's the amygdala (often referred to as the "primitive brain") returning to a primal fear when darkness could bring with it danger or death. Remember, its job is to perceive danger and work to keep us safe from it.

LIMBIC SYSTEM FUNCTIONS

The limbic system serves critical and specific functions; among them, it:
- Holds highly charged memories (both wonderful and traumatic)
- Directly processes smells (the fastest path to a flashback)
- Sets the emotional tone/attitude in the brain
- Promotes bonding and intimacy with others
- Tags events as important and significant
- Modulates libido (sex drive)
- Modulates motivation

PTSD or stress can lead to:

- Decreased motivation
- Appetite/sleep problems
- Social isolation/withdrawal
- Negative perception of events
- Decreased/increased libido (sex drive)
- Moodiness/irritability/clinical depression

The following image of the brain shows the limbic region from a slightly artistic perspective (please note–this isn't Aaron's brain). In this chapter, I want to focus only on a few of the many areas of the limbic region. While this brain model is rather impressionistic, the objective is to give you the lay of the land. So, when I talk about the hippocampus, which shows up here in the red, you'll have an idea from this image where it is.

All along the top line, in a ribbon of green, is the cingulate gyrus. The cerebellum is the green mass at the base of the back of the brain. Shown under all of these is the almond-sized amygdala (one on the right and left sides). Above that sits the basal ganglia in the orange (also one on the right and left).

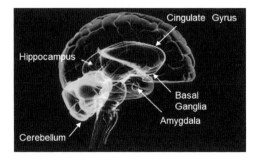

We'll return to Aaron's SPECT images, only now giving more details on how the cingulate gyrus, the basal ganglia, and the cerebellum all contribute along with the amygdala to the PTSD symptoms. We'll compare Aaron's brain against itself both with and without PTSD present to help clarify this.

PLEASE NOTE: In order to show what a non-PTSD brain can look like, you'll first see Aaron's brain AFTER treatment for his PTSD. Then to show what PTSD can cause within the brain, next you'll see Aaron's brain prior to being treated.

THE CINGULATE GYRUS

The cingulate gyrus runs along the full top midline of the brain (a side perspective follows). In Aaron's case, (as with all the rest of my cop research clients) only the forward tip was overactive. Even so, that was enough to cause intrusive thoughts of the incident to seemingly run 24/7. Along with those intrusive thoughts, the "inner judge" questioning (i.e. what you did or didn't do) kicks in, along with all of the reactions related to those thoughts, including guilt/anxiety.

Remember that it's normal to recount a traumatic event rather obsessively for a while after it has passed. This quiets down if the incident doesn't generate PTS or PTSD. If PTSD does happen, one symptom that can occur is this relentless recalling of the incident and sudden, high-disturbance reaction[3]. That will ease off once the PTSD has been fully treated. Then if a memory does come up, it's not as highly charged. It also typically requires a purposeful attempt at recall in order to retrieve it from the brain's archive where it's been stored.

Post EMDR Treatment

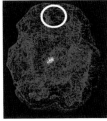

The Cingulate Gyrus: Normal Functioning
- Enables one to be cooperative with others
- Allows for cognitive flexibility (i.e. adaptable)
- Connects & interfaces with the basal ganglia & frontal cortex
- Enables one to shift attention (doesn't get stuck on thoughts/behaviors)

The Cingulate Gyrus: With PTSD
- Oppositional/argumentative reactions to others
- Increase in second-guessing, guilt and/or worry
- Cognitive rigidity (can't let go of things, may hold grudges)
- Difficulty shifting attention (gets stuck on thoughts or behaviors)
- Interfaces with the amygdala and coordinates with it to re-experience PTSD related emotional, visual, mental imagery.

Pre EMDR Treatment

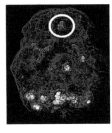

This is what a clinical case of OCD looks like from a side view (left temporal lobe perspective).

The part I've circled illustrates the small section that was overactive for Aaron with his PTSD. While he had some similar symptoms of OCD he *didn't* have OCD.

The cingulate gyrus is one of several areas of the brain implicated in Obsessive Compulsive Disorder[4] (*OCD*). One result of OCD is that thoughts seem to get stuck and repeat themselves over and over again.[5] Also, certain behaviors can become compulsive[6]. This occurs when the cingulate gyrus becomes overactive.

You can see that there is a significant difference between the OCD brain's SPECT image and the PTSD brain's image. You (or your loved one) may have noticed that "somebody has become just a little rigid." Even so, the fact that the behaviors are similar doesn't necessarily mean you have OCD. You may have traits that mimic OCD. This can be responsible for officers (typically undercover officers) with PTSD stocking guns in strategic places (i.e. one in the garage, one in the bathroom, one in the bedroom, one in the car, while packing two concealed)—and that's on a day off!

Many people with PTSD suffer panic attacks during the unwanted obsessive recollection and re-enactment of the traumatic event/s. The section of the brain involved in these are the basal ganglia.

THE BASAL GANGLIA

The basal ganglia is responsible in part with highly skilled movement by interfacing with the cerebellum to coordinate such ability[7]. It's also one of the areas (in connection with the amygdala) responsible for panic attacks for those struggling with high levels of anxiety or PTSD. In both cases panic attacks can occur at any time, including during sleep. In the case of PTSD, panic attacks may kick in with just a reminder of a traumatic incident.

There are two ways that panic attacks can hit a person by way of situational triggers.[8] One is through an *external* trigger, for instance, being a passenger in a car after having survived a helicopter crash. The other way is with an *internal* trigger, such as a nightmare. This commonly ends up with the person in the ER believing he's having a heart attack. Then once everything checks out just fine, the ER doc suggests a visit to a "shrink."

This is not to say you should avoid the ER. Any time you think you're having a heart attack, *always* head to the ER. The one time you don't could buy you the farm. Unfortunately, the triggers of a panic attack, whether external or internal, may not be apparent at the time. The cause can be so subtle that the conscious mind can't perceive it, even though the amygdala within the limbic system does. Whether you recognize the trigger or not, the amygdala does. It then springs into action and the panic attack is off and running (more on the amygdala in the next section).

Another PTSD symptom arising from an overactivated basal ganglia can be that sense of being overwhelmed that can take you right out of the game. Putting words to it this would sound something like: "I CAN'T DO THIS!"

Seeing how overactive Aaron's basal ganglia was it's easy to understand why he felt overwhelmed by just the thought of taking care of his own son if anything happened to him. You may recall that he also had problems dealing with conflict. That showed up with his shutting down and withdrawing from his wife and son.

Withdrawal often comes in the form of isolating from interactions with others, or avoiding discussions around difficult topics. The avoidance can also happen on duty out on the streets. For instance, an officer with PTSD might avoid patrols or stops in tough areas of the city. When PTSD is the issue, these results of being overwhelmed don't reflect laziness if that individual had a good work ethic prior to the condition.

The withdrawal and avoidance stem from the fatigue and being overwhelmed that an overactive brain creates because of the hard work it has to do to maintain the over activation. Along with mental fatigue, the rest of the body may experience a lack of stamina as well. This is especially true if it's not getting enough sleep. The brain knows when the mental and physical systems are vulnerable. Fatigue in these systems causes even the most skillful Warriors and Rescuers to lose confidence and stamina. Low or non–existent reserves of energy pull them out of the game.

General Patton once said, *"Fatigue makes cowards of us all."* He was right.

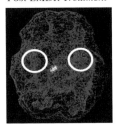

Post EMDR Treatment

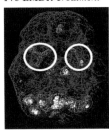

Pre EMDR Treatment

The Basal Ganglia: Normal Functioning
- Integrates feeling and movement
- Sets the idle speed & anxiety levels
- Suppression of unwanted motor behaviors such as jerks
- Helps to render the sense of pleasure by processing dopamine
- Enhances motivation (i.e. in the "11th hour" kicks you into gear)
- Helps control movement especially highly skilled movements (i.e. tactics/weapons skills by networking with the cerebellum)

The Basal Ganglia: With PTSD
- Tremors
- Headaches
- Panic attacks
- Conflict avoidant
- Fine motor problems
- Anxiety/nervousness
- Muscle tension/soreness
- Physical sensation of anxiety
- "Worst case scenario" syndrome
- Low/excessive motivation (or a combination of both)

THE AMYGDALA

Located deep in the left and right temporal lobes (see the circles in this SPECT image), the amygdala, which means "almond" in Greek, is intricately involved in the symptoms of PTSD. It's critical to many brain functions and perhaps most importantly, to the processing of emotions such as anger, fear[9] and pleasure. The amygdala is also critical for helping to perceive emotions accurately in others.

For the person with PTSD, the amygdala causes an exaggerated response to generalized negative input.[10] In other words, it's running at DEFCON 5 all the time.

Until recently, neuroscientists thought the amygdala was solely responsible for perceiving danger and moving us into hyperdrive to respond quickly. Now research is indicating that the amygdala may act more as a hub to activate other parts of the brain to accomplish such things in concert with each other.[11] Either way, the amygdala is monumentally important to the chain reaction of fight/flight/freeze reactions.

Post EMDR Treatment

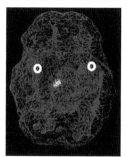

Pre EMDR Treatment

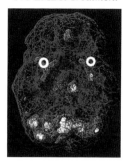

The Amygdala: Normal Functioning

- Arousal
- Memory
- Emotional responses
- Hormonal secretions
- Autonomic responses associated to fear

The Amygdala: With PTSD

- Hyper Arousal
- Re-occurring Traumatic Memory
- Emotional responses
- Increased Stress Hormonal secretions
- Autonomic responses associated to fear

In nonstressful times, the amygdala receives informational cues from three other parts of the brain—the thalamus, the somatosensory cortex, and the hippocampus. The sensory thalamus takes in all information from sight, smell, sound, and touch and sends it all to the somatosensory cortex. This identifies objects and the concepts of the things it's taking in (i.e. baby...cute, rattle snake...not cute). The somatosensory cortex then sends information on to the hippocampus, which then relays the context of the input (i.e. the gist of the story) to the amygdala saying, in a way, "So, what do you make of this? We've got a cute baby smiling at us...nice."

The prefrontal cortex (PFC), located right behind the forehead, is the seat of reasoning and higher thinking. In normal times, it also takes in assimilated information from the areas mentioned above and then formulates a logical plan. It thinks of cause and effect, impulse control, and reasons why you might not want, for instance, to pick up and hug a cute baby whose parents don't know you.

However, in the case of a perceived emergency, the process is abbreviated. Then the amygdala only receives input from the sensory thalamus, thereby cutting out all other pieces of the matrix. Then the amygdala makes assumptions based on limited information.

In such times, the Warrior and Rescuer's amygdala typically clicks into training without having to think. However, it won't be able to stop and phone home to the PFC. It's the PFC, in partnership with the hippocampus, that would be able to later explain the rationale that led an officer to decide for instance, to fire in self-defense. While we train for rapid response, the brain is unable to attain all of the memory when a CI is happening. In fact, it can't even do that under normal circumstances. For instance, can you recall exactly how many times you used your turn indicators and exactly where you turned those on each time as you drove this past week?

THE AMYGDALA ON DUTY (ACT NOW, DELIBERATE LATER)

One piece of exceptional research illustrates why the brain speeds up response time in critical incidents. Dr. Bill Lewinski, the co-founder and executive director of the internationally renowned Force Science Institute, has done numerous scientific studies on the time frames involved in different kinds of lethal contact (shooting) incidents.

This study underscores the significance of mere fractions of a second to an officer facing an armed subject and how precious time is in the kill zone. The pictures below, from the study, graphically show the findings when Bill Lewinski measured time with digital video with a stand-draw-fire-run shooter.

He found that in a standing position, facing an officer, with arms down but hands concealed behind the back, a subject can draw his gun, fire, turn 180º and run away from the officer in 50/100ths of a second. Breaking this down from (1) being in a facing-the-officer-stance, to (2) pointing the gun at the officer, to (3) then firing at the officer, then (4) dropping gun off target (as the suspect is pivoting to prepare to run) took an average of 42/100ths of a second. The fastest took 32/100ths of a second.[12]

My thanks to Dr. Bill Lewinski and Force Science Institute for the use of these pictures.

In the crucial milliseconds of the unfolding critical incident, a number of atypical things play out in the officer's brain, all intended to insure survival. As the amygdala takes charge of operations momentarily, going "radio silent" with the PFC, something else is going off-line back in the limbic system right next to the amygdala.

The hippocampus momentarily "goes to black" and is not able to take on memory to reformat the incident into a *past* event once time has passed. (More on this in a bit).

In the heat of battle, *if* the amygdala were to take the time to relay forward a deliberation with the PFC on why, *"it might be a good idea to weigh the merits of taking the shot at this particular time,"* while the hippocampus is chipping in, *"Wait! I want to get a picture of this to add to the scrapbook to remember it by--it may come in handy!"* ...it could end up as "game over in sudden death." By that time, the officer would be too far behind the reaction curve to ever catch up.

THE DOWN SIDE OF A SPEED-OF-LIGHT RESPONSE

While this rapid-fire response can be lifesaving in the actual event, it can block the ability at a later time to access a narrative recounting of what the officer remembers, or a logical rationale to explain his actions (say during a post-shooting investigation).

Needless to say, it's worrisome to know that *something* told you to click into fight-to-stay-alive mode, yet not be able to articulate exactly what that something was in the wake of the incident. When in the perceived lethal-contact situation, you can't always make slow, rational choices that can be neatly explained later. The human brain doesn't function that way in a crisis situation.

The fact is that the limbic system can and will decide to go to DEFCON 5 even before you fully grasp the seriousness of your situation. On the down side, however, it can also react in fight/flight mode when the situation is not as lethal as first perceived.

This can, for instance, happen on a regular basis for officers returning from the Middle East theatre. Down shifting one's brain from *down range* can be an extremely difficult transition after being in combat. The returning asset's brains are typically hypervigilant. This is a classic set up for having increased startle and/or self-defense reactions against innocent movements or sounds.

BACK IN FROM THEATRE

The note below, which I received from one of my military assets when he got home, describes a good example of how post-theatre de-escalation can be accommodated. He had checked in with me on his return home from his third deployment. He didn't have PTSD, but the increased startle response and hypervigilance were present, as they are with all returning from active sectors (at least, initially) in the Middle East. (Excerpt used with permission)

> May 31, 2011:
>
> *"As for my health, dear lady, I'm doing okay. Last summer it was a blessing that Jenny and the boys went to see her parents not long after I came back in from Afghanistan. I was pretty wired up coming out of theatre. Not jumpy but freaking hyperalert all the time. Nature of the beast. I had spun down by the time they got home. I find I do fine as long as I get my regular PT in every day. I'm swimming 1600 meters 6 days a week and doing TKD 3 times per week. The TKD is especially helpful as I can let the violence out in the air..."*

It was ideal that he had quiet time to himself shortly after his return to allow his brain to recalibrate and quiet down. He and his family were able to reconnect before the bloom came off of the homecoming. Once his wife and kids were away, he busied himself with projects around the home (his usual routine after a long tour of duty) and he exercised. Note his choices of physical training: swimming (rhythmic) and TKD (aerobic). More will be said about exercise choices in Chapter 4.

This military asset had a graceful re-orientation back to life so he could settle inside and allow his amygdala and basil ganglia to settle down. It was a smooth transition for his brain. Unfortunately that isn't always the case.

THE PTSD COSTS EXACTED FROM INFORMATION PROCESSING

The hyperarousal described above was first identified as a trait of "war neurosis" (the term Freud used in 1915 to refer to PTSD). Then, in 1941, the psychiatrist Abram Kardiner described soldiers with this diagnosis as having difficulties processing incoming information. (This issue of information processing will come into play again in the chapter on EMDR).

Kardiner explained that a narrowing of a soldier's attentional field would occur and then they would hyperfocus on perceived indicators of potential threat or danger. He noted that this kept them in a chronically elevated state of over arousal.[13] Today the term for this is "hypervigilance" and it ties directly to the physical responses in the chain reaction of fight/flight/freeze. The last sector of Aaron's PTSD brain we will look at, his cerebellum, relates to this.

THE CEREBELLUM

The term "cerebellum" comes from the Latin term meaning "little brain." In fact, this part of the brain is a type of "Mini Me." It's the second largest area in the brain, and we're just beginning realize how very diversified its role is.

For decades our understanding of the cerebellum was limited to the role it plays in motor control. It networks with the spinal cord and basal ganglia, both of which also play key parts in movement. In more recent years, however, research has discovered the cerebellum carries out visual, cognitive, speech and sensory input functions also.

Post EMDR Treatment

Cerebellum: *Now acting normally*
- Cognitive functions (i.e. planning)
- Involved in sensory information processing
- Involved in verbal fluency and correct grammar
- Involved in the learning and remembering of movement
- Executes movement timing in conjunction with basal ganglia
- Develops complicated movement memory through trial and error without conscious thought (i.e. like riding a bicycle)

Pre EMDR Treatment

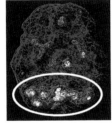

Cerebellum: *Now overactive can instigate:*
- Increased startle response ("learned" at time of traumatic event)
- Increased aversion response to unpleasant physical and visually emotional stimuli

The ability of the cerebellum to learn and remember movement may relate to posttrauma reactivity, particularly when we think about a critical incident as being, as far as the brain is concerned, a real-time training event.[14]

In the chronic Monday morning quarterbacking that follows the event, the brain recalls the event and the response over and over, potentially leading to the unconscious integration of reactions in real time when given similar stimulus.[15]

If an officer was ambushed or violently assaulted from the left hand side, the cerebellum will learn from that experience. It will mentally rehearse the physical reaction to that kind of attack every time the brain relives the incident. This then can become an automatic response that's been over rehearsed subconsciously due to the replay of flashbacks, nightmares and intrusive memories.[16]

This over-practiced defensive tactic then becomes an imprinted reaction. One of the most common manifestations of this that I see in clients are startle/defensive reactions when they sense unexpected movement or someone coming up to them, even if outside of the officer's field of vision.[17] This is especially true when the person is coming from the same direction as the past attack.[18] These reactions and startle responses have the potential to pose grave physical dangers to Warriors/Rescuers and those around them.

The cerebellum also has a part in self–protective reactions to physically and emotionally unpleasant input. Its role in such cases is in activating an aversion response to painful physical contact and highly upsetting images. Both of these the brain knows it would be better off not taking on.[19]

THE INNOCENT TRIPWIRES TO "DANGER CLOSE"

In a near-miss situation, one of my officers was nearing the top of the stairs going to the second floor of his house. He was looking down and preoccupied when his little, curly topped, angel-faced 4-year-old daughter, in a playful attempt to surprise Daddy, jumped out from around the corner at the landing and screamed.

Right on cue, Daddy's heightened startle response kicked in, nearly causing him to fall backward down the stairs. Just before he grabbed his daughter around her fragile little throat, he suddenly realized where he was and whom he was attempting to fight. It wasn't the one who had been on high ground trying to kill him and his team; it was his baby girl, who just wanted to play with him. He collapsed, sitting down on the stairs horrified by what he'd nearly done.

In such occurrences with PTSD, the first reaction to a sudden sound or movement is fear. The second is rage, sometimes literally blind rage. If the tripwire you unintentionally hit brings on a full-blown flashback (think loss of present awareness times three), the end result can be devastating.

In the wake of a near miss like that one on the stairs, self-loathing and shame usually arise. Your startle defense responses can make you seem to others, and feel inside your own soul, as though you've become a monster.

The thought that comes with that negative belief (you may know it by heart) is, *"They'd all be better off without me."* Believing you're a monster makes you feel you have no place in your family, your circle of friends and colleagues, in society and even in the human race. And that leads to the dangerous loneliness and isolation I referred to earlier. For us creatures of the herd, this belief can mean death.

Yes, that ever-present abyss you must look into also looks back into you. And yes, tragically, a minority do fall in. Even so, getting PTSD and having trauma-based reactions to innocuous stimuli (due to an injured brain that can't discern innocent from lethal triggers) are quite simply not the same thing as being a monster. The telling trait that testifies to the fact that you're not is your feeling of remorse and grief after such incidents. "Monsters" quite frankly don't have the capacity to experience those feelings. They can't empathize and they can't experience remorse.[20]

It may be good to ponder for a moment exactly how a good and loving father could nearly end up with his hands around the throat of the little apple of his eyes. Most of the time, PTSD is brought on by fighting to save a life or witnessing the harshest realities and traumas the world can dish out, and to do this so that civilians won't have to. While coming down with PTSD is a crapshoot, almost everyone pushed beyond the breaking point ends up broken.

Lt. Col. Grossman addresses the fear of being a "monster." He points out in his book *On Combat* that it wasn't until the start of WWI that battles began to continue around the clock and go for weeks—even months—on end. The battle on the Normandy beaches in WWII was a nonstop fight for two months with no rear lines to fall back behind. Soldiers were exposed to unremitting war with deaths, injuries and continuous combat surrounding them. After 60 days of constant fighting, 98 per cent of all surviving soldiers became trauma casualties.

Lt. Col. Grossman underscores how we learned the hard way in WWI and again in WWII that the human mind could not keep up with the newly devised war machine. We also learned something else: The remaining two per cent coming out of that living hell were just fine. According to WWII researchers Roy Swank and Walter Marchand, these were "aggressive sociopaths." They are the natural killers.[21] They don't get PTSD because it's not in their neurological composition to have the capacity to develop the condition.[22]

If there's a silver lining to having PTSD, it's this: By virtue of having this injury, you're factored out of that two per cent. In other words, PTSD won't turn you into a monster, but it can at times cause you to act like and believe that you are one. Now, *that* has got to stop and Chapter 4 should help with this.

For now, it's important to understand why the memories of trauma can cause this kind of horrifying reaction to occur.

"NOW" VS. "THEN"

Besides taking over "operations" in times of crisis, the amygdala also acts as a librarian of memories. Like the hippocampus, it too decides what memories will be shelved and where. The difference is that the amygdala focuses on tagging the most critical memories.

Imagine a library located in a region prone to earthquakes. Inside, the librarian is pushing around a cart full of books on a variety of topics, such as cooking, interior design, great artists of the 14th century. All these can be shelved to be accessed when needed at a later time. However, that librarian has lived through several big earthquakes. For this reason, she decides that the books *How to Survive An Earthquake for Dummies* and *Emergency First Aid* should stay on the cart. This way they'll be more easily accessible, just in case the earth starts rocking and books start falling.

A key factor relevant to the amygdala deciding where a memory is shelved is the level of intensity of the emotions connected to the original event. The most intense emotions are those having to do with survival (i.e. fear) or exceptionally joyous life events (i.e. birth of a baby).

Brain researchers currently think the memories of a traumatic event/s that generate PTSD get maintained differently by the amygdala. They are kept "right there" in the amygdala for quick access, just as librarian did with the emergency books on the cart. This has that ready-access advantage to enable faster reactions to a threat the next time.[23]

Additionally, the amygdala doesn't seem to have a sense of time regarding such memories, except in the present tense.[24] Instead of distinguishing between "now" and "not now," the amygdala is a one-trick-pony. "Now" is the only option it can play with unresolved/unprocessed traumatic memory. This impacts the nature of the trauma-based memories that get held in the amygdala, because they're locked in the present tense and not able to be reformatted into the past. As long as they're maintained in that way, they remain on the "HAPPENING NOW!" cart rather than shelved on the "back then and over now" region.

That frozen-in-time aspect of PTSD is what generates the flashbacks, nightmares, intrusive images and physical reactions, all as if the incident were still happening.

Unlike the amygdala, the hippocampus is the archive and librarian for non-traumatic memories; it has a sense of time, space and proper perspective. It knows when remembered events happened and what they have taught us.[25]

That means the hippocampus is able to maintain the storyline and the chronological placement of the traumatic event/s as a type of "incident chapter" in the book of one's life. It's then able to make narrative and chronological sense of memories it has absorbed after having formatted them into a not-now, past-tense historical (no longer traumatic) event. It also acts as a librarian as it reallocates memories to different locations in the brain.[26] As a result, the brain is able to retrieve the learning points from the memory to then put into use within life.

PTSD IMPACTS THE STUFF OF LIFE

Besides causing symptoms such as vigilance, trauma re-enactments and avoidance of conflict, PTSD affects other critical survival skills based in the limbic system of the brain.

These effects impact our worldview, our relatedness to others, and our responses to the typical trials and tribulations of daily life. Recognizing these as a part of the possible PTSD injury helps you make sense of why you don't always feel or act like yourself and possibly, as if you were cut off from others.

It may be hard to fathom that optimism is a critical survival skill. But remember that optimists, who keep fighting and don't easily lose hope (like those in the world such as Cptn Ernest Shackelton and Lt. General Hal Moore) are more likely to survive (and bring others out with them) than pessimists, who give up the fight and lose all hope. As you know by now, PTSD leads to over activation of many regions of the brain, which can lead to sleep deprivation and resulting chronic fatigue. These conditions can bring about a downward spiral in mood and worldview that makes optimism difficult to maintain.

ISOLATION AND THE CALL OF THE MAN CAVE

PTSD symptoms, such as hypervigilance, uncontrolled anger and flashbacks, are often visible, noisy and dramatic. However, others, such as hopelessness, are harder to perceive. Yet it's the quiet ones that are potentially the most deadly.

Bonding and attachment are critical to humans' survival from the moment we're born. We're creatures of the herd because we can't make it on our own. That's why I believe that the most dangerous symptoms of PTSD are social isolation and loneliness. That denotes the lack of attachment to others. Without a sustaining social support network, it's far easier to lose hope and perspective.

Men are most vulnerable to this tendency to pull away from the herd. They have to fight the strong urge to isolate and withdraw when wounded (especially when it's an inner wound). The *"call of the man cave"* is mighty. I'll come back to this in a later chapter because it is so important. For now, suffice it to say that PTSD can become life threatening when one is isolated or attempts to go it alone.

FLASHPOINT ANGER

As you've seen by now, PTSD affects not only the person who experienced the traumatic event/s, but also their families and loved ones. The two symptoms that render the most difficulty to those closest at hand are the moodiness and irritability of the loved one with PTSD.

A disproportionate level of anger is commonplace in a life that's struggling along with PTSD in tow. The brain is chronically under siege and can't tell the difference between friend and foe in day-to-day life. Just as the PTSD brain can't distinguish between lethal and innocent movements or actions, it also can't discern friend from foe.

The brain with PTSD becomes indiscriminately defensive, like an injured animal that fights the rescuers attempting to help. When the limbic brain is "injured," it takes a defensive posture even in the absence of viable threat or danger. With this position, negative interpretations of events, usually a misreading of the good intentions of friends or family members—are inevitable. Add to that, children who drop toys, slam doors, scream or pop balloons, because to the PTSD brain it's hard or completely impossible to distinguish those sounds from gunfire or an RPG attack.

This chronic irritability and flashpoint anger can suck the lifeblood, along with any sense of fun, out of a family, out of friendships and out of the heart and soul of the one with PTSD. It's exhausting having to endure this level of vigilance and stress. And it comes at a very high cost.

THE 24/7 WAR AND THOSE WHOLE LIVE WITH IT

It's natural for those without PTSD to imagine that their symptoms come and go, that life is normal most of the time, until the symptoms happen. In this view, PTSD would be like any chronic condition such as asthma. In certain conditions—high pollen count; stress; illness—the person has an asthma attack. At other times life is perfectly normal. In certain circumstances, such as a child jumping out at you on a stairway landing, the person with PTSD has an attack. At other times, life is calm and normal. Would that it were so.

The SPECT images of Aaron's brain *before* EMDR treatment clearly show overactivation and indications of PTSD. However, during the imaging process, Aaron was not consciously thinking about the infant he couldn't save or the mother screaming at him in the hospital. Conditions were created carefully to ensure this.

Neither Daniel nor I wanted to re-traumatize Aaron in the process of this study. The most common research structure would require him to listen to a recorded recounting of his trauma during the SPECT imaging process. We were concerned that tactic might induce a trauma reaction.[27] So instead, Daniel suggested we have Aaron take a standardized, computerized, concentration test[28] during the SPECT imaging procedure.

The significance of the results of Aaron's SPECT imaging before EMDR in that setting is that they showed us how PTSD runs in the background, no matter what one is doing. PTSD is active when you're fully focused on a standardized, computerized concentration test, when you're asleep, when you're watching television, when you're driving (more on that later), when you're working out, when you're shopping for food, when you're making love. In short, PTSD is "on" 24/7, 365 days a year. It never takes furlough, block leave, R & R or any sort of leave or vacation time.

As stated earlier, Lt. Col. David Grossman wrote about what six weeks of being in a war zone will do to 98 per cent of the Warriors stuck into the battle. So what happens when the war comes inside? Those Warriors/Rescuers go on to live with the internalized war going on in their brains all the time. They're dealing with it constantly, sometimes for months, for years, for decades, without "liberty."

The nonstop quality of PTSD is tragic for the Warriors and Rescuers stuck in this internal war. Equally as tragic are the effects on those they love, who never signed up to live in a battlefield. This is the last thing that any would wish upon their children, their significant others or their friends and family. That causes perhaps the greatest heartache of all for my clients.

And yet again, ironically, this is good news. If you are struggling with regret for your family, as well as for yourself, it means *you* are still "in there." You are still human, still loving... because "monsters" aren't able to ache for anyone.

PHOTO CREDITS:

1. In the Wake of the Ambush © Karen Lansing 2012
2. Human Brain – Limbic System: © MedicalRF.com/Getty Images
3. The SPECT Images ©Karen Lansing & Daniel Amen, taken at the Amen Clinic in Fairfield, California (The Amen Clinic: http://www.amenclinics.com/clinics/).
4. "Why is the suspect shot in the Back?" Pictures used with permission by Force Science Research Institute & Dr. Bill Lewinski.

ENDNOTES:

1. D. Grossman, Bullet proofing the mind. Audio, Callibre Press. 1st Ed. 1996.
2. D. Amen, M.D. Amen Clinic Website, Summaries of brain functioning in key sectors that are impacted by PTSD:
   http://www.amenclinics.com/brain-science/cool-brain-science/a-crash-course-in-neuroscience/cingulate-gyrus/
   http://www.amenclinics.com/brain-science/cool-brain-science/a-crash-course-in-neuroscience/basal-ganglia-system/
   http://www.amenclinics.com/brain-science/cool-brain-science/a-crash-course-

in-neuroscience/limbic-system/
http://www.amenclinics.com/clinics/professionals/how-we-can-help/brain-science/cerebellum-cb/
http://www.amenclinics.com/brain-science/cool-brain-science/a-crash-course-in-neuroscience/prefrontal-cortex/

3. L. M. Shin, A. M. Kossllyn, et. al. "The role of the anterior cingulate in posttraumatic stress disorder and panic disorder." Archives of Genera Psychiatry, vol. 54 (3): 233-241.

4. L. Friedlander and M. Desrocher. "Neuroimaging studies of obsessive-compulsive disorder in adults and children." Clinical Psychology Review, vol. 26, Issue 2, January 2006, 32-49.

5. S. Ursu, A. V. Stenger, K. M. Shear, et al. "Overactive action monitoring in obsessive-compulsive disorder: Evidence from functional MRI." Psychological Science, vol. 14, 4, Jul., 2003, 347-353.

6. C. M. Adler, P. McDonough-Ryan, et al. "FMRI of neuronal activation and symptoms provocation in undedicated patients with obsessive compulsive disorder." Journal of Psychiatric Research, vol. 34, Issues 4-5 July 2000, 317-324.

7. V. Braltenberg and D. Heck; F. Sultan. "The detection and generation of sequences as a key to cerebellar function: Experiments and theory." Behavioral Brain Science, June 1997 (2), 229-277.

8. The Diagnostic and Statistical Manual of Mental Disorders, 4th ed. (DSM-IV-TR). The American Psychiatric Association, Washington, D.C: 2000. http://www.psych.org/MainMenu/Research/DSMIV/DSMIVTR/DSMIVvsDSMIVTR/SummaryofTextChangesInDSMIVTR.aspx.

9. J. LeDoux. " Emotions circuits in the brain." Annual Review of Neuroscience, vol. 23: 155-184, 2000.

10. S. L. Rauch, P. J. Whalen, et al. "Exaggerated amygdala response to masked facial stimuli in posttraumatic stress disorder: A functional MRI study." Biological Psychiatry, 47, 2000. 769–776.

11. R. M. Todd and A. K. Anderson. "Six degrees of separation: the amygdala regulates social behavior and perception." Nature Neuroscience, No. 10; Oct. 10, 2009.

12. W. Lewinski. "Why is the suspect shot in the Back?" The Police Marksman, Nov./Dec. 2000, http://www.forcescience.org/articles/shotinback.pdf.

13. A. Kardiner. The Traumatic Neuroses of War. Hoeber, New York: 1941.

14. W. T. Thach. "A Role of the Cerebellum in Learning Movement Coordination." Neurobiology of Learning and Memory, 70, 1998, 177-99.

15. R. B. Ivry, R.B., R. Spencer, H. N. Zelaznik, and J. Diedrichsen. "The cerebellum and event timing." Annals of New York Academy of Sciences, vol. 978, Dec. 2002, 302-317.

16. W. T. Thach, "A Role of the Cerebellum in Learning Movement Coordination." Neurobiology of Learning and Memory, 70, 1998, 177a.

17. D. Timmann, C. Musso, F. P. Kolb, M. Rijntjes, M. Jüptner, S. P. Müller, C. Diener, C. Weiller. "Involvement of the human cerebellum during habituation of the acoustic startle response: A PET Study." Journal of Neural Neurosurgical Psychiatry, 65, 1998, 771-73.

18. L. C. Kolb. "Neurophysiological hypothesis explaining posttraumatic stress disorder." Am J Psychiatry, vol. 144, 1987, 989-95.

19. E. A. Moulton, I. Elman, G. Pendse, J. Schmahmann, L. Becerra, D. Borsook, "Acersion Related circuitry in the cerebellum: responses to noxious heat and unpleasant images." The Journal of Neuroscience, vol. 10 Mar. 2011, 31.

20. B. M. Hicks and C. J. Patrick. "Psychopathy and negative emotionality: Analyses of suppressor effects reveal distinct relations with emotional distress, fearfulness and anger-hostility." Journal of Abnormal Psychology, vol. 115(2), May 2006, 276-287.

21. D. Grossman and L. W. Christensen. On Combat: The Psychology and Physiology of Deadly Conflict in War and in Peace. PPCT Research Publications, 2004, 12-13.

22. H. Cleckley. The Mask of Sanity (5th ed.). St. Louis, MO: Mosby, 1976.

23. B. Rothschild. "Post-traumatic stress disorder: Identification and diagnosis." (Reprinted for Soziale Arbeit Schweiz), The Swiss Journal of Social Work, Feb. 1998.

24. B. A. van der Kolk. "The body keeps the score: Memory and the evolving psychobiology of post-traumatic stress." Harvard Psychiatric Review, vol., 1, (5), 1994, 253-265.

25. S. Otani (Ed). Prefrontal Cortex: From Synaptic Plasticity to Cognition. Kluwer Academic Publishers Group, The Netherlands, 2004, 108.

26. W. C. Leon, M. A. Bruno, S. Allard, K. Nader, A. C. Cuello, "Engagement of the PFC in consolidation and recall of recent spatial memory." Learning Memory, Vol., 17, Cold Spring Harbor Laboratory Press, 2010, 297-307.

27. R. A. Lanius, P. C. Williamson, M. Densmore, J. Gupta, R. W. J. Neufeld, J. S. Gati, R. Menon, "Brain activation during script-driven imagery induced dissociative responses in PTSD: a functional magnetic resonance imaging investigation." Biological Psychiatry, Vol. 52, Iss. 4, Aug. 2002, 305-11.

28. C. K. Conners. "The Conners' Continuous Performance Test II." IPS (International Psychology Services), 2000.

CHAPTER 4
THE HIGHWAY MARKERS LEADING HOME

"Don't be afraid of embracing disappointment you feel, old or new. Don't be scared of unreasonable joy either. They're the highway markers home. I've gone on ahead..."

Brent Curtis and John Eldredge
The Sacred Romance

By moving through this book page by page, you're doing the work of getting to know the terrain of this place called PTSD. By now you may recognize that the behavior and symptoms you've experienced yourself or have seen in someone you work or live with are, in fact, signs of PTSD or one of its affiliates. If you're experiencing any symptoms, you also now have a good idea of where in your brain they are coming from. In other words, they're on the map. Hopefully by now you're not as lost or thinking you're as isolated as you may have originally believed.

Now, in this chapter, you'll get a compass and map for what lies ahead.

The terrain should be making more sense and the way through it may not seem as foreboding. Others have been this way ahead of you. I've witnessed many heal and end up doing their jobs and living their lives even better they had before they encountered PTSD. They became stronger and deeper inside once they'd made it through.

As you move forward, remember that you've got a Warrior's heart buried in there amidst the rubble. You're going to need that. Recall what I said in the beginning: PTSD will leave you stronger or weaker, but never the same. So again I tell you, choose strength. Even when you may feel anything but strong...choose strength. That must become a moment-by-moment, day-by-day decision. The tools in this chapter and the next can help you, but they're not a magic wand. You must resolve to get back home, to do your part on this journey and to strive to do it well.

EMDR

From the start of treatment for duty-induced PTSD, clients are in training. They're being prepared for the phase of treatment when the trauma work is done. Once that's completed, they're preparing to integrate all of that new learning into their lives beyond treatment.

The success of everything relies upon the heart of the Warrior/Rescuer, the abilities of the therapist, the strength of trust in their joint working alliance, and the foundational preparation in the first stages of treatment.

EMDR was created and founded by Dr. Francine Shapiro using a standardized protocol with three parts: (1) assessment of past events that have set the groundwork for the current symptoms; (2) the current situations/triggers that activate the disturbance; (3) the template to establish for appropriate future actions. These three parts together contain a total of the eight phases involved in the EMDR therapy model.[1]

The beauty of EMDR is that it's incredibly adaptable. At the heart of her creation of EMDR, Dr. Shapiro was an observer and innovator, and she has encouraged those traits in those trained in this model of treatment. It was with trepidation that I amended her original protocol to fit my population, until a comment she made after seeing a presentation that Dr. Amen and I did on our police study.

In her keynote address the next day, Dr. Shapiro said, "It was a beautiful example that Karen Lansing was giving yesterday of having used the standard protocol to work with the policemen that was getting the results that Dr. Amen was showing on the brain scans. She used the standard protocol with three additions she added in order to help access the information that needed to be processed. And her understanding of the police allowed her to put those additions in which would be different than the additions someone might work in with a firefighter, or with a sexual abuse victim, or with a phobia client, or with a substance abuse client...whatever it might be."[2]

Dr. Shapiro knows that the therapist must trust the solid construct of EMDR and at the same time understand their clients' needs in order to render the best practice to them.

Below is the thumbnail sketch of the treatment protocol jointly devised by my officers and me, which I then refined through trial and error. We worked and fine-tuned until we landed on a course that performed optimally for them. Not all of it is original to us, such as the terms used for the three stages (Protect, Direct, Connect, which came from Diane Myers[3]), EMDR therapy, as well as logging, and the basis for a technique my officers and I devised called, "Going to Baseline" came from Dr. Shapiro's design[4]. The EMDR Peak Performance Protocol,[5] designed by Dr. Sandra Foster and Dr. Jennifer Lendl, has also been critical to us, especially in sessions out on the weapons range.

So I have arranged the eight phases in EMDR Therapy[6] into three stages specifically to meet the needs of my officers. (For a full description of the eight-phase protocol, please go to http://www.emdrnetwork.org/description.html). The adaptations that we tend to use in session are specific to the nature of traumas; the terms we use are shorter and more specific to our work as well. Even so, this doesn't change the nature or process that unfolds with EMDR.

STAGE 1. PROTECT: INTELLIGENCE GATHERING & STAGING

The first stage begins with an intake, which includes a thorough history, assessment (includes screening for neurological concerns, such as seizures/traumatic head injuries or other clinical diagnosis that may rule out EMDR as a viable option); education, training, safety, stabilization and resiliency (EMDR phases 1 & 2). Because of the training in containment techniques to manage symptoms, by the end of Stage 1, officers frequently say they feel so much better that they aren't sure they need EMDR after all. This is what stabilization and increased resiliency should look and sound like. Once those are accomplished, Stage 1 is complete and it's time to go operational, in Stage 2.

STAGE 2. DIRECT: GOING OPERATIONAL

Stage 2 is comprised of the EMDR trauma work that corresponds to Dr. Shapiro's phases 3-7.

The number of critical incidents being dealt with dictates how many EMDR sessions will be in order. OIS incidents may require 3-4 sessions (each dealing with different aspects/ integration of re-training); these include interactive video scenario range sessions, if necessary. We've found that even when a significantly large dance card of incidents is involved, the course requires only four to six EMDR sessions. I've never had to do more than eight EMDR sessions, including weapons-range sessions, with any client. The containment techniques taught in Stage 1 are important in this second stage, should any fragments of memory come up between sessions that need to be managed by the officer until his next session.

After the EMDR sessions, we add in clinical cross-checks to assess for any need for fine-tuning to reprocess fragments of memory that didn't come to the surface during EMDR. You'll see examples of these in Chapter 9.

STAGE 3. CONNECT: POST OPERATIONAL & CLINICAL CROSS-CHECK

With the trauma-based memories neutralized in the previous stage, the work in Stage 3 is focused on the integration of what's been learned tactically and working to merge those learning points into real skills by coordination with tactical/weapons trainers. With OIS officers, we do straight range sessions and move up to interactive video firearm range sessions including shoot/don't shoot scenarios.

If an officer has been on extended sick leave/sickness absence, then monitoring the transition back to light or full duty is important. For any leave of over four months, I recommend at least two full shifts with an *FTO* to help the officer reorient to being out on duty. It also serves to ensure that any new computer programs, policies and procedures have been fully reviewed.

Graduation out of therapy comes in this stage and should be done in a titrated manner. When an officer realizes, as he's driving to his session, that he's got nothing to talk about, that's a good indication things are winding down. Then sessions can be scaled back to every other week with the logging still being maintained for review in sessions. Next, a once-a-month-session schedule can be set. Finally, follow-up check-in sessions once every three months can be set up. Tune-up's of any trauma-based memories/fragments can be attended to. These will not typically generate a significant level of distress. If all holds between the three-month check-in's, then the officer is "good-to-go."

AMBUSHED BY INTERNAL STUFF

I'm out on "graves" with Reggie. Soquel Street is empty as we make our way towards downtown, when suddenly he pulls the unit around in a full 180º. I'm clueless as to what had caught his eye—I had seen nothing. As it turned out, he had seen movement in the parking lot of a law office on the opposite side of the street and decided to check it out. Sure enough, there was a questionable activity going on in that location.

That's what being a trained observer *from the uniform out* means. You Warriors and Rescuers are gifted at spotting things the rest of us miss, and that ability becomes stronger over time as skills increase...it's great. However, what you're typically not so good at noticing is the stuff that goes on from the uniform *in*. Taking notice of internal reaction is not as comfortable a bit of ground to venture on to.

Even the really obvious stuff, like fear, can be hard to pick up. For example, when officers who've been in a shooting fill out the PDS assessment for PTSD, the question comes up, "Did you feel afraid for your life?" Commonly they honestly answer "No," and not because they're trying to be macho. They really have no memory of that fear. It may have appeared for a fragment of a second, but other things by then had to take priority.

At the time of a shooting, (1) the officer's brain clicks into training, and (2) he becomes too busy trying to stay alive to notice the fear. So without their awareness, that fear gets stowed into a cubby hole in the brain's deep limbic system because it would just get in the way if it manifested in the midst of a CI. If left buried and unattended to, that fear that's fused with the trauma-based memory gets frozen into the present tense and often starts to show itself in strange and sometimes mysterious ways.

In the stage of EMDR treatment where trauma work is done, the fear (or other emotions) attached to the actual CI will surface. That's okay, because an EMDR session is exactly where and when it should surface so it can meet its final resolution (end). Initially, when the fear is accessed, it's intense. Then its intensity and strength reduce more and more. Eventually, because EMDR helps the brain work through the trauma-based memories, the disturbing reactions attached to the incident, such as fear, are neutralized (reprocessed). They no longer exist at a measurable disturbance level.

AVOIDING DEPRESSION AND MODULATING STRESS

Prior to resolving the targeted CI however, the brain is still struggling with a chronic state of Code 3/Blues & 2's. With PTSD, it becomes so hyper-focused on watching out for danger that, in the course of a day, it filters out many of the positive events, large or small. For the one with PTSD, a lot of positive things can get completely lost even as they're occurring, and a depressing, glass-half-empty view of life takes center stage. We have found brain changes due to PTSD[7] and depression (none of them good). Not only that, but PTSD itself can result in depression, which only complicates things even further.

Just as in weapons and tactical training, we create automatic responses by repeating actions over and over; the brain turns repeated thoughts and moods (such as stress and depression) into habits as well. We know for instance that exercise has a positive impact on brain function and mood. Making exercise a part of a life pattern can change how the brain functions, whether young, middle aged or elderly. This can happen with brains with or without PTSD. Both positive and negative actions can instigate change mentally, physically or both.

To understand this, and because it's highly relevant to the condition of PTSD, we need to review the functions of neurons and synapses, which you probably learned about in high school biology (who'd have guessed it would be important to you now?). The neurons relay electrical and chemical messages in the form of impulses throughout the brain. The synapses are essential for escorting the impulses across the gaps between neurons. Both act as neurological messengers.

This matters to you now because difficulties occur for the neurons and synapse when the brain is under a high level of sustained stress, i.e. PTSD or, is dealing with a case of depression. Those two mood disorders weaken the neurons and synapses and literally cause them to atrophy.[8]

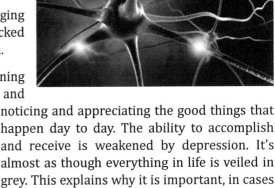

It's not unlike having the supply lines bringing food, ammunition and medical supplies attacked or shut down completely in a hostile region.

For the brain, the results of this weakening include great difficulty getting things done and

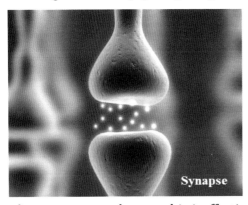

noticing and appreciating the good things that happen day to day. The ability to accomplish and receive is weakened by depression. It's almost as though everything in life is veiled in grey. This explains why it is important, in cases of PTSD, to avoid depression if possible.

PTSD often leads to the same grey veil across life, so with depression added into the mix you're getting double-teamed. In fact, PTSD can mimic depression so well that it's often misdiagnosed as depression. Being placed on antidepressants when you are not depressed is ineffective and can have troubling side effects, especially if you suddenly stop taking the medication. That said, if depression develops along with PTSD, medication should be seriously considered as a part of the treatment plan.

Suffice it to say, it's best to avoid the combination of PTSD and depression, if at all possible. It's also important to set up a system to enable stress modulation. Finally, we need to also start building the skills needed for the upcoming EMDR sessions. All three of these objectives can be facilitated with the first of two interventions my officers and I found effective. The first technique is called logging.

THE LOG: BECOMING A TRAINED OBSERVER IN A NEW WAY

As already stated, Warriors and Rescuers focus more attention on external cues than on internal reactions to situations and events. You're not all "robo cops" running around with cyborg internal circuitry, but most of you do have a limited bandwidth of acceptable reactions: happy, angry, hungry. Of course, you know you've got more going on inside than that, but you sure don't typically discuss it out loud.

If an officer is able to become a trained observer of inner reactions but refuses, he is probably not a good candidate for EMDR. However, often the refusal to do this technique is simply nervousness about somehow becoming all soft and fluffy. Calm down. I assure you that this technique makes my officers better at reading their reactions to things out on the ground. Signs that they'd normally have missed because they weren't paying attention to that small, quiet voice that was picking up on critical cues.

Logging is such an important technique that I train my officers how to do it in the second session of our work together. I hand them a small, pocket-sized spiral notebook. This is their Log and I instruct them to carry it with them "like a piece in a bad neighborhood." In other words, always.

HOW TO LOG REACTIONS

Logging works on a scale of 0 – 10, with 0 = no reaction at all and 10 = the strongest possible reaction. It's always a good idea to code your log events, in case you leave your notebook in the canteen or the roll call/parade room. No one but you needs to know the meaning of those entries, so be creative and concise. And remember, you're logging, not journaling, hence the small-sized notebook.

To get a sense of the how to use the log, imagine you were cut-off on the drive home after picking up your two-year-old daughter from preschool. The fact that this near miss could have injured or killed not just you, but also your child, might cause you to become enraged. You may become as angry as you could ever be. That would place you at a solid 10 on the scale. You would enter the reaction and the rating, in this case, "anger @ 10."

Models used for illustration

That evening after dinner, if your daughter climbed up on your lap and wrapped her arms around your neck and told you she loved you, you'd notice more reactions, probably a sense of joy and love. Both reactions are strong, so perhaps you'd enter it as "joy @ 8.5 and love @ 10."

You can see that the 0-10 scale rates the intensity of both positive and negative reactions. If you weren't angry at all about getting cut off, then you'd be at a 0. If you didn't feel any joy or love with that little show of affection, then you'd be at a 0.

Besides rating your emotional reactions, it's important to note any physical reactions to events, no matter how subtle. So you learn to notice physical sensations that occur, such as where physically you feel the reaction of joy. Let's just say that you feel that in your face–that it's like a relaxing around your eyes. Even that needs rating. So you give it a 7. Then you do the same check-in with your reaction of love. Maybe you feel that in your chest and you rate it a solid 9.5 in strength. To complete the log for that, you enter the date and time as well.

This is what your log might look like:
April 13, 2011 @ 17:30 +/- (Hug from Ashley)
Joy @ 8.5   Love @ 10.
Face/Eyes @ 7   Chest @ 9.5

Enter the location of any log-worthy reactions when appropriate. Sometimes things consistently happen at a certain place or doing a specific activity. For instance, intrusive images occur most commonly for my officers when (1) driving alone or (2) working out alone or (3) in the shower alone. Other reactions you have may show patterns like that. This can be very useful information.

Imagine, for instance, that you notice that on your drive to work, whenever you get on the freeway, you are seeing the scene or thinking about the incident even when you don't want to, perhaps because you're on a straight away that demands less focus than side streets. Then, because you're getting better at paying attention to internal cues, you might also realize that you're having both mental and physical reactions. Then you'd note and rate all of them on the 0-10 scale as soon as you safely could. The Log entry might look something like this:

May 14th @ 17:45 p.m.
Lex Res. ... That Dunkirk Ave 5150
dread @ 7 + nausea @ 4.5

This indicates that as your were passing Lexington Reservoir on 5/14, you visualized that suicide call you were sent out to on Dunkirk Ave. The log entry records that you re-experienced the response of dread @ 7 and you also had a flash of nausea at a strength of 4.5.

INFORMATION IS POWER

Seeing the pattern of what you're doing and where it's happening through the log enables you to figure out a strategy for derailing the activation of the traumatic material and keeping it from coming up when you don't want it to. You can take an inventory of your options based on those patterns. For instance, when you get to Lexington Reservoir, you may decide at that point in the drive to put in a favorite DVD or an audio book. By strategizing in this way, you are taking control.

It should be stated here that logging is not burying stuff away; it's containment. The Log is like a clear glass jar, not a hole in the ground. When you write entries into your Log, you're saying, *"Okay...I see you, I've noted you and when I'm ready we're going to deal with you...but for now I'm containing you and sticking you on the shelf and out of the way."*

The reason I included the information on the neurons and synapse is this: If you don't derail those intrusive images and thoughts, those neurons and synapse involved in bringing them up become stronger and better at doing that. It's as though every time they push that memory to the surface, those little things are pumping iron. If you interrupt them from carrying that information to your conscious awareness, they stop lifting those weights and that pattern will weaken. That's a good thing for you.

SOMETHING ELSE TO DO WITH REACTIVITY

Once your brain begins to think more frequently on that 0 - 10 scale, even if you can't log at the time of a reaction, you can note important information and you can become more able to more quickly shift gears. For instance, if you find your reactions shooting up to a 6 in reaction to something that you know shouldn't be more than a 2, you can act right then to alter course rather than get swept off the rocks. My officers often recount their internal conversation that sounds like this much of the time: *"My anger's just shot up. Wow, I'm up at a 6 with this! It's not that big a deal. I'm going to swing down to a 2 before I do something that I wish I hadn't."*

Having a more structured, objective means to measure and note *Log Worthy* reactions moves you from being like a field mouse in tall grass not knowing where the next predator might appear...

or

To being a hawk up in the thermals looking down to see things from a safer and more empowered position.

The view's much better from up here.

If you're logging a symptom reaction, you can take an almost clinical perspective rather than become upset. As you make the log entry, you might think, *"Well now, isn't that interesting–an 8 on anxiety"* and feel relief at being able to just notice it, put the Log back in your pocket, and go on with your day. You know it's written down, so you're not running away, burying it or surrendering to it. In fact, you are choosing to distance yourself from the intensity and to face the battle when you and your therapist agree that you're ready to engage. Until then, you take a measured, objective, management posture.

FLASH-POINT ANGER MANAGEMENT

Ethan was ironing his children's school uniforms for the next school day. It was sometime past 20:30. They'd eaten late because his wife was in the hospital recovering from surgery, so it was a one-man show that week.

He was beyond exhausted and rushed when an outbreak of sibling rivalry flared up. He had already ordered the kids to bed several times, so this fight over the remote control sent him over the falls. He started screaming at the top of his lungs. With iron in hand, he felt an incredible urge to hurl it through the kitchen door and right into the TV screen in the living room. Instead, he tightened his grip on the handle of the iron and did not move around the ironing board in order to run into the living room.

One simple thought played through his head that had come from our doing a Log review two weeks prior to that night. "Distance is my friend…don't move." This saved him and his children from a far worse meltdown that night that might have involved things breaking and possibly even uncontrolled physical aggression.

Ethan had noticed from his earlier logging that he'd progressively become more agitated and aggressive. He was stepping into situations such as this with the children and his reactions were beginning to scare him. That concern however, was overshadowed by his fear of where his thoughts would go at those times. These were terrifying him. This pattern became clear in his logging, so we were able to respond to that information by setting up straightforward response options. The one he'd found most effective was distancing and not moving to take any physical action.

LOGGING ANGER

My officers commonly tell me they are keenly aware of how disproportionate their anger has become with PTSD. What should be at a 2 or 3 can quickly escalate to a 6 or 8 when the brain feels it's under siege all the time.

Prior to developing PTSD, Ethan never had a history or tendency toward domestic violence/aggression. And now, after treatment, he is again on solid ground. He's a very loving husband and father who's very involved in his kid's lives. However, in its hard-hitting early stage, PTSD changed him. He'd been appalled by his thoughts and his escalating reactions during that time. Initially, he was too ashamed to tell me about these things. He did, however, start logging and rating his reactions. Finally, he had enough logging information compiled to realize that it was getting worse and he couldn't rein things in on his own. As he learned to trust me, he brought it up in session. Thank goodness.

For logging your anger incidents, I recommend that you first date and briefly note what triggered the anger reaction. Record and rate any forewarning physical indicators you noticed, such as clenching jaw/fists, face becoming hot/flushed, racing heart, tingling in arms/hands, tightness in chest. Whatever the physical indicators are, they're your early warning signs, telling you to be thinking about your preventative measures and options immediately.

Once the physical reactions are noted, then rate your anger response level on the 0-10 scale.

Then rate what you think would have been an appropriate level of anger or perhaps just frustration or agitation—you decide. After that, do a private tactical debriefing on how you would do that scenario differently given a "groundhog day" opportunity. Examples of possible alternatives are:
- Refuse to discuss the issue at that point, but instead give yourself time to calm down/think.
- Design immediate exit strategies to put in place to insure safety for yourself/others.
- Distractions: Those of you who are cops and have to neutralize potential violence are probably extremely skilled at this ability, so try it on yourself. Just remind yourself, "I don't have to go there right now. Instead I can do—."

If you have fear of becoming uncontrollably violent, the best first reaction is to remove yourself from the immediate area. It's a good idea to keep your cell phone on you to have a means of calling one of your safe people or leaving a message for your therapist. Even if the person you call doesn't pick up, sometimes just hearing that person's voicemail salutation and then leaving a message can be a break in the chain reactions that can lead to trouble. As an aside, if you call your therapist, be sure to leave a message. As you can well understand, hang-ups are worrisome to us.

Never get behind the wheel of a car if you're close to your tipping point. A walk around the block with the dog or just sitting in the car if the weather is bad are better options than pulling into traffic and having to take whatever other drivers might dish out to you on top of anything else.

Finally, there are anger management groups, books and courses that can expand on the options above. If anger management is proving to be more difficult and less containable with these items listed above, keep seeking more methods. It is especially important to discuss this issue with your therapist so that this can be worked on in sessions and/or so that referrals to additional resources can be made.

TOLERATING UNREASONABLE JOY

Having discussed powerful negative reactions, we come to an important and perhaps surprising point. Your logging needs to include positive reactions, too. This is critical to that first goal of beating back any potential development of a pattern of automatic negative thoughts. So, for example, that bear hug from your two-year-old is Log worthy material too, so that it is not easily forgotten. When you review your log, that good stuff continues to remind you that it's occurring.

Although it can be difficult—and, yes, frightening—to dare to feel joy and hope in the midst of PTSD, it is crucial that you at least tolerate them, and on occasion, let down your shield to let them in. By doing this, you develop what we refer to as *positive affect tolerance*[9] and it's critical. You do this by focusing your full attention to positive and good things when it is safe to do so. You've done this in the past, but with PTSD, your brain is under siege and has a very hard time "putting down the club and shield" to smell the roses. This is why the dark becomes even darker as time goes on. Atrophy happens.

So, your little girl climbs up and is looking into your eyes and she's smiling. Notice that and smile back. Then she delivers her great big hug and you smell her hair—she smells slightly of baby shampoo because her mother just gave her a bath and washed her hair. Deeply breathe in that wonderful clean-baby smell. And if this kind of little exchange usually ends with a tickle, notice the sound of her laughter and what you feel in your face (usually a smile) and chest (often like a weight being lifted). Just enjoy that moment with your daughter and force yourself to drink it in totally. In other words: delight in your child!

All of those things you take in require neurons and synapses to pick up and relay. These good things are the kind of input you need to be taking on-board to strengthen those messengers and escorts of positive reactions. The more you do that focused investment in these kinds of gracious "traveling mercies," the stronger they get. The stronger they get, the better your mood will be for a short period of time. Lasting improvement comes during the

Direct and Connect Stages, but it starts here. Remember that repetition teaches the brain habits. By focusing on positive reactions, the brain begins, bit by bit, to create points of light in a difficult and dark place.

This business of feeling good feelings will be hard-going at first. In fact, it may feel like you're just going through the motions, but that's because of the atrophy. In fact, if you can feel a lift for even a second or two, that's improvement. You build on that and work to get those seconds to extend into moments, and on and on from there.

Poet Raymond Carver captures this in his poem "This Morning."[10] He describes waking to a beautiful winter morning. The sky and the sea are an incredible blue and he decides to go outside to walk and to drink in all that nature has to offer. We pick up in this excerpt as he's having to do battle to take in the beauty all around him...

Where I gazed at the sea, and the sky,
and gulls wheeling over the white beach far below, all lovely
All bathed in pure cold light.
But, as usual, my thoughts began to wander.
I had to will myself to see
what I was seeing and nothing else.
I had to tell myself this is what matters, not the other.
(And I did see it, for a minute or two!)

For a minute or two it crowded out the usual musings
On what was right, what was wrong – duty,
Tender memories, thoughts of death,
how I should treat my former wife.

All the things I hoped would go away this morning.
The stuff I live with every day.

What I've trampled on in order to stay alive.
But for a minute or two I did forget everything else.
I know I did.
For when I turned back I didn't know where I was.
Until some birds rose up from the gnarled trees.
And flew in the direction I needed to be going.

Carver's description drives home what a struggle joy and taking in beauty can be even without PTSD. It is hard work to discipline our minds to focus on and take in solely what exists right there before us. Without that ability, which for most of us was lost just beyond childhood, we lose out on so much. For Warriors and Rescuers, that ability has been turned into scanning the environment for unfriendlies, or burning structures, or patients—even off duty.

It's time to work at regaining that early-life ability and to hold on for even briefly to what else is "out here" that can pull you out of what Carver described as those "usual musings."

This is why it's important to log the little things you notice that normally pass you by. If you're near the coast, a moment of noticing the light dancing on the water may be Log worthy. Or a bird singing its heart out as you're stopped at a light with the window rolled down. Every day you need to collect as many positive observations as negative ones (more of the positive if possible). Aim for four to six observations a day. The more you look for sources of "unreasonable joy" the easier it gets for your brain to spot them.

LOGGING AS CONTAINMENT AND PREPARATION FOR EMDR

Logging serves all the functions mentioned above: It allows you to (1) recognize and measure reactions; (2) strategize for more control of symptoms; (3) dial down over-reactivity; (4) manage flash-point anger; (5) build an increased awareness of need for family and officer safety; (6) strengthen positive neurotransmission by neurons and synapse; (7) scale back negative hyper-focusing.

In addition to those benefits, rating and logging your reactions help if or when you begin EMDR sessions to work through a target event. In the EMDR trauma work session, we will use the same 0–10 scale to measure the Subjective Unit of Disturbance (SUD). Your practice of logging, using that scale and your observation skills will simplify that process for you.

Once in the second stage of treatment and doing EMDR, logging becomes, of all things, a road map. The Log tracks and points out any need for "finish work" on a CI that is not quite sewn up. It also tells us what incident is next on the dance card—the one tapping you on the shoulder by means of intrusive images, nightmares, and other attention grabbing techniques.

Logging is an amazingly simple technique and so very useful to treatment. However, what logging *cannot* do, is cure PTSD. Even so, it can continue to come in handy out beyond the finish of treatment. Officers who have completed treatment with me often return to the logging practice if they experience suddenly reoccurring anxious or agitated moods that they can't trace to anything. The logging technique of noticing, rating and recording (using the 0–10 scale) stays with them, and so does that high-end training of being a more skilled trained observer.

EDUCATING THE CHILDREN

Just as helpful as it is for you to know and understand PTSD and what to expect on this treatment journey, the same can be said for those you care about...friends, family, and especially your children. Remember the near-miss incident of the officer whose little daughter jumped out at him at the top of the stairs? To as age-appropriate extent as possible, you can educate your children on PTSD-related concerns. You can also prepare them for changes in routine or behavior that may be necessary during Stages 1 and 2.

Of course, kids are going to make noise, fight with each other and playfully pop out from behind things, no matter how often you caution them. Even so, making children aware of the dangers of certain behaviors is the better part of wisdom. Lest you think you can hide this injury from your kids, let me remind you: the children often know something is wrong with Daddy or Mommy— without knowing *what* is wrong—before anyone else. So be proactive.

In a family meeting, you don't need to go in depth about the parent's PTSD, but you can say as much as you need to help them and to caution them about shouts and ambushes. This is especially true if (1) you think your children already know something's wrong, or (2) they're old enough to understand the condition. This is a family-by-family decision. Good communication can be good prevention. If you and your spouse or loved one are unsure about what to say and what to avoid, you might talk to your therapist. But given that, it's always up to the parents to decide what's best for their family.

A CAUTION ON JUDGING YOUR PROGRESS

The "brain injury" that results in PTSD is different for each person and so is the healing of the injury. This is a process of rebuilding "muscle" in the brain, and you know that takes time. Some days will just be better than others. Some days you'll feel you're making progress, others you'll feel like you're not. Don't be hard on yourself because of unrealistic expectations. Just keep focused and do the work.

The techniques you learn in this book facilitate that process. In Chapter 5 you gain two new tools to deal with intrusive images or thoughts and to start the process of dialing down the power of flashbacks. So…the way lies ahead of you now. The end may not be in sight just yet but it's out there.

Time to roll…

PHOTO CREDITS:

1. The Magical Compass: ©iStock.com/zulufriend
2. Synapse: ©iStock.com/Eraxion
3. Neuronal System: ©iStock.com/Sashkinw
4. Wood Mouse: ©iStock.com/Andrew_Howe
5. Red-Tail Hawk in Flight: ©iStock.com/DanCardiff
6. Daddy's Girl: ©iStock.com/Linda Yolanda
7. Light on the H20: Name withheld for security purposes...Thanks Sam!
8. Road By Night: ©iStock.com/WillSelarep

ENDNOTES:

Opening quotation taken from Brent Curtis and John Eldredge. *The Sacred Romance: Drawing Closer to the Heart of God*, Thomas Nelson Inc., Tennessee, 1998, 128.

1. F. Shapiro. *Eye Movement Desensitization and Reprocessing (EMDR): Basic Principles, Protocols, and Procedures,* 2nd Ed. Guilford Press, New York & London; 2001, 76.
2. F. Shapiro. Plenary Address, "Adaptive Information Processing & Case Conceptualization," EMDR International Conference, Boulder, Colorado, 2003.
3. D. Myers. The four-phase construct of "Protect, Direct, Connect, Select" was developed by Diane Myers, (unpublished manuscript). Originally devised for survivors of natural disasters, I've augmented it slightly by removing the "Select" phase since there's no need to select resources such as FEMA in a final phase of duty induced PTSD treatment. Phases 1-3 fit extremely well for the treatment plan purposes in my Warrior/Rescuer client population.
4. F. Shapiro. *Eye Movement Desensitization and Reprocessing (EMDR): Basic Principles, Protocols, and Procedures,* 2nd Ed. Guilford Press, 2001, 89, 125,
5. S. Foster; J. Lendl. "Eye movement desensitization and reprocessing: Four case studies of a new tool for executive coaching and restoring employee performance after setbacks," *Consulting Psychology Journal: Practice and Research,* Vol. 48, Issue 3, Summer 1996, 155-161.
6. F. Shapiro. *Eye Movement Desensitization and Reprocessing (EMDR): Basic Principles, Protocols, and Procedures,* 2nd Ed. Guilford Press; 2001; 91-220,
7. M. A. Friedman. "Post-Traumatic stress disorder," *The American Journal of Psychiatry*, vol. 155, no. 5, p. 8 http://wwwacnp.org/g4GNr01000111/CH109.html
8. R. S. Duman, J. Malbers, J. Shin Nakagawa, C. D. Sa. "Neuronal Plasticity and Survival in Mood Disorders," *Biological Psychiatry*, 2000; 48:732–739.
9. A. M. Leeds, References given in an EMDR training, "Positive Affect Tolerance and Integration Protocol" on June 17, 2006.
10. R. Carver. "This Morning," *Ultramarine*, New York: Random House, 1986.

CHAPTER 5
TAKING HIGH GROUND & ADVANCED CONTAINMENT

"The pictures were burned into my mind…They were happening right here, right now. My subconscious didn't know it wasn't actually real."[1]

Michael Ferrara,
Highly Decorated Ski Patrol, Paramedic, Search & Rescue

At the closing of Chapter 4, I suggested that you consider as a safety measure the education of family members about PTSD symptoms. This was not suggested to imply that symptoms are destined to become increasingly or consistently worse. In fact, in the first phase of treatment the opposite should occur. However, there can be the possibility of increased symptoms on occasions during treatment. If this happens these should be transitory and brief in nature and there are tools that you can use to deal with them effectively.

While logging and anger management can be foundational for containment and for tracking progress during treatment, some symptoms may require more advanced observation skills and containment options. The two described in this chapter can significantly help with more intrusive or overwhelming types of symptoms—flashbacks and intrusive thoughts. In addition, you will learn about three life patterns that can help override the isolation, the negative worldview and the destructive allure of the moth-to-flame activities that some enact to attempt to override their PTSD.

TAKING ON A WINNING MINDSET

The terrifying thing about an avalanche of overpowering feelings brought on by a flashback or intrusive thought is that you feel as if everything in its path will be either swept away or buried. But is that actually always true? This photograph shows another possibility. Look closely at this picture and you'll see that there's high ground to the right. With enough early awareness of the oncoming avalanche, you may have just enough time to clear out of the way. The terrain on the right is scalable…it's doable. The critical question is, can your brain move from helpless to proactive in order to get your body to react?

This is the point that one needs to arrive at with PTSD. If symptoms such as flashbacks are sweeping you away, you need to understand one important fact: It doesn't have to go that way every time. There are things you can do to increase your lead time due to early indicators. There are things you can do to get to high ground so that you don't get hit.

Containment techniques require actions on a number of different fronts: (1) verbal, (2) visual, (3) mental (cognitive), (4) physical and (5) relational. As time goes by, the frequency, intensity and duration of flashbacks abate and perhaps even cease. Even so, during treatment for some, these may come and go during Stage 2. This of course depends on the individual. These containment techniques have proven successful for my clients, but there is room for creativity and individuality. You may find approaches that work far better for you. Some of the best interventions come from client ingenuity. As long as the technique is safe, legal and not abusing of any substances, I encourage you to use your imagination.

The first group of PTSD symptoms listed in the DSM IV-TR are those that instigate re-enactment of a trauma.[2] These are:
- Flashbacks (acting or feeling like the event is happening again)
- Intrusive, upsetting memories of the event
- Nightmares (either of the event or of other frightening things)
- Feelings of intense distress when reminded of the trauma
- Intense physical reactions to reminders of the event (e.g. pounding heart, rapid breathing, nausea, muscle tension, sweating)

This chapter focuses on those symptoms (except for nightmares, which I discuss in Chapter 10) and how to contain them.

FLASHBACK CONTAINMENT:

One afternoon I was in session with a client and we were doing the pre-EMDR, listing of what CIs were going to be put on his "dance card." By this time he'd been trained in all containment techniques, but as he named the third CI, I could see him slipping away (avalanche style). He began speaking, but not to me. It was to a fellow officer who wasn't in the room.

I called to my client and ordered him to look at me, to look at my face (verbal, visual and relational) but he couldn't unlock the 1000-mile stare focused on the floor to the right of him. I then took hold of the soft rubber ball that I keep on the table between my chair and my client's chair and I moved that across his field of vision.

I ordered him to look at the ball and lock on to it, to follow it up as I raised it to eye level. He was able to start to disengage out of the flashback's pull because he could hear me (verbal), and his eyes followed the ball's movement. Then I told him to nod so I could know he was hearing me. He did (verbal and relational). Then I told him I was going to toss the ball to him and he was to catch it and toss it back to me. I then tossed the ball to him and he caught it. The 1000-mile stare had changed. He had to focus on the ball in order to catch it, and then to focus on to me in order to toss the ball back. He did this and then smiled. I smiled back (visual and relational).

We played catch with a couple more passes until his awareness was fully back in the room with me. Then we stopped. I had him do a couple of rounds of "tactical breathing" (explained below). Then we debriefed on what had just happened (mental) and I had him practice "going to baseline"(to be discussed later). We did this several times so he could learn how to pull himself back into the present more efficiently on his own.

That exchange involved a number of different intervention modalities so that my officer could regain contact with real time to become grounded:

1. Verbal - giving spoken commands
2. Auditory - listening to things around you
3. Visual - placing an object into the field of the 1000-mile stare to interrupt visual locking up
4. Physical - instructing the officer on what I wanted him to do as a physical action
5. Relational - we played catch back & forth to get him fully reoriented to me and my office
6. Mental - once he was back-in-the-office with me, I reminded him that it was a past memory that felt like the present but that it was a historical event all the same. At that point I also asked what happened just before he started to slip into the flashback so that he could recognize his unique "early warning system" indicators... Very Important.
7. Breathing - deeply in through your nose and slowly out through your mouth. Breathing in through your nose helps to loosen up your chest so it's easier to inhale. It's common for one's chest to tighten up as they're going into/through a flashback and that only increases the stress reactions.

Having flashbacks or intrusive, upsetting memories of an incident (sometimes referred to as emotional flooding) in session creates opportunities to coach an officer through containment options. I classify that in-session work right up there with practicing for weapon jams in trainings on the weapons range. In truth, this is taking far more time to describe and type out than it takes to do in real time. In real time this whole exchange with my officer took around 90 seconds to run through items 1–5 above. Beyond that, tactical breathing took around 12 seconds for each complete inhale-hold-exhale cycle. This intervention took us around 36 seconds in total.

In brief, Going-to-Baseline is a method to generate positive experiences by bringing up a great memory with lots of sensory input to counter the strong sensory memories of traumatic events. When my officer went to Baseline in the session recounted above, I gave him all the time he wanted with that great memory during that session. That took about five minutes, which is not a big loss of time in the grand scheme of things and great practice in what to do if a flashback occurs outside of sessions.

Once learned, none of these techniques are dependent on having someone there to direct you in them. If, because of your advanced skills for reading the signs (more on this in a bit), you pick up on indications of an oncoming flashback, there are many things you can do on your own.

GOING SOLO WITH ANTI-FLASHBACK TACTICS

1. Mental: You can initiate your own internal self-talk about how the flashback is only a memory that isn't aware of that fact yet. This means that at every opportunity you need to start thinking and talking about traumatic memory in the past tense rather than the present tense. How we think and talk about things does play an important role in how they're automatically perceived.

Even if you're alone, you can still use verbal cues by reminding yourself that it's only a flashback but it's not happening anymore. If you feel yourself slipping into a flashback you can say something such as, "I'm not going there now." That can be attached to a metaphorical concept. In my client base we call it "refusing to get on the express bus to perdition." The empowering aspect of that is in knowing that even if a bus comes along, stops and opens the door, you don't have to get on.

2. Verbal: If you initially have difficulties gaining traction in order to get yourself out of flashback, you should consider going over some verbal instructions with your spouse or partner. Let them know that if they see you "slipping away," or if you suddenly start reporting-in about what's occurred down range or in that CI in the present tense (*i.e. "things are raining down everywhere–I can't get through to my team")*, then they can to take verbal action. Tell them to remind you in a strong, clear voice that this event happened however long ago and that it's not happening now. Have them remind you where you are and that you survived, that it's over and you are not there any longer. *This doesn't diminish the significance of what occurred, or the meaning it has to you because those things do matter. It's just putting it into the correct designation of being a past event.* Again, if alone, you can still use verbal cues by reminding yourself that it's a flashback and that it's not happening in the present/now.

3. Visual: If you feel your eyes glazing over, the first thing to do is to control your visual field. Move your head and eyes rather than allowing them to freeze or lock up. Find something to concentrate on and focus on its details, such as a doorknob, a stain on the wall or the scene outside the window. Notice the details but don't fixate. To ground yourself even more, reach out and touch whatever it is you're focusing on.

4. Auditory: Work on listening to the sounds around you, such as traffic, or the fridge running, or birds. Again, focus on the details—you can try to count how many birds are singing, or how many cars are passing.

5. Physical: The sense of touch and movement can powerfully ground you in the present moment. Reach out and touch something; if you're at home, kick your shoes off and slide your feet on a carpet or a cold floor. Shake your hands and arms or jump up and down briefly. Moving helps to disengage being physically locked down and encourages mental movement as well. IMPORTANT: If you have the urge to break something, DON'T. Fight that urge. It only scares people around you. It isn't a good habit to start and if you've been doing it, knock it off. It's not a good thing to link relief to causing breakage or being violent.

6. Relational: Your ability to reach out and engage someone, even a pet, when you feel yourself slipping away can bring you back to the present. That said, if the loud uncorking of champagne in a posh restaurant sends you under the table, the relational part will have to be initiated by whomever you're with. My experience with clients is that no sooner are they taking hard cover than they're out of the flashback. That would then be a good time to state that you've just lost your contact lens or that your napkin has slipped onto the floor and you're retrieving it before the main course arrives. Be creative and think ahead.

7. Tactical Breathing: At the onset of a flashback, your chest tends to tighten and breathing becomes shallow due to the stress reaction. To counter that and avoid slipping away, use this breathing technique. To the count of four, breathe in slowly through your nose. Hold your breath to the count of four. Then slowly exhale through your mouth to the count of four. Breathing in through your nose helps to loosen tightness in the chest, so it's easier to inhale.

Important: Listen for sounds around you such as traffic or the sound or the fridge running. If you're outside and it's too quiet to hear traffic, then listen for birds. Try to count how many there are singing.

IN CASE OF FLASHBACK—AVOID TOUCH

It is noteworthy that when my clients go into a flashback in session, I don't touch them. When the timing is right, and after warning them, I'll toss a soft foam ball. It's important that before anyone throws anything to you, or touches you during a flashback, that they warn you. During a flashback you may believe that it's INCOMING! time again. That's not the time to get walloped by some object out of the blue. So if that "catch & toss" becomes one flashback response strategy you choose to make use of, go over these things with family or close friends.

If you're close to someone with PTSD and reading this, look back to the above exchange I had with my officer as he was going into flashback. You'll see the following: (1) I gave him specific instructions to visually follow the ball I'd put in his field of vision; (2) I checked to make sure he was hearing me by his response to my verbal instructions; (3) I informed him of what I was going to do next and what I wanted him to do in return. There were *no* surprises for him in anything that I did. A simple phrase to repeat to yourself if you're faced with a friend or loved one in flashback is, *"Flashbacks are not a good time for surprises."*

Concern about violence in a flashback is viable. This needs to be discussed and alternative options must be worked out to insure safety for everyone. Again distance can be your friend. If you're post-deployed military, rethink carrying a Benchmade auto folder or other knife when in the house or among friends at a gathering.

Additionally, if the trauma involved being attacked/ambushed, you will recall from which side. You need to inform those close to you, who just may be present if you go into flashback, which side *not* to approach you from. This is critical information to share, because the amygdala believes, "Whatever comes at me is trying to kill me." Needless to say, if attacks came from multiple directions, this would still be the case. You're going to have to think ahead tactically about what's the best means for pulling yourself out of the flashback (i.e. visual, movement, use things to ground you) and plan your strategies.

EARLY SIGNS – SEEING IT COMING SOONER

The sense that flashbacks come on without warning is common for those with PTSD. That belief increases the sense of helplessness in controlling flashbacks. Your newly trained skills coming out of observations and logging will be strategically important in changing this. It also would be wise to establish a pattern of conducting your own "post-flashback debriefing" to gather clues about what occurs just prior to the full onset of a memory avalanche. Again, your Log can come in handy for this, be sure to enter any and all information you can recall.

Here are the types of observed "pre-flashback" indicators I've gathered from my officers:

1. Hearing changes:
- I heard my heart beating in my ears
- Tinnitus in my right/left/both) ear/s got louder and louder
- Sounds around me started to sound distant/quieter/went silent altogether
- It sounded as if I was under water…a whooshing sound/garbled aspect to noises around me

2. Visual changes:
- I started to get tunnel vision
- My peripheral vision started to go black
- I felt my eyes lock onto (*something in the surrounding area*) and I couldn't move my gaze

3. Somatic (body) changes:
- I felt dizzy
- I felt numb
- I felt my jaw clench
- My mouth went dry
- My arms/legs suddenly felt weak
- My chest became tight…it was hard to breath in
- I suddenly felt sick…like I was going to throw up
- There was a sudden tingling in my hands/arms/legs/face…
- I felt something like lightening/electricity surge through my whole body
- I felt cold/hot all of a sudden (this may be in specific location i.e. face/hands, etc.)

Unfortunately flashbacks don't always come pre-announced by such indicators as those listed above. Sometimes they hit suddenly as though someone's just lobbed a flash-bang right into your brain.

SUDDEN ONSET FLASHBACKS

It was a quiet Sunday afternoon and the entire family was home. AJ's wife asked their teenage son if he'd climb up on a chair to replace a burned out light bulb in the kitchen that had gone out earlier that morning.

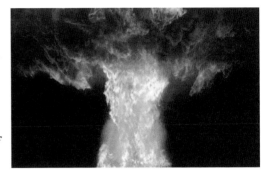

As AJ was at the kitchen counter making sandwiches for everyone, Jordon brought in the chair and replaced the bulb. He then jumped off the chair and landed a few feet behind his father.

AJ suddenly whirled around and grabbed Jordon by the throat slamming him up against the wall as the chair went flying off to the side. AJ's wife watched in shock and horror as her husband's right fist pulled back and was primed to slam into their son's handsome but terrified face. She shouted as loudly as she could, "AJ, it's Jordon! Don't hit him! It's your son!"

The post-flashback debrief we did in session just two days after this incident told us which CI was going to be the first we'd be doing EMDR with in the rapidly approaching Phase 2. AJ knew exactly where that sensory input had dropped him into. It also was able to help AJ understand what set off his reactions, which he felt horrified and terrified about.

The flashback landed him into the memory of a foot patrol he'd been on in a highly troubled sector. AJ had passed a house that had a 4-ft. cement wall surrounding an overgrown front yard. Just as he went past, someone who'd been concealed behind the overgrowth had come over wall and had landed hard just behind him. Spinning around, AJ turned just in time to see a metal baseball bat closing in on his head.

Should a flashback come on the heels of a certain smell (the fastest way to a flashback), a sudden movement or a loud noise, the physical reaction (diving for hard cover/moving to engage in physical combat) will happen too quickly to be able to curtail initial reactions.

There are two things that can bring you back out of that. The first is to train your brain to realize you're in a flashback (just as you can realize when you're sleeping that your having a nightmare and you're not really there). This dovetails with the internal self-talk you should start having that underscores that flashbacks are memories from the past and not currently happening.

The second thing comes from what we've been able to gain from flashback debriefs. We discovered that these types of incidents, back when they occurred, often had radio contact during those encounters as they were actually occurring in the past. Typically the officer wanted contact with dispatch/other officers even if they couldn't initiate it at the time. This has meant in most cases my officers are able to pick up verbal commands during their flashbacks. In AJ's case what he locked onto was his wife's screams and the words, "It's your son!" That was what stopped the entire sequencing of his defensive tactics in their tracks.

This again underscores the potential benefits of education for family members. It also calls for proactive situational awareness regarding things that can set you up for such rapid-fire flashbacks in those innocent day-to-day life occasions.

This suggestion of formulating preventative accommodations can bring on a bit of resistance at times. It can seem to go against the soldier's own m.o. The gist of such resistance can sound like this: "No one should have to change their behaviours because of my stuff…" or, "I don't want to give into this s--- …I should be able to override it instead."

While these are all fine and lofty sentiments, it may be better to choose one's battles wisely in the early stages of this journey (preferably ones you have a chance to win at present). Additionally, instigating containment for control over symptoms should be seen as short-term. You're not being asked to marry them—just to date.

This battle with flashbacks should not last forever if you're in with a highly skilled therapist who knows what he/she is doing clinically. This is true even if you've had the flash-bang type response for years. AJ's inciting critical incident had occurred over 15 years earlier. In fact, his #1 goal that he wanted out of our work together was to be rid of his magnified startle response.

AJ'S POST TREATMENT OUTCOME

In AJ's case EMDR was highly effective in defusing the magnified startle response and sudden flashbacks in his life once we neutralized that incident described above along with another that involved a near miss with death.

As we were winding down and finishing up in Phase 3, AJ came into session one day with an ear-to-ear smile on his face. He told me a "little incident" had happened late the previous week and he ceremoniously pulled out his Log to recount it to me.

He'd been waiting for two other officers on his team to arrive for a run that previous Friday and was standing in a hallway with his back to a long window that looked out onto a parking lot. He was in conversation with two other officers (who were facing both him and the window he was standing in front of) when the others from their team arrived outside. Those two out in the parking lot decided it would be funny to bang on the window to see AJ jump (his startle response was renowned to all in his life).

Just prior to these two outside starting to pound thunderously on the window, the others, who'd been talking with AJ inside, had seen what was coming. The funny thing was that when the sudden banging and rattling occurred, AJ saw the other two officers who were facing him jump (even though he realized afterwards that they'd been expecting the noise that came). He, on the other hand, didn't jump at all. Instead he turned around and looked out the window at his other teammates and smiled and waved to them. They smiled and waved back. Then AJ pointed to his watch to indicate that they were late.

In that session AJ stated, "This thing, in the past, would have just ruined me for the rest of the day."

No longer were there panic-then-rage responses, a racing heart rate or the sense of shame and embarrassment. AJ's Log entry recounted that training day incident in this way:

4/4th: Training Day (window pounding)

Fear: Anger: **Happy** to see "Tweedle Dumb & Tweedle Dumber"
                              arrive *(not their real names)*

@ 0   @ 0   **@ 9**

It should be noted here that sleep deprivation can increase the startle response significantly. If once fully treated for PTSD that magnified response returns out of the blue on an odd day/night, assess the amount of sleep you've recently had (or not had). If you haven't been severely re-traumatized, (even then it's extremely rare to come down with PTSD again if you're doing good maintenance) it's more than likely related to lack of sleep.

Sleep deprivation dampens down the brain's ability to inhibit the startle response, so this sudden onset of its increase is a fairly straightforward thing to fix. Catching up on and maintaining adequate amounts of sleep is the priority.

HOW INTRUSIVE IMAGES/MEMORIES/THOUGHTS GET THROUGH

In moving to containment of intrusive images/memories/thoughts of traumatic events, it will be important to understand how these gain access to "brain time" in the first place. As previously mentioned in Chapter 4, there are places and activities that are primed for ushering up these CI related intrusions. In fact, these tend to occur far more often with my clients than flashbacks do.

Driving, working out and taking a shower are the three most common places my clients report (but these intrusions can happen just about anywhere) and they have some attributes in common. One is being in a relatively undistracted, relaxed state while typically alone, and the other is the occurrence of bi-lateral stimulation in the brain that they can all instigate. This is where both the right and left hemispheres are getting alternating stimulation that occurs by means of visual, physical or even auditory sensory input that the brain takes in.

This same bilateral stimulation happens in REM sleep. That is accomplished when our eyes move back and forth during that stage of sleep. In doing that, both the right and left hemispheres get alternately activated (right – left – right – left…). When this happens with normal non-traumatic memory, it's as though a book opens, enabling access to the story inside. With the help of the hippocampus, the amygdala proceeds to make sense of the story as context, connections and learning occur. At times, solutions to problems are even found during that state of sleep. This is where the phrase, "sleep on it" comes from. Once that adaptive learning process is done, the normal, non-traumatic memory is then taken off the librarian's cart and allocated into other places within the brain.

How intrusive images and/or memories come to us in day-to-day activities is accomplished a bit differently, but with the same bi-lateral feature. For example, when we drive, both of our eyes are seeing things out the front field of vision as well as the peripheral fields. Our peripheral vision is aware of things moving by on both sides of the vehicle...trees, cars, kids, streetlights, etc. Similarly, when working out, both sides of the body are moving. In the shower, unless yours is a rather uniquely constructed model, both sides of your body are getting hit with warm drops of water.

The bi-lateral stimulation needn't be in perfect rhythm. If you've ever watched a dog or a baby's eyes moving during REM sleep, you'll notice those movements are keeping anything but perfect time. Difficulties arise whether awake or asleep, when the amygdala has a big trauma-based memory or multiple traumatic memories stuck in there, overstaying their welcome. These are the images/memories/thoughts that will be pushed up to the surface when you end up in that quiet, solitary state coupled with bi-lateral stimulation. This is because the amygdala labels them as PRIORITY.

Most of the time, these kinds of intrusive images/memories/thoughts won't cause the loss of awareness x 3 that flashbacks do. Even so, your brain will be preoccupied with thoughts or images of your traumatic event/s and their nature is typically disturbing. Then you're dropped back into recalling a place/time you don't want to be...again.

This difficulty caused the creation of this handy little containment technique to be factored into the protocol my first generation officers and I devised. We call it "Going to Baseline." It simply means being brought out of that disturbing image, memory or train of thought and back to a normal baseline. It's done by fighting fire with fire—a wonderful memory verses a terrible one, or a great relational and moving pattern in life verses an isolating and locked down one are two different ways to go to baseline.

#1. GOING TO BASELINE WITH A GREAT MEMORY DU JOUR

As incredible as the amygdala is, it can't multitask with two opposing images or memories at the same time. Remember that the most wondrously, incredible (emotionally charged) memories of your life story are stored in there, just as are the most emotionally charged horrifying, terrible memories. But the gate is narrow. That's a good thing. While memory flooding can occur with multiple memories of a like-kind, this happens only because they're chain-linked together with similar strong responses such as terror, horror, sadness, etc. These things bind similar types of trauma together like one miserable, dysfunctional little family.

Opposing positive memories, however, are not birds-of-a-feather with the trauma-based ones. So when these two different memories try to get-out-the-gate, vying for your attention, they don't go in single file, chain-linked style. Instead, opposing memories make a run for the gate and try to crowd the other one out. Additionally, the same low impact type bi-lateral stimulation that you're receiving when you drive, workout or shower helps to usher both types of memories to the surface.

The conscious decision you must make then is to decide to choose the good memories over the bad or the ugly to give your attention to. You then become the "Gate Keeper" and you decide which one is going to get through. There's a method to this containment technique that will require some "lay-up" work first and it's very important that you follow these instructions.

1. You'll want to get out your Log and turn it over to the back cover and open it up. At the top of that very back page you'll want to write "Memories du Jour." I have you do it this way for two reasons. First, your Log is with you all the time, and second, putting these baseline memories in the very back makes them easy to find so you don't need to fish through your logged entries to find them.

2. Underneath that you're going to want to number and write down the names of 10 -12 of your most amazing memories that you've ever had. The number here is important. You're going to want to rotate around to different memories or else if you keep doing the same one over and over again, you're going to neutralize it. That's what you'll want to do in EMDR with your traumatic memories, but not with the splendid ones.

Don't write out the memories…just what you would call them. For example…
- Our son's/daughter's birth
- The hardest and best laugh we ever shared
- The best sunset I ever saw (in Spain/Greece/BVI)
- Winning the Gold medal in the All Stars in Jr. High Little League

The objective is not to remember a whole day (or heaven forbid the whole labor and delivery!) but rather, the most glorious moment within that entire event. So…if you wrote down "the trip to Italy," then you'd want to narrow it down to the most favorite day, then the most favorite part of that day, then the most incredible moment in that part of the day.

3. Here you'll need to get someone you really trust to sit down and try this next part out with. I want you to describe to them in great detail the story of that boiled-down-to-the-best-most-incredible-magnificent-memory. Do it so that they can almost reach out and touch it, breath it in, see the colors, hear the sounds. I'll walk you through one of these Baseline memory containment trainings from a session with one of my officers:

First tell me what you're seeing…the scene you're looking out on in that memory:
I'm standing out on the cliffs overlooking the sea on the island in Greece. I'm looking out over the village and beyond…out to the bay and its sunset.

What colors do you see?
Crimson, pink and brilliant yellows and orange…it almost hurts to look at the sky it's so intense.

And what are you hearing?
The sea birds off in the distance…but closer in the little children down in the village walking along the street…they're laughing.

What does the air smell like?
Freshly baked bread…it's wafting up from the village like it does every evening. People come in on their way home from their days to buy bread for dinner, or they'll send the children down to the bread…it smells like life! I can smell it at a 9 right now…incredible!

And what's the air feel like?
There's a soft breeze but it's warm. I'm in a t-shirt and shorts; it's totally comfortable.

And how would you describe what your reaction is to all of these things you're taking in right now?
It's…it's hard to … no … it's quiet…it's quiet inside. It's peaceful and content. It's perfect.

And where do you feel that physically?
In two places...in my neck and shoulders. They're totally relaxed right now. That tightness is gone completely. In my chest...it's easier to breath. Ha! I can still remember the smell of that bread!

DEFUSING DISTRESS OR BODY PAIN WITH MEMORY REMINDERS

Once we've gone through this good memory the first time, we then will work on gaining back this improved and positive mood and/or physical relief a couple of times before the end of session. If it can be done "on demand" without needing to go through the memory, then better still. This can facilitate a more rapid response if the officer gets hit with a distressing mood/body memory pain outside of sessions.

There's flexibility in this intervention however. If on-demand shifts are difficult, or you just want to do that walk down memory lane, the option is still there. Just quickly access whatever the memory du jour is for that day and override the negative one that's attempting to gain dominance.

The above Baseline intervention is not hypnosis and there's no trance inducement involved. The memory is bringing up well preserved sensory/body memories attached to the scene that are positive in nature. A client's mood can shift to the positive end of the spectrum rapidly in the brief time this exercise is being done. It's not unusual to get positive reaction ratings of 7–10 on the 0–10 scale when the officer came into session originally at a 2–5. Conversely, the negative things they came in with will go down measurably.

THE WORDS "REMEMBER WHEN"

What we found in devising this technique was that going through it with eyes closed for the first time in containment training sessions really strengthened the details of the scene (not recommended while driving of course). Next, we found that talking the story through out loud (even if no one's there to hear the story) with eyes open could make it stronger and more able to focus on than just thinking about it silently (although in a pinch you do what you must). The last, but most important bit of instruction is this: the whole idea behind the *Memory du Jour* is just that. You choose the memory-of-the-day at the very start of your day (or night). If you have an intrusive thought or image, you then go into the fight-fire-with-fire m.o. You have whatever memory you want to click into pre-selected, so you're good-to-go.

If and when the need arises to refuse to take that "express bus to perdition," then you're ready to refuse and then to choose another route. Instead, take the other bus...back to Greece, or to the top of "El Cap" or surfing that best wave you've ever had (green room and all) where it seemed to last forever...go there instead.

IMPORTANT THINGS TO DO:

1. ***Use Good Judgement:*** You need to be prudent on when and where you use this containment technique. My clients have used it quite commonly in the car as they're driving alone. We've never had any accidents created by thinking of the positive versus the terrible memories while driving (although there have been a couple of close calls when the terrible ones have hit). The fact is that drivers think of things as they drive, listen to the radio or have conversations with passengers. That said, you need to be smart and use common sense.

2. *Tell the Memory in the Present Tense:* This is just the opposite of what I've instructed you to do with flashbacks. With positive memories I'll ask questions to get the memory started with a client in a way to intentionally generate a present tense description (i.e. what are you looking out on with that view?...what are you hearing?...what's the air feel like?). That way you're in the scene vs. describing it. This is why my officer could actually smell the bread at a very respectful score of 9. That olfactory memory is still preserved along with sights, sounds, even the feeling of that gentle, warm breeze in the "It's still happening now" in the amygdala.

3. *Start with the Visual Memory First:* This I suspect is a guy thing. Men are highly visual creatures. Once you've got the scene clearly in sight then you can pretty much go with whatever sensory based memory comes up next (smells, sounds, the feel of the air, the sense you had as you took it all in... etc.).

4. *Notice the Positive Memory's Impact Both in Mood and Body:* It's important to link up with the internal reactions you've got attached to the memory and to notice where you feel those physically (for example, it may be relief of muscle tension in the shoulders/neck). This will enable you to work on getting good at bringing up those positive, calm, upbeat, type physical manifestations, getting them to strengthen and occur faster on demand. This is a great shortcut to getting relief immediately by using the Pavlovian method to accomplish that. Instead of having to ring the bell AND bring the food...eventually the dogs just salivated at the sound of the bell.

Remember, you can "up source" the positive physical reaction with practice and increased skill, perhaps eventually without needing to go back to the *memory du jour*. Then you can kick into that positive response to override the stress and/or trauma driven ones (that also can get generated without going to the CI due to over-practicing). It relies on how well you can discipline your mind and your body to work together with the positive verses negative memories and physical reactions to them.

5. *This Too Shall Pass:* The upward mood swing won't be permanent, but to get the concept of how much sway you can have with your mood is yet another critical piece of high ground to claim as your own. Work at extending the positive mood's staying power as time goes on.

6. *Share the Wealth:* Last, but most important of all, doing the same baseline memory over and over will change it to a past event, thereby making it less opulent. That's *not* what you'd ever want to do with that kind of brilliant memory. Share the wealth among a good collection of memories. At least 10, but better to have 12 (or even more if you've got them!) on that list.

MANAGING INTENSE PHYSICAL REACTIONS

The last cluster of symptoms in the DSM IV-TR list given at the start of this chapter involves a number of physical reactions. Rapid heart rate and breathing, nausea, muscle tension and sweating all, or in part, show up with a sudden reminder of a traumatic event. It's important to get medical assistance to rule out that these may be indicating a medical emergency. However, even enroute to the ER, tactical breathing can slow the heart rate down and help to regulate breathing. Furthermore, going to Baseline can help to relax muscles.

If all of those systems, heart, breathing and body muscles quiet down, then the sweating may, as well. In this kind of a scenario, it would be best to start with tactical breathing in order to bring down the heart and breathing rates and then go to the mental options of thinking up a good memory to go with.

#2. GOING TO BASELINE "IN LIFE"

Ryan's PTSD forced him to have to go off on sick leave, which was, as is usually the case, one of the worst parts of those early days. He was taken out of the game, taken out of daily contact with his support group of other officers. Then he was left isolated and alone during those long days when his wife and kids were carrying on with their lives.

On around the fourth day of this, he found himself yet again on the couch just having burned up an hour and a half of just staring into space. Something was different though...something that had brought him out of the 1000-mile stare. It was his dogs (a relational intervention).

Something struck him so strongly at that moment as he "came to." As he looked down at these two dogs, each one was sitting at his feet, and each one had their heads resting on one of his knees. They were both staring intently right into his face. It was like a focused campaign of empathy.

As he recounted that moment in his Log to me in session that week, he said that this "doggie knee hug thing," they'd never done before in all of their years...ever.

Log Review: Loneliness dropped down in intensity to a 4 from being up at an 8.5.

Now he was noticing that if he sat for too long on the couch they'd come and do the same thing–every time. It seemed like a conspiracy to bring him back into the fold. He began walking those two daily out in the hills. Hours a day they were out there – together. That really did help. They never had to leave for work in the morning. In fact Ryan became their "day job."

FIRST: BE IN GOOD COMPANY

The strong tendency to isolate and withdraw has already been commented on. And while it is important—no imperative—to have a good ring of supportive, trusted friends and family surrounding you, it's hard work to be with others when you're not feeling all that good about life in general. Also, if you're off work on the DL due to your PTSD and/or due to physical injuries as well, then chances are everyone else is working. That means there will be long stretches of time you'll be on your own.

One of the first questions I ask an incoming officer is if there's a *good* dog in his/her life. Ryan would not have been the first client nor the last whose very life relied not just on therapy but on a "good dog presence" in his herd.

In my clinical opinion, good dogs are responsible for at least 50% of the success in keeping my most at-risk clients alive. They're there 100% of the time and they know when one of their "pack" is wounded inside. They "show up" and they stay with them. Good dogs are incredible and I have every belief that they do go to heaven. Cats can be wonderful too, but they're hard to take for runs on the beach.

In Life Baseline is a life pattern skill you take out into the world. This is just simply deciding that you're going to heave your cares over the side for a set amount of time and head out to clear your head. You can choose who you want to spend your time with on these endeavors, but the best companion for this, that we've found (if you're not allergic), is a good dog. They're easy company, full of unconditional love, they adore how you drive and anywhere you want to go is just great by them. Perfect...

SECOND: FIND BEAUTY AND LET IT HAVE ITS WAY

Writer John Eldredge, in his book *The Journey of Desire*, recounts the battle he struggled with to eventually come to terms with the tragic loss of his best friend and co-author, Brent Curtis, in a rock-climbing accident.

John wrote about how in the days following Brent's death, as the anesthetizing effects of shock were wearing off, he found he was closing into himself. He wrote:

"Conversation required more than I was able to give. Frankly, I didn't want to talk to anyone, not even God. The only thing that helped was my wife's flower garden. The solace I found there was like nothing else on earth."

He wrote in his journal amidst those dark days:

"Sitting outside this evening, the Shasta daises swaying in the gentle breeze on their long stems, the aspens shimmering without light, the full moon rising over the pine-crested bluff...only beauty speaks what I need to hear. Only beauty helps.

Simone Weil was absolutely right – beauty and affliction are the only two things that can pierce our hearts. Because this is so true, we must have a measure of beauty in our lives proportionate to our affliction. No...more. Much more."[3]

If ever there is a time when one's "hardware of the soul" needs to be given deep solace by some kind of beauty...the kind that can reach in and "pierce our hearts" (in a good way), it's when you have PTSD or when you're lost within the deepest pain of grief. That said, some caught in the depths of PTSD, especially when coupled with overwhelming grief, can't see beauty to save their lives. This can be extremely dangerous.

Michael Ferrara who's quote opened this chapter, in the *Outside* article that recounted his case of PTSD, described the state he was in after all he'd "seen" on duty and off for 30 long years. Then there came the free-fall he went into following the tragic loss of his best friend. He stated to writer Hampton Sides in that interview:

"I was in a fog of despair. I couldn't see beauty anymore, only darkness."

Sides wrote, *"He withdrew into himself. He couldn't sleep, couldn't think. On his days off, he wouldn't leave the house. The slide show played without cease."*[4]

Being chronically under siege with PTSD will cause "lock down" to happen. This occurs both inside as well as physically. Therefore, another thing that's most crucial to stabilization ironically is beginning to move again. Physical movement helps to unlock the inside's "closing down."

Michael Ferrara got in and got treatment. In fact he received EMDR Therapy. What is relevant to his containment technique of *In Life Baseline* however, is something that Hampton Sides comments on that's worthy of quoting here. I believe it's important:

> *"Ferrara has found a similar restorative power in physical activity that involves a rhythmic, left-right-left-right action, which may physically mimic EMDR. Soldiers diagnosed with PTSD have widely found that vigorous repetitive-motion exercise such as ice skating and rollerblading can be extremely helpful in keeping the disorder's symptoms at bay. For many PTSD suffers though, the most helpful sport of all seems to be Nordic skiing. Ferrara has taken to it with a vengeance. In fact he's made cross-country skiing a central part of his recovery."* [5]

Recall back to Chapter 3 where my military asset chose to swim when he came home. He also doubled that up with tae kwon do (TKD) to keep his martial arts skills honed and, as he'd pointed out, to release the violence into the air. Swimming (low adrenaline and rhythmic) and TKD proved to be a good combination for him as he readjusted to post deployment life.

THIRD: FOREGO THE "CALCULUS OF MOTH-TO-FLAME"

Ferrara had been trying for years to self-medicate his PTSD (pre-meltdown) with high–octane sports done on his off-time from his high-octane jobs. The more deadly, the better the rush. The better the rush, the further at bay PTSD would seem. But it didn't work.

I have worked in some noisy foreign places and have witnessed this same calculus of moth-to-flame take hold of Warriors who are dangling above the flame of PTSD. Some of these choose go out to the tormented regions...they go out to the foreign missions where war resides. They carry with them that same false notion...the more lethal the better. What they learn is that this can't end the war that comes inside. Going closer to the flame just fries the moth.

What Ferrara learned was there's recovery and healing that can't be had through extreme sports and adrenaline. Interviewed 11 months into doing combined psychotherapy and a drug rehab program he said:

> *"I've got joy again...I'm running. I'm climbing. The slide shows have stopped. My eyes are open again - I'm here."*[6]

He's also discovered that endorphins are far and away more effective in his journey (out of PTSD and now in his lifelong recovery from drug addiction) than adrenaline dumping ever could have been. *That's* what I want to stress here...endorphins will out perform adrenaline in this rite of return.

In this chapter and the previous one, I've described logging, going to Baseline, keeping good company, finding beauty and now endorphin producing modes of exercise. These self-driven interventions my Warriors and Rescuers have found help them to override disturbing images/memories/thoughts/physical memories and moods that may come up when working out, driving, etc.

An ounce of determination is better than paying with a pound of flesh any day, so decide if you're willing to out climb and outmaneuver the avalanche. *In Life Baseline* means getting out and moving. It doesn't mean getting on the computer to buy things online or watching a big screen TV to view others moving. It means moving and getting *your own* rhythm back. It means listening to your own breathing and the wind rustling the trees, or to a good tune that builds you up and pushes you on as you run up the next hill. So get out there...start making tracks and take the high ground every chance along the way.

PHOTO CREDITS:

1. Avalanche: ©iStock.com/mmac72
2. Attack!!!: ©iStock.com/Kileman
3. Nuclear crystal ball: ©iStock.com/jgroup
4. Friendship Between Man and Dog: ©iStock.com/papermeadow
5. Man and Dog: ©iStock.com/happyborder
6. Tree with a Luminous Flux: ©iStock.com/eugeniobarzanti
7. Skiing Person on Frozen Lake: ©iStock.com/Pi-Lens
8. Footprints ©iStock.com/druvo
9. Real Friendship: ©iStock.com/ILonaBudzbon

ENDNOTES:

1. H. Sides. "The Man Who Saw Too Much," http://Outsideonline.com/adventure/travel-ga-201101-michael-ferrara-sidwcmdev_153564.html
2. The Diagnostic and Statistical Manual of Mental Disorders (4th edition). American Psychiatric Association. Washington DC. 2000.
3. J. Eldredge. The Journey of Desire: Searching for the Life We Only Dreamed Of, Thomas Nelson, Inc. Nashville, TN, 2000, 191.
4. Ibid., Sides.
5. Ibid., Sides.
6. Ibid., Sides.

Chapter 6 Introduction
ON SHEEPDOGS AND HORSES

Lt. Col. Dave Grossman (US Rangers, Ret) depicts the nature of the job done by Warriors as that of a sheepdog minding over and protecting the sheep. I fully agree with his choice of metaphor and couldn't find a better one if I tried.

In this chapter however, I'll be describing another aspect of Policing/Military/First Responders: That tendency to run alongside, to encourage one of their own kind to keep going...and in many cases to stay alive.

For this I have a different metaphor and it grows directly out of my experience of working (as a "whisperer in training") with horses. These creatures taught me just about everything I know about how to work with Warriors and First Responders (for one thing, all share in common an initial fear of me and who can blame them?). In all cases we become a critical "Herd of Two" within the greater herd of that horse, Warrior or Rescuer's life.

Therefore, I will be talking about the power of the herd and the wondrous formation of the "Virtuous Circle." That amazing skill that naturally grows out of healed brokenness and then can come back around to encircle the injured one/s in the herd to render assistance. My choice of metaphor is not designed to negate Lt. Col. Grossman's construct (and as you've already seen, I include "good dogs" in the herd). Nor am I demoting anyone lower down on the food chain. This is only an attempt to add another aspect to the bigger picture. Sheep dogs and horses have their place. There is a time and a season for both...

"A time to kill and a time to heal...a time for war and a time for peace"
Eccl. 3:3 & 6

CHAPTER 6
WITHOUT A HERD WE PERISH

"Everything in this world has stopped except war...and we are all men of new professions out in some strange night caring for each other."

Ernie Pyle
"Out of Nowhere a Rolling Little Subchaser" (7/22/43)

I got to the ER at the same time as the on-duty lieutenant, Jake, and Sergeant Brian, the president of the Police Officer Association (POA). We met in the parking lot at the ambulance entrance, out of earshot of anyone. They briefed me about the situation: Owen, a sergeant, had been shot by a distraught man with a gun; no one else wounded or dead. Stopping mid-sentence while giving me the details, Jake suddenly choked up. The shock wave hit, now that it was safe to react.

In the dim light, I could see the POA president turn without hesitation and put his arm around his lieutenant's shoulders. There was no shame attached. I'd seen similar scenes play out countless times before, either with officers arriving at hospitals or on scene in the wake of shootings. "The weight of the bars" is mighty when one of your own, under your command, gets injured or killed.

Minutes later, we arrived at the bedside of the sergeant who'd been shot, and the same scene played out again. This time it was the wounded one the shock wave hit. It was Jake, standing next to the bed, who then reached out to him in support. Just as Brian had told him shortly before, Jake was telling this wounded sergeant, that it was okay, that all of his team were fine, that everyone was alive. Each of us knew what the tears were about. They had nothing and yet everything to do with what was now imbedded in this sergeant's body. He was so grateful he was the one who'd taken that bullet.

I stepped into the hall to give these three some time. The wounded sergeant didn't know me yet. The two I'd come in with were doing instinctively what was called for and doing it exceptionally well. I looked up the hall to see one of our Peer Support Officers arrive. I'd worked with Mark, a sergeant, several years earlier dealing with an ambush he and his team had been involved in. Mark is one of the best Peer Support Officers that I've ever worked with—pragmatic, empathetic, trustworthy with confidentiality—rock solid out on the ground—officers respected him. He'd made no secret that he'd once had PTSD and doing that made it safe for others to follow his example and get in for treatment. After exchanging information we both had by that time, we joined the others back in the room. We had a couple of critical incident stress defusings to do that night. This one would be the first.

TRAUMA DUE TO THE FACT - TRAUMA AFTER THE FACT

As you've learned, PTSD and its affiliates result from a traumatic event. This is what I refer to as "trauma due to the fact." The brain scan images you've seen show the visible injury of that event and the array of symptoms that the officer may have to deal with. The journey back to the land of the living can be long and challenging. However, when the trauma results from critical incidents involving use-of-force and lethal contact incidents, such as riots, officer-involved shootings, etc., another type of trauma, which I call "trauma after the fact," can make recovery even more difficult.

This trauma is caused by the post-incident, soul-killing hardships inflicted on officers by elements such as the media, human resource and administrative departments, poor investigative techniques, and the legal system. Loss of privacy, public humiliation, betrayal by those once trusted and the helplessness of being caught in a bureaucratic web create their own deep traumas. Injuries sustained can also take a toll and, in fact, become career-ending. It can seem to an officer that everywhere he'd thought there was solid ground prior to a CI suddenly transforms into unstable and hazardous terrain beyond that point.

In my courses, commanders are always surprised to learn that of out of these two traumas, the trauma *after* the fact is more likely to be fatal to an officer's career than the original traumatic event. They have an even harder time believing that the official events following a CI are far more likely to be deadly to the officer himself than, say, an OIS. It's that second trauma that can finish off an officer's promising career and leave him devastated, bitter and at a huge disadvantage fighting an uphill battle to reach a successful end to his PTSD. This begs the question, "Why?"

The answer is found first within their respective natures...

TRAUMA DUE TO THE FACT:

The first traumatic event had a beginning, middle and an end. It's a past event, even if PTSD has set in and is making it feel like it's still happening. It occurred over a specific length of time, it ended and then the officer/s got out... alive.

The officer knew the type of adversary he was prepared to meet up with; the dangers were not unexpected.

TRAUMA AFTER THE FACT:

This trauma is typically unforeseen, and then it takes on a life of its own. Bungled investigations, scandal-mongering newspapers, tangled red-tape, rent-a-mobs with the officer's name on signs referring to him as a murderer—these are not the dangers officers are trained for. Add to these and the traumatic aftermath typically takes on a life of its own and can go on for months or years. The officer's career may not survive, and in some cases he may end up in prison.

Suddenly, the officer must defend himself against the Rule of Law—and those who uphold it, those with whom the officer has worked alongside to maintain the peace. This is how the system has to work, but it's a terrifying reversal of the order of things for officers.

No Warrior or Rescuer prepares for a shift, expecting that outcome to unfold in her day or night on duty. This lack of preparation powerfully affects the impact of this second trauma.

STREET READY FOR DANGER BUT UNPREPARED FOR BETRAYAL

From their first day in the academy, officers are being physically trained and mentally prepared for what will come at them with when they step into their uniforms and out on the streets. However, nothing can prepare them for what their agency and/or investigative arm may inflict on them if they are involved in a critical incident that requires an investigative level of scrutiny.

I attend to some of the most deeply impacting types of traumas, such as the taking of life, the loss of close friends in lethal contacts/deadly operations, scenes of terrorist carnage, and dead children. I've found that the two most high-risk type of clients are (1) those who've made a tactical decision that ended up with one/more of their team members injured or killed, and (2) those who have been wrongly accused of actions or of sinister intentions behind their actions.[1]

If you are wrongly accused, you need to keep your vision clear regarding who you truly are and all you've done throughout your life that attests to that truth. Most importantly, you need to have loved ones in your life who serve as reminders to you of the truth of who you are.

In Chapter 1, I described a scene of the boats outside my window during a ravaging storm. Remember that the good and great people in your life are the strong lines that can help to keep you from being torn away from the dock. You need to do the best "line maintenance" you can, even though it's hard enough maintaining yourself with PTSD. Despite that, you *need* people standing in the gap with you more than ever if trauma after the fact is in play.

Cases involving protracted investigations and wrongful accusations following an already traumatic CI have a myriad of powerful negative impacts on an officer's life and outlook.

These harmful effects include but are by no means limited to the following:

1). Forced isolation: If there is a protracted investigation, and the officer is placed on suspension, he is cut off from the daily support of his active-duty routine and of being with his team and his peers. As I've already made clear, isolation to any degree is harmful to healing from the original trauma. That becomes magnified when the isolation is enforced.

2). Assignment of guilt based on poor or no science:[2] The lag time of up-to-date research getting into the awareness of investigative entities increases the potential for wrongful assignment of guilt[3]. Beginning in the 1980s,[4] studies of large numbers of law enforcement officers involved in lethal contact incidents,[5] have shown that gaps of memory and perception distortions are extremely common in dangerous and pressure-filled incidents.[6] That science, as well as other studies, is not always integrated in these investigations in order to guarantee Best Practice.[7]

3). Loss of livelihood and financial security, including the officer's pension: If a guilty verdict is reached and appeal lost, the officer faces the loss of his entire career and his future retirement income.

4). Loss of reputation and sense of integrity—a lasting humiliation: In the cases of those wrongfully accused, this can be unbearable.

Hayden's case below is only one of many examples that I can cite of trauma after the fact.

HAYDEN'S STORY

Hayden is one of the most ethical, solid and courageous commanders "out there" I had ever met. The sheer magnitude of the abyss he was staring down would have shaken anyone to their core. The thought of enduring a long investigation and then possibly a trial/court martial, with the potential for a lengthy sentence was almost unbearable.

This was all due to an honest gap of memory (while under the stress of extreme danger) of using an appropriate and justified tactic to restrain a subject.[8] That gap of one to three seconds for Hayden nearly undid just over 20 years of exemplary service. He stood in the crosshairs of a potential conviction for attempting to render a false report because he was unable to recall this action.

The investigative team held to an errant belief that anyone should be able to recall every move they make in a stressful confrontation. The tactic was investigated[9] (it had been captured on someone's cell phone video), and found not to involve unnecessary/excessive force. Then attention was shifted off of the tactic and on to Hayden's not being able to recount doing it. That's what the investigation ended up going after him for. The investigators lacked any understanding of sensory gating (the brain's inability to take in all sensory and memory input, especially under severe stress)[10] and they assumed Hayden was lying.

One morning, Hayden was home alone; everyone was gone for the day. Feeling helpless and without hope, he found himself in the garage. With the quiet desperation that had become his constant companion, Hayden took a rope, threw one end over the rafters and anchored it to a secure base.

Standing on a stepladder, he tied a noose and placed it around his neck. He heard nothing but empty silence and saw nothing but the darkness that closed in around him. Standing ready, his gaze had landed on something that seemed important. He had to fight through the darkness to figure out what he was looking at.

It was his daughter's tricycle, resting right beside the wall opposite him. She'd long since outgrown it, but seeing that hit Hayden like a ton of bricks. It looked so small and so vulnerable in such a big open space. The symbolism was not lost on him, thank God.

In that moment, the reality came home to Hayden of what he would be doing to his wife and daughter if he carried through with his actions. He'd be abandoning them, even though, like him, they were innocent. That realization literally sickened him. He grabbed the noose and pulled it off over his head. He took the rope down from the rafters and hurled it across the garage. Right there, for the sake of his family, he chose strength.

After a tormenting investigation, Hayden was found innocent.

THE POWER OF THE HERD

According to a two-year study (2008-2010)[11] conducted by the Badge of Life[12], a suicide-prevention non-profit organization, the suicide rate for the U.S. military was 20 per 100,000; for police officers it was 17 per 100,000. Both groups had a higher rate of suicide than did civilians, of whom 11 per 100, 000 committed suicide. Although I have not lost a client to suicide, in three cases it came extremely close, despite all the care and precautions I put in place. In all three cases, it was "the herd" that saved these men.

All are alive today because of the pull of the people around them who loved, protected and needed them.

My treatment plan with my officers requires them to formulate a list of "safe people" (preferably two to three). Additionally, I have those names and phone numbers on hand should I need to contact them. My clients have to give me written permission to do this or else we don't work together. That indicates how much importance I place on the herd in the life of every one of my officers.

How you select who goes on the "safe-people list" is a personal matter, of course. The first question I ask in discussing this with an officer is, "Who's your best friend, besides your spouse?" This is someone you'd trust your life with. That is your #1 on the list. Then you go from there to think of who will be your fall-back guy when your #1 is out of town. After that, if you've got a #3, even better.

Along with your family (ideally), these safe people are your "shield line," surrounding you when you need it. To do that, they need to know what's going on with you and that you have PTSD (although those close to you, more than likely, already know).

As you travel this journey, you're going to need occasional shoring up and distraction to get a break from worries and woes. Let them know that. It is critical that the herd is out there, ready to run alongside you, to buffer, support and even protect. Sometimes they may need coaching on how *not* to render harm (see below), but those select few are willing and able to be there for you. You've got to round them up.

In a perfect world, at least one person on your list will have had PTSD and successfully made it across to the other side. If not, in the future you may become that one if any of them develop PTSD on down the line—one day when you're strong again.

Once you have your list of safe people, next you need to set up some kind of a structure for staying in contact with them, if you don't have that already. You might get together for coffee or grab a pizza once a week to check in with any one of these. If you've got running buddies, you could get back into that with one or more of them, along with weight circuits if you're physically able. Weights provide deep-muscle relaxation that can help you sleep (more on sleep in the next chapter). They're great.

Your safe people can provide some measure of distraction from worry and isolation, as I mentioned. And now I hate to be the heavy here, but that does *not* include going out to tie one on. You don't need that kind of drinking buddy running you into the pub with the false notion that he's "helping." With PTSD, you've got to make very good choices about what you put in your head, life and body. And the liquid depressant *isn't* one of those good choices.

THOSE WHO'VE WEATHERED THE STORM

I drove into the parking lot to start the day. It was early and I was the first one in. I opened the car door and noticed two figures sitting at the base of the stairs that go up to my office. One I recognized immediately, and I smiled. I didn't know the other person. That clued me in on what the surprise visit was about. It was another injured one. This is what a "Virtuous Circle" looks like.[13]

Quite simply it means that a successful solution leads to more desired results for success, which generates still more desired results for successes in an interconnected chain. That's how I think of these visits. It's always someone I've worked with who gives me a call or comes by in person. He tells me that there's someone he knows who really could use some help and do I have any time to see this person... soon?

People who have recovered from PTSD gain the eyes to see PTSD in those around them. After recovery, feeling healthy, strong and good humored again, it's hard not to notice. Not only that, but the person who sees this "resurrected one" often approaches them, albeit cautiously. He'll ask how he got all squared away. Was it diet, exercise...what?

Those who have recovered from PTSD won't joke about it when approaching the walking wounded they spot. They know what a lonely and dangerous place it can be. If it's serious, they'll escort that injured one right to my door. They're very good at seeing a potential suicide sitting close to the edge. They expertly take any weapons off them and then bring them in. They wait outside as we meet, and then get coffee with the injured one when he comes out. They make sure he has that post-first-session sense of relief and hope. They stay available; they join the herd. They make up the "Virtuous Circle" and they have saved many lives. It's a wonderful thing to see...how brokenness becomes healed and then goes on to help other broken ones to heal.

TIPS FOR THOSE IN THE HERD

I'd been out on swing shift riding with the team of one of my sergeants. On that front end of the shift I was riding with a delightful young officer (still in the honeymoon phase with the job... such a lot of fun at that stage!). He was telling me how they'd all been really worried about their Sarge there for a while (this one didn't know I'd worked with him). He said to me that they finally got him all straightened out. I asked him, "Wow...how did you do that?"

"We joked and teased him back to his senses...that's how."

In fact, that campaign hadn't helped at all. It had only made their beloved "Sarge" feel all the more isolated and alone.

There is an instinctive drive to get a herd member back into the fold. While there's a period of grace that's allocated to the injured one, eventually the anxiety becomes too great for the team. For one thing, they miss their member and they want him or her back the way they used to be. At that point they will attempt, with the best of intentions and sheer desperation, to drive this limping team member back into their formation. Every time I've witnessed this, it's been done out of affection and concern. Even so, there's a right way and a wrong way.

THINGS TO AVOID:

Getting together for "choir practice" (having a few pints): This is a bad idea (please see next chapter). If the herd wants to get together, great. Just stay away from alcohol for the sake of the one you are helping. Alcohol is a depressant and can lower self-restraint. Not a good combination even without PTSD.

Humor (especially dark humor) about the CI: Humor can be a great outlet that can bring down stress levels and ease tension. This is often the first element incorporated into the campaign, especially in young male-dominated teams.

Humor becomes problematic when the teasing and jokes are centered around the actual incident that led to the PTSD. The intention behind such "interventions" are rarely, if ever, malicious. The underlying hope is that if the incident can be laughed at, it might become less oppressive for the officer involved. Unfortunately, the humor campaign can act like a bolt of lightening to the one who's trying to stay on his feet to contend with the CI and the PTSD.

Taking in action movies: Once harmless fun; however, now the movie may hit a tripwire. One of my clients had been pinned down at night by two armed shooters who were trying to kill him and another officer. The SWAT team was being held off until sunrise, so these two had to hole up behind one lone tree for cover as bullets whizzed by them all night long. Months later, just as he was starting with me, friends from work decided it would be a good idea to get him out to see a "macho guy flick." *Black Hawk Down* had just been released and had a similar theme as that night-from-perdition my officer had endured. When the flash-bang action hit on screen, he climbed over laps of people to get out of the line of fire.

Playing video games: Their visual and auditory replication of war can trigger flashbacks. This was tragically what set off Marine Erick Hall's flashback on one Super Bowl Sunday after he'd been back from Iraq for three years. When the flashback hit, he left on his motorcycle. He was later found dead from smoke inhalation after being trapped by a brush fire in a culvert.[14] Eric had been tormented by PTSD, enduring it in silence and not letting his family know how difficult it was. My hope is that this list of suggestions of activities to avoid can help those with PTSD and those who are trying to be there for them.

HOW TO INITIATE AND MAINTAIN CONTACT

The PTSD brain has a hard time with groups and crowds, as a general rule. However, there is a difference between how men and women react. Research out of the University of Southern California has found that brain activity for men and women under stress is different. Researchers found that under stress, the areas of the brain that read emotion and facial expression increase in activity for women and decrease for men.[15] Since those regions of the brain also relate to being socially engaged, it's easy to see why there are gender differences in coping with PTSD.

For men, one-on-one activities that don't require a whole lot of talking are easier. Fishing, running, surfing, cycling...the cup of java at the neighborhood coffee house are all fine, as long as they are low demand. The majority of men find great comfort in just doing things. It allows them to feel less disconnected only without having to talk much.

Women, on the other hand, when under stress, like to talk, as a general rule. In fact, we de-stress by talking, whereas for our male counterparts, engaging in talk can cause the exact opposite reaction. Where men tend to revert to the man cave, women tend to seek out connections with others. Women, when ready to talk, want to think aloud in conversations. They want to sort through things (often repeatedly). This can be hard for those listening and can push them to attempt to fix the problem just to put an end to it and move on. That, of course, never works.

For the vast majority of women, it's both the journey and the destination that matters. We want to wrestle with and solve things for ourselves in due time. However, over that time we can become difficult company for friends who are trying to be there but are hearing the same things being reviewed.

It's good to be aware of this tendency and to curb the potential for burnout in your circle of friends. Try to control the amount of time you spend going over the same pressing issues (some clients have literally set an amount of time, say 10 minutes, and have set their watch alarms to keep within that!). Try setting up get-togethers that focus attention on other things, such as movies, getting lost in a bookshop on a rainy Saturday afternoon, doing an act of kindness for someone else. Be aware that as you're in processing mode, friends and family are dealing with stuff in their lives, as well. Be there for them as much as you're able.

What I've seen as my officers have recovered from PTSD is an evolutionary progression back into their community of friends, family and peers. It can be a slow, cautious re-entry into the tribe of humankind. It takes time, and often happens in phases. Just remember that the person with PTSD determines the level of connection that can be maintained with the world outside of home. Keep it simple.

There tends to be an ebb and flow to relational patterns with PTSD. Below I've listed the general patterns I've observed with my PTSD clients. Even so, it's good to remember that everyone is unique and there are differences that can present themselves that go counter to these.

Stage 1: Protect
Early on in dealing with PTSD, solace and a sense of security can be gained from isolation. The PTSD brain has so much going on that it just doesn't have a lot of room for much else. Then there's the "dog phase" –(if you are blessed to have one) that easy company of a companion with unconditional love and devotion who can force you to get out into the world.

Stage 2: Direct
Gradually, the officer is ready to have low-demand, one-on-one time with his or her "safe people" friends.

Stage 3: Connect
Moving back into the officer's previous level of social interaction is a gradual progression that just happens naturally over time.

DIFFERENT LAYERS OF RELATIONSHIPS

Not all relationships are created equal. As you deal with PTSD, it's helpful to remember than in every life there are different layers of relationships. This is true in the herd, as well. I think relationships as falling into three basic levels.

Level 1: Acquaintances
Those relationships on the surface of your life. These would be the people who you pass in the hallways or in your neighborhood. You exchange pleasantries of "Hi, how are you," and that's about the depth and breadth of the relationship.

Level 2: Friends
These are those in your life with whom you can go out and swing a golf club at the driving range or call to grab a quick bite at lunch. You may not often, if ever, talk about deep things with them, and you may not connect with each other on a regular basis. Even so, when you, do it's enjoyable and you remember why you call this person "friend."

Level 3: Best Friends/Soul Mates
These reside at this deepest level of your life. Hopefully you've married one and beyond that, if you have one or two others in the span of your lifetime, you've been truly blessed. These know you in depth and still like you! Even if distance and time separate you from regular contact with these prized individuals, once reunited (even just by phone or email), it's like you've never been out of touch. This relationship simply picks up where it left off as if it's not been interrupted at all.

Mentors who have gone the distance to invest in you fit in this deep layer. If they have been great supporters, then they have known you with all of your flaws and kept faith in your ability to grow and strive for excellence. These people are some of the greatest and wisest ones in a life and are exceptional gifts.

In addition to being aware of those layers of relationships, it's also helpful to note your own relational style, whether introvert or extrovert. In general, introverts tend to find social gatherings hard work unless they have a designated job or role (flipping burgers or taking pictures). They tend to be satisfied with their own intimate circle of friends and with them, can even look like extroverts. Introverts usually have a small group of close friends. Extroverts, on the other hand, find social gatherings inspiring and have a wider bandwidth of friendships, most of whom would not be considered truly close.

As you maneuver your way through PTSD, it's helpful to understand the range of possible relationships and their characteristics. You need a herd to run with, especially now. Don't worry about the numbers; concern yourselves with the quality. One thing is true for the vast majority of the humankind: Without a herd we perish.

"Nobody, but nobody, can make it out here alone."

Maya Angelou

PHOTO CREDITS:

1. Border Collie ©iStockphoto.com/tirc83
2. Wild Horses Running Silhouette ©iStockphoto.com/St.MarieLtd
3. US Soldier comforting another after the death of his best friend while a fatality report is being filled out by another soldier nearby (Korea) Courtesy National Archives, (111-SC-202199)
4. Soldier grieving 3 Children burned Iraq: Photographer Victor Calvano/AP
5. UK Riot Police Flames: ©iStock.com/toward76
6. Belfast Court Room 2006: © Karen Lansing
7. Ropes on Dock ©iStockphoto.com/shadowportland
8. Tricycle II ©iStockphoto.com/dalton00
9. Ibid: Wild Horses Running Silhouette
10. Life Preserver ©iStockphoto.com/mevans
11. Life Preservers ©iStockphoto.com/mevans
12. Storm on the Field ©iStockphoto.com/mike_expert
13. Message in a Bottle ©iStockphoto.com/urbancow
14. Rescue Me ©iStockphoto.com/johnhortondesign

ENDNOTES:

1. R. Seides. "Should the current DSM-IV-R definition for PTSD be expanded to include serial and multiple microtraumas as aetiologies?" *Journal of Psychiatric and Mental Health Nursing,* Vol. 17, Issue 8, 725-731, Oct. 2010.
2. E. Nielson. "Salt Lake City police department deadly force policy shooting and post shooting reactions," unpublished paper, Salt Lake City, UT: Salt Lake City Police Department, 1981.
3. J. G. Stratton, D. Parker, J. R. Snibbe. "Posttraumatic stress: study of police officers involved in shootings," *Psychological Reports,* 55 Aug. 1984, 127–131.
4. R. M. Solomon, J. H. Horn. "Post shooting traumatic reactions: a pilot study," *Psychological Services for Law Enforcement Officers,* ed. James T. Reese and Harvey A. Goldstein, Washington, DC: U.S. Government Printing Office, 1986.
5. J. H. Campbell. "A Comparative Analysis of the Effects of Post shooting Trauma on the Special Agents of the Federal Bureau of Investigation," unpublished Ph.D. dissertation, *Department of Educational Administration, Michigan State University*, East Lansing, MI, 1992.
6. D. Klinger. "Police Reponses to Officer-Involved Shootings," *Final report submitted to NIJ, Police Responses to Officer-Involved Shootings* (grant number 97-1C-CX-0029), NIJ Journal No. 253, January 2006.
7. A. Artwhol, Loren W. Christensen. "*Deadly Force Encounters*: *What Cops Need to Know to Mentally and Physically Survive a Gunfight,*" Paladin Press, Boulder CO, 1997.
8. Ibid., Artwhol and Christensen.
9. W. Lewinski, D. Blocksidge, J. Dixon, J. Anderson, L. Hope. "Final findings from force science exhaustion study," *Force Science* News, Apr. 25, 2011, Force Science Research Institute. http://www.forcescience.org/

10. L. Hope, W. Lewinski, J. Dixon, D. Blocksige. "Witness in action: The effect of physical exertion on recall and recognition," *Psychological Science* 23(4), Mar. 7, 2012, 386–390.

11. A. F. O'Hara, J. M. Violanti. "Police suicide–A web surveillance of national data," *Journal of Emergency Mental Health* 2009, 11(1): 17-23.

12. The Badge of Life, http://www.policesuicideprevention.com/id48.html

13. BusinessDictionary.com
http://www.businessdictionary.com/definition/virtuous-circle.html

14. J. Davis. "Parents of marine found dead seek PTSD awareness," *Sarasota Herald-Tribune*, March 12, 2008.

15. M. Mather, N. R. Lighthall, L. Nga, M. A. Gorlick. "Sex differences in how stress affects brain activity during face viewing," *NeuroReport*, 2010; 21 (14): 933.

CHAPTER 7
TONIGHT'S TARGET

By Theodore Knell
"From the Corners of a Wounded Mind"[1]

The first pint tonight will go a long way
To cooling you down at the end of a long hot day
Start a conversation with a total stranger
Piss the wife off
Even raise her to anger.

The second pint is easier to swallow
it will take you that little bit further
make stupid orders easier to follow.

Three pints and you're well on your way
to another forgotten night
followed by another painful day.

The fourth pint is easier to sink
it's the point where old scores will need to be settled
Help you tell others, what you really think.

Five pints and you're about to cross that line
the line where nothing really matters
where you'll drink anything that's going,
except the posy wine.

Six pints or more, and your target is finally reached
just getting here has deadened the pain
softened the loss hidden the guilt and anger,
well a least until you're sober again.

This alcohol induced stupor
the one which now engulfs your body
will eventually provide that much needed sleep
the one where you'll lay
comatose on the NAAFI floor...
until the next day.

Model used for illustration.

102

YOUR BRAIN'S IN TRAINING

If your brain is going to be at peak performance during the EMDR sessions, it needs to be able to fire off neurotransmissions—that is, to send and connect critical info—with efficiency and speed. Your brain needs to go into training and be at its fighting weight for the trauma resolution work ahead. A chemically induced depression of brain activity only slows things down. If you're addicted to alcohol, then that needs to be addressed through a recovery process before you go into therapy for PTSD. This is because excessive use of alcohol will negatively impact the brain.

The pictures below were taken of Aaron's brain as he worked his way through PTSD. The middle picture shows just how hard the brain is working as it processes through and then resolves the trauma that contributed to the PTSD. In that EMDR, Aaron was in the midst of working through the trauma related to the SIDS death. This was the first SPECT brain image taken in the world of EMDR occurring in the brain. It's a still shot of a very active and dynamic process occurring neurologically. As you can see, there are areas firing off in different sectors of the brain as all aspects of the memory (sight, sound, physical and emotional) were being reprocessed. This is why you need to take care of your brain. You're going to need it in this passage through and out of PTSD.

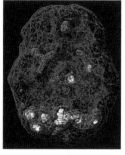
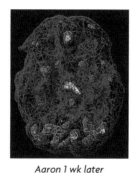
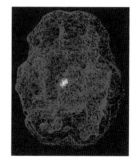

Aaron with PTSD	*Aaron 1 wk later* *During EMDR*	*Aaron 6 wks later* *No longer PTSD*

SELF-MEDICATION WITH THE WRONG STUFF

With the intense demands that are put on an overactivated brain with PTSD, it's understandable that the brain hungers for some rest from it all. In fact, it could be viewed as a neurological craving. This makes the use of a drug that causes the brain to quiet down and go offline a natural choice. Besides providing down time from overactivity, taking alcohol before going to bed seems a natural way to cope with the difficulties that PTSD causes in getting to sleep.

However, there are a number of problems with drinking alcohol regularly for either of those reasons. The first, of course, is that tolerance develops over time, so you need to drink more and more to get the same effect. The second problem is that while alcohol may make it easier to float off to sleep, it doesn't allow for the full five cycles of sleep to occur. With alcohol in the system, you can only get into the lighter first and second stages of sleep, which leaves you still feeling tired in the morning, even if you've managed to get eight hours of sleep that night. Lack of sleep is very common with PTSD, and this chapter will deal with it.

The third problem is that excessive use of alcohol creates a chronic slowing down of brain activity that can have a significant impact on brain function. This drop in brain activity remains long after the blood-alcohol level has gone down.

Take a look at what SPECT images show us about excessive alcohol intake. These brain images compare a healthy non-alcoholic brain to an alcoholic one. Those holes in the alcoholic brain are not loss of actual "grey matter," so don't interpret them as literal holes in the brain. Instead the holes reflect lack of brain activity. Still, it's a lack of brain activity! No small concern.[2]

Top of Brain Perspective   Underside of Brain Perspective

 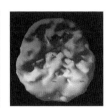

1. Non Alcoholic   *2. Alcoholic*   *1. Non Alcoholic*   *2. Alcoholic*

The point these images make is not subtle. They explain why it's a good plan to factor out over-indulging in alcohol in order to prepare your brain for the rigors of EMDR.

It warrants repeating that alcohol is a depressant. While most brains can take the occasional light- to-moderate exposure to alcohol, the key words when it comes to drinking alcohol are "occasional" and "in moderation." The good news is that in most cases, the brain can recover activation if alcohol use is discontinued, depending on the extent and duration of alcohol abuse or addiction.

TONIGHT'S OTHER TARGET… SLEEP

Out of all the symptoms of PTSD, one of the most frustrating is difficulty sleeping. Like air, sleep is essential for just about everything. It is critical for our very survival.

When it comes to PTSD, sleep plays the leading role. We've learned that PTSD isn't, at its base, a trauma-based memory problem. Instead it's a dysfunction of sleep, especially REM sleep. That's where memory gets reprocessed and learning from events is integrated (resolved). In PTSD, it's in the lack of adequate, fully functioning REM sleep that the wheels come off.

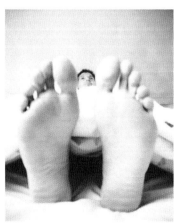

Model used for illustration

With PTSD the brain commonly isn't getting enough sleep; more specifically it's REM sleep that is lost. When REM sleep does kick in, it seems that nightmares either (1) chase the sleeper in a reign of terror or (2) chase them out of REM sleep altogether because "Dream Land" isn't a very friendly place to be.[3]

SLEEP—THE DO-IT-YOURSELF THERAPY

Dr. Ernest Hartman, a professor of psychiatry at Tufts University School of Medicine and director of the Sleep Disorders Center at Newton-Wellesley Hospital in Boston, has an intriguing way of viewing REM sleep. He states in his article, "Making Connections In a Safe Place: Is Dreaming Psychotherapy?" that REM is structured very much like psychotherapy.[4]

Hartman explains that both dreaming and psychotherapy involve the "freeing up of associations," that is, freely and safely "thinking outside of the box." This creative flow of consciousness during sleep, which has the potential for being unchecked by reality-based reason, comes with the prevention of physically acting things out in real time. This is caused by the body's chemically induced state of temporary paralysis during REM sleep. This is a very handy benefit for those who like to fly in their dreams. Another parallel is that both sleep and therapy enable a person to make connections on different levels, such as perspectives on things, thoughts or ideas, lessons learned and emotions.[5]

The most interesting parallel between sleep and therapy is seen in the wake of acute trauma. It's in the aftermath of trauma, Hartmann points out, that both therapy and dreaming provide a safe place where connections can be made between the traumatic event and relevant memories, issues and themes. Making these connections lets the brain integrate the traumatic memory into the greater context of one's life. Remember that this is where the hippocampus comes in, providing the context. This allows that trauma-based memory to become less disturbing and then ideally, neutralized over time.[6]

In the course of that process, the amygdala habituates, or normalizes, that trauma with the help from the hippocampus. That allows the brain to learn from the trauma and become all the wiser for having survived those life lessons.

Another sleep researcher, Dr. Robert Stickgold, is a professor out of Harvard—a brilliant and kind man. (I sat in on a lecture by him about sleep and memory and he's really quite wonderful. If you want to view that lecture, you can find it at http://www.youtube.com/watch?v=WmRGNunPj3c.) He breaks down what sleep does for us into three simple benefits:

1. Extracts the gist of memories of events in life; that is, it gives us the take-away lessons
2. Discovers the "rules" of our lives—what works and doesn't; how life goes
3. Fosters insight

Dr. Stickgold described in that lecture how a research fellow named Erin Wamsley, Ph.D., working under his supervision at the Center for Sleep and Cognition, discovered additional dream functions:

Dreaming helps us to:
1. Integrate new and old memories
2. Imagine possible futures, through solutions and new directions[7]

All five of those functions combine to create the meaning in our lives. All that from sleep!

This discussion about REM sleep is closely tied to EMDR, because it's during that stage that critical processes occur, which help process and then normalize traumatic memories. It is important for those with PTSD to get some level of improvement in sleep. So first, we'll look at what is "normal."

WHEN SLEEP IS NORMAL

Sleep's five stages all generate very specific brain waves and body responses. A transition into sleep starts before Stage 1, when **Beta** waves (active in concentration, stress, attention, fear and learning) transition into **Alpha** waves, present when you are relaxed or not working.

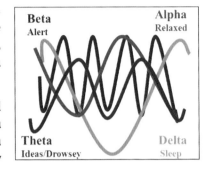

Stage 1 of sleep is the transition phase from relaxed wakefulness—Alpha waves—to light sleep (**Theta** waves) and lasts 5–10 minutes. It's easy to wake a sleeper in this stage, and they may not even know they were asleep.

The deadly "micro sleep" that occurs at the wheel of a car is a good example of how stealthily this transitional stage can come on. Theta waves have a range. At the lower level is a relaxed state in which the brain is able to multitask and form solutions and ideas. On the other end of the Theta wave range is light sleep. This is also where sudden jerks of movement can occur and where you may startle out of sleep because of that feeling like you're falling. This happens because the brain's motor areas are being activated spontaneously.

Stage 2 lasts approximately 20 minutes. Here the brain goes into bursts of fast and rhythmic brain activity (called "sleep spindles") and then slows way down into Theta waves. During this stage, the body's temperature and heart rate go down.

Stages 3 and 4 dovetail together. This is the transitional phase that moves the brain from light, Theta wave sleep into deep sleep (**Delta** waves).

By Stage 4—dreamless sleep—Delta waves occur most of the time. Dreams actually do occur, but they lack the detail and associations (connecting up of things) of REM dreams. Stage 4 is the most physically restorative sleep. Without it our bodies develop painful problems such as body aches or more serious, the condition of fibromyalgia (see chapter notes). This is also the stage where sleepwalking and bedwetting typically occur. Important hormones are released in this stage, including prolactin and the human growth hormone. Stage 4 lasts about 30 minutes.

Stage 5 is REM sleep. Breathing rates increase as does brain activity. As brain activity goes up, the body's voluntary muscles become paralyzed. While dreaming and nightmares can occur at all phases of sleep, the real substantial and extended dream state occurs during REM sleep.[8] The nature of dreams change depending on what stage in the sleep cycle they occur in. J.F. Pagel, MD, a sleep specialist and researcher, gives a good description of these. Dreams that occur in Stages 1 and 2, as well as the deep, non-REM sleep stage, are short, simple and have fewer associations to them than dreams in REM sleep.

I refer to these as "flashbulb" dreams or nightmares because they can come and go so quickly.

These carry little, if any, storyline and are described as being "more diffuse (e.g., dreams about a color or an emotion)."[9]

 A normal non-PTSD sleep cycle can look like this:

1	Stage 1 10 mins	Stage 2 20 mins	Stage 3 10 mins	Stage 4 20 mins	Stage 3 10 mins	Stage 2 20 mins	REM 30 mins	Stg. 2/4 10 mins
2	1	2	3	4	3	2	REM	2/4
3	1	2	3	4	3	2	REM	2/4
4	1	2	3	4	3	2	REM	2/4

 With PTSD this is what a night's sleep can look like:

1	Stage 1 10 mins	Stage 2 20 mins	Sleep interrupt: *Sound of car noise*	Stage 1 10 mins	Startle awake		Stg 1	Stg 2 10 mins
2	1	2	3	Sleep interrupt	1	2	3	REM > nightmare awake
3	Fully awake > get up > watch t.v. on couch … doze in and out of Stage 1							Stg 2
4	Sleep interrupt	Go to bathrm > more t.v.	1	2	3	4	3	2	REM Wake-up time

Recall of such dreams will be scant or non-existent. REM sleep is closer to the end of the sleep cycle, more highly activated and those dreams can be bizarre or chaotic in nature, with storylines fed by details and associations from our lives. This is where the working aspect of dreaming occurs, in which connections are made and learning can happen.[10]

In the normal pattern of sleep, Stages 1-4 at the start of the night run for around 10-20 minutes, with REM carrying on for around 30 minutes. As the night progresses, Stages 1-4 get shorter and REM sleep becomes longer. By the last cycle, it can last up to one hour.

The general idea is that sleep with PTSD is hell …longing for heaven.

It is essential, in PTSD treatment, to address sleep problems at the outset. Without good sleep, the brain is compromised, which impacts cognitive function, mood, insulin levels,[11] energy, world view, levels of isolation and hopelessness.

WHEN COUNTING SHEEP JUST ISN'T ENOUGH

A good number of websites offer information on wise sleep practices, which you may have read already.

These include recommendations such as:

- No caffeine after 4:00 p.m.
- No eating a meal just before going to bed
- No aerobic exercises 4 hours or less to bed
- No TV or Internet surfing one hour before bedtime
- Go to bed and get up at the same time each day

The reality for most people with PTSD is that while these are worthy of attention, they won't solve completely the problem of insomnia arising from a combination of shift work, family life and PTSD, but they can help.

ENVIRONMENTS JUST PLAIN HOSTILE TO SLEEP

It's not unusual for PTSD Warriors and Rescuers to have pre-existing sleep problems before having developed PTSD, due to shift work (daytime sleep cycles in billeting shared with nighttime sleepers), environmental factors, such as 24/7 noise, security lights, and disruptive off-duty entertainment, including video games, movies, SKYPE calls home with major time differences. Those chronic sleep disturbances set up behavioral patterns in the brain even before the chemical and activation changes occur due to PTSD.

An article in the January 2011 issue of *Stars and Stripes* disclosed a sharp rise in long-term sleep problems in the past 10 years among military troops returning home. Not only that, a Pentagon study indicates that insomnia in both the U.S. Army and Marines doubles after deployment.

Dr. Alan Peterson, a researcher, studied the effect of deployments on sleep habits. He reported, "The noise, the living conditions, the risk of threat are all factors that make it difficult for anybody to sleep. And the longer a person goes with disrupted sleep, bad habits and patterns can set in."[12]

Dr. Karin Thompson, a psychologist at the Veterans Affairs hospital in Memphis, TN., and co-author of *The Post-Traumatic Insomnia Workbook*, has also seen how improving sleep benefits veterans with PTSD, especially those with hypervigilance. In her sleep clinic, Thompson teaches vets to reset their central nervous systems by creating a sleep schedule; avoiding alcohol, which harms the sleep cycle; waking up at the same time every day; and beginning to relax one hour before going to bed by taking a bath, for example, or doing yoga. She advises vets not to watch television or surf the web while in bed. "The bed," she says, "should be for sleeping and sex only."[13]

While preparing for that "golden hour" before bedtime is a good foundational intervention, it may not be enough. Over time I've worked with some incredibly creative and outside-the-box-thinking officers. Some have discovered innovative sleep aids that are not included or endorsed in the normal list or recommendations. These can be the ones what actually work best for them. Imagine the scene below:

You get home, struggling to keep awake on the drive from work. Finally, you fall into bed. The lights go out and that's when your brain decides to kick into overdrive. It starts unpacking the worries you're facing, everything you need to remember to do, what you didn't get done. And as if that's not enough, then the scene of your critical incident/s shows up when you close your eyes. You've tried yoga, breathing techniques and mental imagery and for whatever reason, they just don't work for you.

On top of that, the tinnitus in your right ear is now blaring like a shrill alarm. The quieter the house is, the louder it gets. Between your racing mind and the loud ringing in your ear, there's no peace to be found on this night or any other, for that matter. It's a familiar dance.

Once you finally manage to slip off to sleep around two hours after hitting the pillow, you suddenly startle awake. *What time is it?! Have I slept through the alarm?*! Grabbing the alarm clock, you squint to see what time it is…you've only been asleep for 15 minutes. Now with your heart racing, you hit the pillow: you're wide-awake. Then the thoughts start again— what you forgot to take care of before you ended your shift, the phone call you have to make in the morning, and there's that fatal car collision popping in one more time…

This is the tormenting dance of the exiles of sleep.

But why does this happen? Why is it that you can barely keep awake on the drive home at the end of your shift but once in bed you're wired? Why does your tinnitus go to the maximum volume once things have quieted down?

Regarding the tinnitus, there are two possible contributing factors. First, tinnitus is always sounding off day and night, but with daily life background noises, it's easy to not notice it. Second, tinnitus can increase in volume when your stress level rises.

Feeling wired when you head for bed becomes an intricate part of the dance. An established history of having nothing but the night as your tormentor will raise your stress level. Then the thoughts and concerns that come in to fill the horizon when all you want is sleep will add to that.

ATTAINING A QUIET PLACE TO SLEEP

Another sleep problem for Officers/Warriors/Rescuers is the lack of a quiet place to sleep. There are the small machines that make white noise that many people use to drown out ambient noise. Even better, one sergeant I worked with introduced me to a great little white-noise app for his cell phone that worked well. With that one little find, he was able to get measurable relief from the volume of his tinnitus. The menu on the app had sound options that were helpful in lowering his stress level.

One added trick that a number of my officers have tried during that hour before bed has been to read something like a magazine with short articles and to turn on the white noise app on their cell phones right next to them well before they head off to bed or drift off to sleep. This soothing noise and low-impact reading has proven to be a calming one–two punch as well.

A common problem those who have insomnia share is the fear of sleeping through the alarm. The deepest sleep you get with PTSD insomnia typically comes in the later part of the last sleep cycle. The cruel irony is that once you're starting to get some *real* sleep, it's time to get up, which is extremely hard to do.

The worry in the back of your mind about oversleeping can cause you to jolt awake to check the time. This tends to raise the heart rate and pull the brain into having to be awake enough to figure out what time it is, what day it is and what time your shift starts, etc. Once it's established that you have another five hours before it's wake-up time, you're fully awake (and then rather cranky).

After passing the white noise app idea to other officers, we've discovered another advantage of the app. These are commonly coordinated with the phone's alarm feature so that the white noise stops once the alarm sounds. With the app running then, if you waken concerned about the time, you'll know immediately that if the white noise is playing, you haven't missed the alarm. That factors out the panic of needing to check the time. This has been highly praised by my officers and excellent white noise apps can be found online for free. To doubly prevent worry, officers usually keep the old alarm clock just as a safety net.

White noise also softens or overrides the little bumps in the night that might bring a PTSD hyper-vigilant brain to full attention and cause the heart to race, again derailing sleep for hours.

THE A-B-C'S OF REINING IN RACING THOUGHTS

Another obstacle to good sleep—the intrusive or racing thoughts—is a different matter altogether. These require what's called a thought-stopping strategy. When we are awake, Theta brain waves can kick in as we drive, especially on the freeway. This same brain wave that can covertly move us into sleep can also initiate free-flowing thoughts. The familiarity and repetition of a well-established skill done in a relaxing place without distractions or intense focus can usher in Theta waves. In non-PTSD brains, what typically comes to the surface are the "issues du jour." With PTSD, however, what typically comes up are the more ominous and unwanted thoughts.

Thought-stopping techniques are pretty simple. Reading at bedtime is a common one. Another, while it may break the recommended rules of proper sleep hygiene above, is watching TV for a short time before bed. This can work with two strategic amendments:

Do Not: Watch news or high-octane action movies, and **do not** play video games.
Not all TV viewing is created equal. In 1980, a young Ph.D. candidate by the name of Radlick wrote his doctoral dissertation on how watching TV impacts brain waves.[14] He discovered that content and complexity were the key factors in determining which brain waves were generated. Radlick found that watching TV shows that were not complex set the brain into a relaxed Alpha wave action and did so more readily than did reading. In other words, mindless content slows the brain into Alpha waves, while reading isn't as effective due to the concentration and mental work required.

Control What You Do Watch: Go For Light Humor & Happily-Ever-After Plots:
Research has identified the Alpha brain waves as the indicators that the brain is in a passive, relaxed state during TV viewing. It's also where the brain becomes more suggestible. Watching a romantic comedy on DVD that you've seen over and over again works (I keep one or two in my kit bag wherever I am). This is the adult version of bedtime stories for kids that settle them down for the night. Just like fairy tales, in romantic comedies they always "live happily ever after." The thing to remember is that you're not doing this pre-sleep viewing for entertainment. You're doing it to get your brain into that Alpha and then Theta wave easy transition so you can let yourself drift off and call it a day.

Make It Easy to Slip Off to Sleep
The key with any thought stoppers is that you need to make it really easy to turn out the light, if your reading or turn off the TV (remote control is a must). You'll undo the benefits if you have to get out of bed to shut something off.

One of my officers put his TV on a 20-minute timer because he figured out that it only took him 10 minutes to slip off to sleep when watching TV. Five minutes after he went into Stage 2 sleep, the TV would simply take care of the rest. That worked extremely well for him.

To summarize then, while I have deep respect for sleep researchers and clinical specialists in PTSD insomnia, sometimes the client knows best. Be creative and see what works best for you.

USING SLEEP MEDICATION

With PTSD insomnia, the second challenge after attaining sleep is being able to maintain it up to the time to get up. That is the hardest part of chronic sleep problems for most. If you fully awaken when you should be asleep and can't fall back to sleep within 15 minutes or so, and you lose an hour or more of sleep, you've still got a sleep problem. If you have a regular sleep time, and if you have trouble maintaining sleep, you probably find you have a "bewitching hour" when you wake up fairly consistently. Mine was typically around 2:00 a.m. and I'd be awake until 5:00 a.m. or so.

Before turning to sleep medication, first you need to assess your sleep environment for contributing factors like temperature, noise, lights that shine in from outside, road noise and, of course, the quality of your bed and pillows. Also consider your diet. There are foods that you can have for dinner that can help encourage sleep (see chapter notes for a website on that topic). Finally, unless you're dealing with an injury, you should be working out at least 30 minutes several times a week.

If all of those things check out or have been corrected and you're still not able to maintain sleep, then it's time to talk to your doctor about medication. PTSD generates chemical changes in the brain with the increase of stress hormones and these affect sleep. The usual suspects are adrenalin and cortisol, but there are a few more. There comes a time when one just has to fight fire with fire.

One thing that is clearly apparent with PTSD is that once more regulated sleep begins to occur again, symptoms lighten up and mood can measurably improve, especially energy and a sense of hope. That doesn't take long.

One of my officers who competed in marathons came into session one day, and he looked great. His color was good, he had life in his eyes and he was smiling. The previous week he'd started to get more sleep for the first time in well over 16 years. He reported that his long run over the weekend was "great!" He'd only planned to do 10 miles but he just couldn't bring himself to stop there because he was feeling so good, so he went on to do 15. He wanted to go farther but daylight was fading so he headed for home feeling "joy at a 10." This is how dramatic the turn around can be with just one or two nights of good sleep.

MEDICATION HAZARDS & REM REBOUND

Sleep medication, when incorporated into the mix with PTSD, should be non-addictive and a temporary solution. Ideally you should be able to use it until you're no longer PTSD and then to titrate off gradually as your ability to sleep without medication takes over. It should enable you to experience as normal a sleep cycle as possible. That means that you're able to experience all stages of sleep, including REM. You should be aware that some, but not all, sleep medications restrict REM sleep. It's up to you and your doctor to discuss different options carefully.

If you've been deprived of adequate REM sleep for even a couple of weeks and then begin full-cycling sleep again, you may experience what's referred to as "REM rebound." In a nutshell, without enough REM sleep to reprocess all the things that usually get attended to in this stage of sleep, they pile up. When REM sleep is able to occur, this backlog of things comes barreling through. Vivid, chaotic nightmares of sometimes-epic proportions may hit. If you're not prepare, it can be worrisome, to say the least.

The good news is that this rebound effect shouldn't last for long. How long you've been REM-deprived will decide the duration of the rebound. It can go from one night to several weeks. After that, things should quiet down. You may still have nightmares, but they'll not be as intense as with the REM rebound. (See chapter notes for a bit more on this).

THE PROBLEMS WITH AMBIEN

"I was prescribed Ambien over there (the sandbox), and good God, I will NEVER take that or anything like it again. It got so I couldn't sleep without it. And it was scary how many people were put on Ambien in OEF. We were all strung out on one med or another just to function. The docs had a revolving menu of drugs to try on you to get you to a place where you were able to work.

Some worked, some didn't, it was all personalized trial and error. Even after we got home, it took me at least six months to start sleeping relatively normally."[15]

This comment by a soldier underscores a very serious situation that I have seen and you need to be aware of it. Some physicians prescribe sleep medications without knowing their potential side effects or, more worrisome, whether it has addictive qualities. You need to discuss medication with your doctor, pharmacist or chemist and get information on all medications you're taking (especially whether it's addictive, and if so, how long does it take for that to happen?). If they do not give you adequate information, get on to the Internet and do your own due diligence. This is critical to your well-being.

While Ambien works well for many who take it, it is highly addictive. After one month of nightly usage, you're hooked, as the soldier's report above describes. I've had officers who've had to go into detox due to the medications they'd been prescribed before I started work with them. Ambien is the most common of those.

For that reason, I've put together a non-medical-professional review of sleep medications on my website at www.copwhisperer.com. Go to the tab for "PTSD and Aches in the Night". The medication list is early on that page. I update it regularly, so won't go into detail on medications here.

MEDICATION FOR PTSD INSOMNIA AND NIGHTMARES

Antidepressants have not been shown to be effective with PTSD insomnia and nightmares. Maher, et al, found that Prozac (fluoxetine), Aropax, Paxil, Seroxat (paroxetine), and Zolof (sertraline) showed no evidence of reducing nightmares and only a marginal effect on insomnia due to PTSD.

There is, however, a new medication called Prazosin—originally developed to treat high blood pressure, which has been tested on veterans with combat-related PTSD. It has been shown to have significant impact on reduction or even elimination of nightmares. It also increases sleep—and especially REM sleep. Even more encouraging is that it is not addictive.

Comments from the VA medical professionals are that Prazosin is delivering. The January 2011 *Stars and Stripes* article I referred to above reports, "[A] University of Pittsburgh researcher has investigated sleep therapies that eliminate Vets' nightmares, including Prazosin, a medication that controls nightmares by depressing adrenaline....The early results are startling," she said, suggesting these therapies can reduce the anger, irritability and poor concentration associated with PTSD.

I am cautiously optimistic. However, there are as always side effects with medications. The more apparent one with Prazosin is the potential for dizziness, especially at the beginning of usage. Since this is a blood-pressure medication, the lowering of BP is responsible for that potential side effect.

As I stated at the beginning of this chapter, sleep plays a leading role in PTSD, and it needs to be addressed as a major concern in any treatment plan. If medication is required, it needs to be one that's a viable long-term prescription. Sleep problems take a significant amount of time to correct. That said, medication shouldn't be considered a permanent solution to PTSD-induced insomnia. Being freed from that condition is.

WHEN SLEEP *IS* THE NIGHTMARE

Though I was never an infantry soldier, escape and evasion were always in the back of my mind as a pilot, and twice in recent years I have awakened, naked and crawling in the snow.

I've been forced to lock my doors and take other measures to keep myself from freezing to death on a nighttime excursion."[16]

David

The earliest case of REM Behavior Disorder (RBD) I ever came across was in my first generation of cops. All had severe cases of PTSD. These guys were the ones who taught me that the more severe the sleep dysfunctions, the more severe the PTSD. Years later, research bore out that fact. [17] [18]

Models used for illustration

Reggie moved silently along the outer rim of the meadow. Slow, slow...then stopping for those long extended periods of time. Artfully done. All in order to convince the enemy that what they thought might be movement in that moonless night was nothing but the breeze they were upwind from...just the breeze...gently rustling the tall grass. Feeling that breeze on his face gives him comfort. He's in an optimum position.

Downwind...still...unseen...silent...patient... Picking up again...slow...balanced, knowing that they're right over there...he has heard them... he's counting...locating...at least two but maybe three. And then someone makes their last mistake. Slicing through the dark silence a branch cracks under the weight of something substantial just to his right. They realize too late that he's upon them. Reggie pivots ever so slightly and fires.

Then he's awake. Just in time to see the backsides of three mule deer take panicked flight crossing his arch of fire. They head across the field that lies to the north end of his house from where he then hears his dogs sounding off inside. Sitting down in the tall grass as he watches the bedroom light go on, he tries to figure out how he can explain this to his wife.

As a young MFT intern, I had come across one or two cases of sleepwalking. Those were child's play compared to the things I started to encounter with what my combat-vets-turned-cops and one or two of my undercover officers were doing in their sleep. It turns out that this is a male- dominated sleep disorder. I have had officers who've wakened at the kitchen sink cleaning a gun or going through the house systematically to "clear" rooms. The officer depicted above, discharged his weapon because he was "operational" around the perimeter of his property in his sleep. Thank goodness it was out on acreage in the country, but still! These types of sleep behaviors can be deadly, and I can guarantee that this fact has not been lost on my officers who've experienced this type of nocturnal return-to-duty.

WHAT IS RBD?

RBD has been the subject of research for decades, and if you look it up on the Internet, you'll see it's often connected with serious neurological illnesses. This need not be worrisome to you, because that connection occurs in cases where RBD is a seemingly stand-alone condition *without* a pre-existing presence of PTSD. Research in 2001 by Husain, Aatif, Miller and Carwile underscores this distinction, finding that although the RBD syndrome is sometimes associated with neuralgic disorders, psychiatric conditions (such as PTSD) were "not typical" of those cases.[19] In other words, don't assume RBD is a harbinger of worse things to come if you've got this occurring along with PTSD.

Consultation with and assessment by a physician is highly recommended should nocturnal acting out of dreams start occurring. With RBD, the incidence and prevention of injury are important. In fact, one of the criteria for a diagnosis of the condition is a history of nocturnal injuries experienced by "self" caused by moving about or injuries to "other" (that is, one's bed partner). All injuries are inflicted when the instigator is not awake. If these are happening to you in your sleep, your primary-care doctor and therapist should be made aware. Additionally, the question should be asked about setting in place a Plan B. These would be self-initiated, safe obstacles. These would be similar in nature to David's "behavioral" m.o. he so wisely instated once he found he was heading out into below-freezing temperatures that could kill him.

Typical activities during RBD include kicking, punching, leaping, night wandering, as well as the activities described at the beginning of this section. The person may wake up during their actions or not. The dreams are typically extremely easy to recall in vivid detail at that point in time.

The cause of RBD is not fully known, but researchers have made some progress. Animal research (Jouvet & Delorme, 1965)[20] identified lesions in the brain stem causing the condition, which blocks the brain's ability to inhibit movement activation during REM sleep.[21]

According to research, PTSD nightmares,[22] distinct from RBD,[23] may result from brain chemistry that causes an overlap of sleep phases.[24] This seems to happen between REM sleep,[25] which does not allow body movement, and another sleep phase in which the body chemistry shifts and allows the body to move.[26] The nightmares can occur when the shifts in sleep phases are out of sync.[27]

No matter what the cause, being awakened by the sound of your significant other's screams as she is being punched is very alarming. This is often the stuff of motivation for finding a means of correcting the problem, and rightly so.

AT THE END OF THE DAY

I hope that this chapter has given some useful options and information that can help you to find tonight's target...rest and sleep. I hope you can make your way to awakenings that find you at the start of your days rather than cast into the middle of long and tormenting nights.

And most of all...may you sleep well.

CHAPTER NOTES:

Foods and Sleep
There are foods that are touted as being able to help sleep along. For more information on this so you can experiment with this for yourself, you can start with this website: http://www.sleepdex.org/foods.htm

Mom Was Right
It's true: hot milk actually has been found to facilitate sleep. Properties in milk encourage the body to relax. Serotonin in milk is a naturally produced hormone that converts into tryptophan and that causes most people to feel drowsy. The calcium in milk is also a natural relaxant.

It's important not to allow the milk to boil, as that neutralizes the serotonin. Also it's better to use skim milk, which is lower in fat content but still has all the calcium of whole milk. Higher fat in milk puts a greater workload on the digestive system, which can keep you awake. To make your mug of milk more appetizing, try adding either honey or a little bit of vanilla extract with a pinch of sugar.

REM Rebound
From a medical student's perspective on REM Rebound, I'm including this below. I found this on the website http://bostonianinny.blogspot.com/2008/02/rem-rebound.html.

If you log onto that site, take his unilateral dismissal of sleep medications with a grain of salt. He's referring to meds that *are* addictive, but as you now know after reading this chapter on sleep that's not always the case.

When I was dealing with my own PTSD, my doc (an ex-USAF Fighter Pilot) literally saved me with a prescription of Amitriptyline (taken as a low 5–10 mgs right at bedtime). I was on it for around 18 months and it wasn't addictive. Once I was finished with PTSD, I worked off of it over the course of 10 days and I never had any difficulties. All to say, not all medications are evil and as stated already, you need to do your homework.

Force Science Newsletter Transmission #177

Opening our inbox on provocative questions about cop fatigue

Readers of *Force Science News* offered an outpouring of opinions about the two provocative questions regarding police fatigue posed in Transmission #174, sent 3/25/11.

> **"My body is in a constant flux"** On days off, I have to sleep nights and be up all day for my family. When I go back to work I have to sleep days and be up all night for work. So my body is in a constant flux of having my sleep pattern do a 180-degree flip every few days. The only way to do it and keep peace in the family is sleep deprivation.
>
> So how would the agency regulate that? Tell the officer he can't listen to his spouse, or can't live with his family during his work-week? No, police need to look at what the fire agencies have set up: some officers would work while others sleep, then trade out. In a large emergency, everyone would roll out.
>
> *Sgt. ----- (WA) PD*

A crazy idea? In any 8-hour shift, whether it is days, evenings, or midnights, I find there is a brief time where my body becomes fatigued and it's dangerous to drive or deal with a high-stress incident. Why not institute a 10- to 20-minute power nap and lift the restriction on sleeping on duty? I suggested to a commander friend who was about to be promoted that he take this issue to the chief. He asked, "Are you crazy? They will never consider me for a promotion again!"

[Name withheld] Oakwood (OH) Public Safety Dept.

Fibromyalgia (FMS) is a physical condition tied in with sleep dysfunction. It involves physical pain that can range from a sore, stiff neck to high degrees of pain throughout the body. In extreme cases even just feather-light touch to the skin of an affected region of the body can be painful. Please see my website page *"PTSD & Aches in the Night."* At the end of that webpage are other internet links to FBS resources/information.
http://copwhisperer.com/Cop_Whisperer_Enterprise/PTSD_%26_Aches_in_the_Nite.html

PHOTO CREDITS:

1. Lonely: © iStock.com/urbancow
2. "Aaron's" SPECT Images © Karen Lansing & Daniel Amen
3. Alcoholic & Non Alcoholic SPECTs © Daniel Amen
4. Man Lying in Bed With Feet Sticking out of Blanket: ©iStock.com/Brainsil
5. Wide Awake at Night: ©iStock.com/Ace Create
6. Elevated view of the head of a young man asleep in bed ©Stockbyte/Getty Images
7. Sheep: ©iStock.com/zkoritni
8. Insomnia: ©iStock.com/almagami
9. Hot Summer: ©iStock.com/rudigobbo
10. Man at Night with Teddy Bear: ©John Rensten/Getty images
11. Army Soldiers on a Hill ©iStock.com/ninjaMonkeyStudio
12. Magic Hour: ©iStock/Soubrette

ENDNOTES:

1. Theodore Knell, *From the Corners of a Wounded Mind*, Night Publishing, 2011 http://theodoreknell.com.
2. Amen Clinic, SPECT Images of a normal brain and a brain using alcohol chronically.
3. R. J. Ross, W. A. Ball, K. A. Sullivan, S. N. Caroff, *"Sleep disturbance as the hallmark of posttraumatic stress disorder,"* Am J Psychiatry, vol.146, 1989, 697–707.
4. M. Nishida, J. Persall, R. L. Buckner, M. P. Walker, "REM Sleep, Prefrontal Theta, and the Consolidation of Human Emotion," *Cerebral Cortex, Vol.* 19 (5), May 2009, 1158-66.
5. M. Ritchey, F. Dolcos, R. Cabeza, "Role of Amygdala Connectivity in the Persistence of Emotional Memories Over Time: An Event-Related FMRI Investigation," *Cerebral Cortex, Vol. 9* (11), March, 2008, 2494-2504.
6. E. Hartmann, *Making Connections in a Safe Place: Is Dreaming Psychotherapy?* Dreaming, Vol. 5(4), Dec. 1995, 213-28.
7. R. Stickgold, E. Wamsley, *Sleep, Memory and Dreams: Fitting the Pieces Together,* Lecture presented by Dr. R. Stickgold, http://www.youtube.com/watch?v=WmRGNunPj3c , June10, 2010.

8. Sleep Stages; http://sleepdimension.com/Sleep-Stages.php Sleep Dimension, 2008.

9. J. F. Pagel. *Nightmares and Disorders of Dreaming*, American Family Physician, Apr.,4, 2001.

10. D. Foulkes. *Dreaming: A Cognitive-Psychological Analysis*, Hillsdale, NJ.: Erlbaum, 1985.

11. K. Spiegle, K.; K. Knutson; K.; R. Leproult, R.; et al. "Sleep Loss: A Novel risk factor for insulin resistance and Type 2 Diabetes," *Journal of Applied Physiology*, Vol. 99(5) Nov., 2005, 2008-19.

12. S. Robbins, "Seeking Better Sleep," *Stars and Stripes*, Feb. 5, 2011.

13. Ibid.

14. M. S. Radlick. *The processing demands of television: Neurological correlates of Television Viewing. Unpublished doctoral dissertation*, Rensselaer Polytechnic Institute, Troy, NY, 1980.

15. Ibid. Robbins.

16. Quote used with permission by David (last name withheld by request), author of http://www.mnwelldir.org/docs/mental_health/ptsd.htm

17. T. D. Warner; R. Schrader; M. Koss, et al. "The Relationship of Sleep Quality and Posttraumatic Stress to Potential Sleep Disorders in Sexual Assault Survivors and Nightmares, Insomnia and PTSD," Journal of Trauma Stress, Vol. 14(4), Oct., 2001, 647-65.

18. A. Germain; D. J. Buysse; M. K. Shear, et al. "Clinical Correlates of Poor Sleep Quality in Posttraumatic Stress Disorder," *Journal of Trauma Stress,* vol. 17, 2004, 477-84.

19. A. M. Husain; P. P. Miller; S. T. Carwile. "REM Sleep Behvior Disorder: Toential Relationship to Posttraumatic Stress Disorder," *Journal of Clinical Neurophysiology,* Vol. 18 (2) March 2001, 148-57.

20. M. Jouvet, F. Delorme, *Locus Coeruleus et Sommeil Paradoxical*; CR Soc. Biol 159, 1965, 895-99.

21. L. D. Sanford; A. R. Morrison; Graziella Mann. "Sleep Patterning and Behaviour in Cats with Pontine Lesions Creating REM Without Atonia," Journal of Sleep Research, Vol. 3, {4}, Jan., 20, 2009.

22. B. R. Lydiard, M. H. Hamner. "Clinical Importance of Sleep Disturbance as a Treatment Target for PTSD," FOCUS, "The Journal of Lifelong Learning in Psychiatry," Vol. VII, No. 2, Spring 2009, 176-83.

23. T. A Mellman, A. Kumar, R. Kulick-Bell, M. Kumar, B. Nolan, "Nocturnal/Daytime Urine Noradrenergic Measures and Sleep in Combat-related PTSD," *Bio Psychiatry,* vol. 38, 1995,174–79.

24. J. A. Hobson, R. Stickgold, E. F. Pace-Schott, "The Neuropsychology of REM Sleep Dreaming," *NeuroReport*, 1998, R1-R14.

25. J. Debiec, J. E. LeDoux, "Noradrenergic Signaling in the Amygdala Contributes to the Reconsolidation of Fear Memory: Treatment Implications for PTSD," *New York, Academy of Science Annual,* vol.1071, 2006, 521–524.

26. C. Gottesmann, "Noradrenaline Involvement in Basic and Higher Integrated REM Sleep Processes," Program pf Neurobiology, vol. 85, 2008, 237–272.

27. J. R. Strawn, T. D. Geracioti Jr., "Noradrenergic dysfunction and the psycho-pharmacology of posttraumatic stress disorder," *Depress Anxiety,* vol. 25 2008, 260 –271.

Chapter 8 Introduction
"FIRST KILL"
Theodore Knell
An excerpt from "First Kill," *From the Corners of a Wounded Mind*

Finally it ends
And in the early morning mist the killing ground falls silent.
Standing alone and drained,
Combats torn by close calls and covered in blood
I survey the fruits of countless months of training.

Models used for illustration

I have had my first kill,
my second, even a third kill,
but realise nothing has really changed.

Have I made a difference in this battle?
Yes...but not in the war.

I have merely robbed the world of yet another father, husband, brother, son,
And like a hammer blow to the head the reality of my actions hits home.

Tomorrow there will be another battle
And whether I win or loose

The killing will go on.

"STRANGE BEINGS"
Theodore Knell

Who are these strange beings?
Trained warriors...my comrades...my brothers
whose special calling turns my world upside down?
A feeling of guilt rushes over me as I watch them working
frantically to save a life, that life which minutes before I had
tried so hard to take.
Torn, I'll share in their sorrow if they should fail but feel anger
should they succeed, robbing me of my kill.
Whether saving my brothers in the heat of the fight, or
wandering the killing ground when the battle is done in search of my enemy's life
to save, their task is endless. They spend each day covered in blood and every night
grieving for those they couldn't save. These are our "Medics," half soldier...half saint.

CHAPTER 8
THE COST OF THE KILL

My bibles on lethal contact are Lt. Col Grossman's books *On Killing* and *On Combat*. In Sections VI and VII of *On Killing*, he renders an accurate description of the salient aspects of lethal contact and its aftermath. (Please Note: Due to the graphic nature of some of the material in those sections, it may not be appropriate reading if you have untreated PTSD). I won't repeat what has already been done so well by far greater minds, but encourage you to read his books.

This chapter will briefly review Lt. Col Grossman's list of post-killing stages Warriors may experience. Along with that review of his comprehensive list, I will include accounts from my OIS officers/soldiers. You may have experienced none, some or all of these post-killing stages. Everyone's unique, and every shooting is unique.

• The Concern Stage:
"All the way in I was thinking, what if I can't do it when the time comes?"

• The Killing Stage:
"My training clicked in and I didn't have to think...it happened just like I was taught."

• The Exhilaration Stage:
"I realized that I'd survived and that I hadn't failed my team, my wife, my kids...I was coming home that night. For a brief time I felt totally high. That worried me later."

• The Remorse Stage:
"Every Christmas I find myself thinking about his family, knowing that he'd have killed me if I hadn't killed him...but still...his family is without him every Christmas because I shot to survive."

• The Rationalization Stage:
"If we hadn't stopped them they'd have gone on to murder more of our guys...next time it could have been us they had the drop on."

• The Acceptance Stage:

"I spent over 15 years struggling through that firefight, wondering if, had I done this or not done that, would he have made a different choice? I see now that we both had our choices to make every step of the way. I've let go of that thought that I controlled it all...I didn't. What I controlled was what I did in response to what he did in response to what I did in response to him... It happened and it's over. Now I feel like for the first time since that night, I'm not leaving myself behind in that incident anymore. It's done and I can let it go."

In summary of these above stages in *On Killing,* Lt. Col. Grossman states:

> *"Some are psychologically overwhelmed by these emotions and they often become determined never to kill again and thereby become incapable of further combat. But while most modern veterans have experienced powerful emotions at this stage, they tend to deny their emotions, becoming cold and hard inside—thus making subsequent killing much easier.*
>
> *Whether the killer denies his remorse, deals with it, or is overwhelmed by it, it is nevertheless almost always there. The killer's remorse is real, it is common, it is intense, and it is something that he must deal with for the rest of his life."*[1]

In the wake of having to take a life, deep wells and currents can work beneath the surface of what may appear to be "solid ground" in OIS cases. These can change everything in the course of a career, so because of their power these will be brought to light.

WHEN THEORY BECOMES REALITY

There are a number of things you can do in order to mentally prepare for that moment when the concept of taking a life moves from the one-dimensional paper target on the range into the three-dimensional reality out on the ground. The magnitude of that shift is impossible to describe, even for those who have endured it. While no amount of knowledge can fully prepare you for it, the more you understand, the less surprised you'll be. One of my officers described this distance between the concept and the concrete reality of taking a life when he stated to me in session one day, *"Killing another human was theory to me for years...Until my shooting made it real."*

If you already have had to take life to save life, you may or may not be struggling with the post-shooting aftermath. I have known shooters who were not psychopaths but who knew what they had to do and why. They didn't like it, but they dealt with what came at them and they were able to move beyond the incident with little if any need for support.

If, on the other hand, a killing still haunts you, know that it can and should be resolved. I've worked with lethal contact trauma spanning multiple wars (Vietnam, the Mid East theatres, the ravages during and following the troubles of Northern Ireland), and the peacetime war that continues in the U.S. streets. In all my years of treating trauma induced by lethal contact, one thing has been consistent: Reaching resolution around killing is rarely an easy journey, but it is a very attainable destination. While the journey can take different routes, three *waypoints* are constants and they can all lead you to becoming a more skilled and resilient Warrior.

First, the trauma must be neutralized. Second, if there's any tactical learning to be gained out of the shooting incident, that must be accomplished. Third, healing around the natural revulsion for human killing must be worked through. The killing will never be shifted from necessary to good. Nor will it ever be forgotten. But with work and time, peace, resolution and a newfound inner strength can replace torment left behind in the wake of an OIS. This is what healing looks like.

It is also extremely helpful to find others from your own or a similar career discipline who have been in shootings and have navigated successfully through the terrain that lies ahead of you. Since there are different reactions post shooting, you may need to speak to several shooters in order to find one who had similar reactions to yours. You can always learn from knowledgeable guides, especially if a shooting becomes part of your story.

It's also important to know ahead of time the normal reactions that can occur during an IOS (even ones that seem "really out there" typically aren't). This last item is extremely helpful since thinking you're going 'round-the-bend in the wake of a shooting is not one of those things you need added to the list. To help avoid that concern, the section below reviews some of the research that has been done, beginning in 1986, on reactions that can commonly occur during the incredible stress of deadly force.

GAINING MORE CLARITY POST-OIS

"Now we see things imperfectly, like puzzling reflections in a mirror, but then we will see everything with perfect clarity. All that I know now is partial and incomplete, but then I will know everything completely..."[2]

I Cor 13:12a

In 1986 and 1989, the earliest OIS reactions studies were published in scholarly journals by Drs. Solomon[3] and Horn.[4] In 1997, the first non-academic book about OIS reactions was published by Dr. Alexis Artwhol & Loren Christensen, bringing the subject out of the confines of LE administrative and psychological journals and into the hands of police and the public. Since then, we've gained more understanding due to scientific research and the honest reporting by OIS officers of what transpires in those critical moments during shooting incidents.

Even so, many agencies still have no idea of what can occur during an OIS. Over the past seven years, I have witnessed the shift from having no knowledge of this important information to having it become a segment of the firearms training courses in places such as the UK, but there's still much to be done.

This past week, I completed a training of a close-protection team in one foreign mission. The team included officers from seven EU countries.

Some knew of this research and a few didn't. The same still can be said for the U.S. law enforcement population as well. Thankfully, however, due to the training and education available now through entities such as policeone.com, Calibre Press, and Force Science Research Institute, those unaware of the research are in the minority. For that reason, the material in the next segment may be very familiar to many of you. However, in case it isn't, I will review key research that is extremely important, foundational knowledge.

IN THE MIDST OF A SHOOTING

In the mid 1980s to 1990s, OIS incidents were on the increase. As this occurred, thanks to the increased use of Kevlar vests, more officers were able to survive shootings. Furthermore, officers were more willing to describe their experiences afterwards. In their excellent book, *Deadly Force Encounters*[5] Dr. Alexis Artwhol and Loren Christensen report on their findings from interviews with 72 officers involved in shootings. This was a critical addition to the newly evolving research on post-shooting reactions.[6] Since then, their research has been replicated.[7]

This brain-under-pressure research began to show consistently that the brain behaves differently under highly stressful and/or lethal contact conditions than it does under normal circumstances.[8] This difference can impact decision-making, reactions, memory and perception.[9]

The authors found that, out of the 72 officers interviewed:

88% had diminished sound
82% had tunnel vision
78% clicked into "auto pilot"
65% had heightened visual clarity
63% experienced time in slow motion
61% had memory loss of segments of the event
60% had memory loss of some of their actions
50% experienced dissociation (i.e. feeling surreal or having out of body experiences)
36% had intrusive, distracting thoughts
19% had memory distortion
17% experienced time in fast motion
17% had intensified sound
11% experienced temporary paralysis

This work, along with other similar studies, indicates strongly that conditions such as distortions of perceptions, distracting thoughts and gaps of memory occur in the heat of rapidly unfolding, potentially deadly CIs. The research showed that as the brain hyperfocuses on what it considers critical for survival, it "gates" out other aspects of sensory input it considers non-essential for survival. The result is often amplified sensory input, such as visual clarity, magnified sounds, etc.

There can also be incorrect or skewed perceptions and gaps of memory. In addition, of course, the human brain doesn't recall everything that happens even in non-traumatic events of life. One major difference between normal and critical incident memory gaps however, is that if we forget where we lay our keys, it usually doesn't end up with a charge for an attempt to pervert the course of justice, or for murder.[10]

Hayden, the officer under investigation for possibly not using a justified tactic to restrain a suspect, never did recall the tactic he used. That memory was lost to him because it was competing with another critical (and more familiar) physical memory, such as becoming fatigued and weaker in an extended physical confrontation.[11] During the EMDR session that dealt with that incident, Hayden remembered the stress and fatigue on that fateful night. That critical information had been buried under the trauma that, by its very nature, tends to fill the psychological horizon until it is neutralized and moved into the "It's History" file.

Gaps in memory even for a brief time, as in Hayden's case, can have a major impact on investigations, especially if conducted by uneducated or untrained investigators who expect 100% recall of a critical incident. Beyond that impact, however, is the wake that spreads out from a memory gap that has another deep and negative consequence for the officer. This negative effect can endure well past even a positive outcome of an OIS investigation.

FRAGMENTED TRAUMA-BASED MEMORY

During the extreme stress of lethal contact or other types of critical incident, memory of sensory input is not absorbed by the hippocampus as it normally would be. This restricts the input from being fully received and joined up in a cohesive story that makes sense. It also causes memory of different aspects of input to become fragmented and disjointed. For this reason, some trauma-based memory will be vivid, such as the huge muzzle and the color of the gun, while other memories will be vague or non-existent, like the face of the person holding that gun. This is illustrated by Robin's story.

ROBIN'S STORY:

Robin saw the panicked civilian (the RP) *waving her down at the sidewalk opposite the Safeway and Straw Hat Pizza. When she pulled into the parking lot, he began frantically shouting and pointing to a man who was standing in the parking lot approximately 45 yards away.*

"He tried to kill me! He's got a machete and he tried to kill me!" the RP *kept shouting. Robin positioned her unit at an angle that would render cover. She then got out on the opposite side of her unit, keeping it between herself and the RP. The large subject whom she now could see was indeed holding in his right hand a long object wrapped in paper. She ordered the RP to stay to her left behind the engine block and to get down. He complied.*

She then attempted to engage the subject verbally. By that time he'd turned away with his back to her, but he was still in the same place. She called to him and asked what was going on, and suddenly he whirled around, pulling the paper wrapping off to expose a machete and charged toward her vehicle. He hurled the machete, which hit the patrol unit and bounced off the trunk. Then with both hands now free, he lifted his shirt and pulled a weapon out of his belt. Closing the distance, the suspect pointed the gun directly at Robin.

On her part, Robin had drawn her weapon when the suspect had whirled around to start toward her. He had not responded to her commands to "Freeze! Drop the gun!" She was clearly aware of seeing the butt of the gun when he lifted his shirt to reach for it. Even with his speed of movement, and all she had to think about in that second, she accurately identified it as belonging to a Luger. In those next closing seconds, the thought came vividly: "If he goes just two feet to the right, I can't do this!" As it turned out, he stayed on a straight course, and in the end, she had to shoot.

Afterward, Robin didn't experience isolation or lack of support from her department. In fact, they paid to have her flown out of the area to see a therapist who worked with her until they mutually agreed that she was "over" the shooting. In the wake of the investigation, it was decided that all her actions had been justified. It seemed that Robin's life would return to normal.

Despite that, Robin experienced no sense of closure about the incident. Although she'd known she had to take the shot, what tormented her was her last thought—"If he moves two feet to the right, I can't do it." Actually, it was the four words "I can't do it" that kept haunting her.

This tactical decision not to shoot if he'd veered to her right during that rapidly unfolding event made no sense to her. It was causing her to question her ability to do her job. In the 18 months following the shooting, she changed. Due to a serious back injury sustained immediately after that incident, Robin finally filed for disability retirement. But she admitted to me years later that even without that injury, she'd still not "have made it." Her confidence had eroded away. The thought "I can't do it" echoed in her mind every time she put on her uniform, every time she even thought of reporting for duty. "I can't do it...I can't do it...I can't."

THINGS ARE NOT ALWAYS AS THEY APPEAR

In the context of the three stages reviewed at the beginning of this chapter, given just this information about Robin's case, it could appear that her sense of being overwhelmed that had developed over time would be centered on not ever being able or willing to shoot or kill someone in order to protect life. However, there was a subtle difference in Robin's situation.

The key for Robin, as it turned out, had everything to do with the thought, *"If he moves two feet over...I can't do it."* Eventually that memory fragmented and Robin forgot the first part of the thought. She became stuck over the course of time on the last part: *"I can't do it."*

This is how fragmentation of memory, due to the way the brain processes information under severe stress, can undermine an officer's self-confidence. An incomplete, disjointed perspective of the incident and of her reactions in it constructs a flawed self-perception and *a negative belief.* That then can undermine a life.

In the EMDR work Robin and I did on this incident after the dominating traumatic image became less disturbing, more memory fragments found their way to center stage to be reprocessed and understood. For instance, midway through an EMDR set, a visual memory of a teenage boy in the picture window of the Straw Hat Pizza came to the surface. Robin suddenly broke into tears, realizing immediately that a teenager was facing Robin from inside the Straw Hat Pizza and had watched things going sideways.

During the incident, Robin's brain instantly had registered the danger this teen was in as he stood wide-eyed behind a pane of glass. He was positioned just to Robin's right of the unfolding events. Had the suspect moved just a couple of feet to Robin's right, this boy would be in the backdrop and had she shot and missed the suspect, her bullets could possibly have hit the boy.

Memories that came back to her in that segment of the EMDR session then started to complete the fragmented puzzle. The report had mentioned a witness who'd seen the events from another position but hadn't heard Robin's verbal commands. No wonder, he'd been watching from inside a building at least 40 yards away. In the post-OIS haze, the severe pain from the back injury, and the stress of the investigation, Robin had not known where the witness had been or why he hadn't heard her yelling commands. Now she knew: it had been this teenager standing in harm's way.

During that incident, Robin's amygdala did its job by rapidly calculating what she had to do in fractions of seconds. It did not connect the reason behind the tactical thought for the decision with the hippocampus or the prefrontal cortex. That "disconnect" kept her from understanding why she'd worried about things possibly drifting to the right. She had no context for that thought until the fragmented memory came to the surface in the EMDR session.

Finally, after putting that piece of the puzzle about the arch-of-fire concerns into place, she was able to let go of her belief that she had a lack of competence or, worse yet, cowardice lying-in-wait inside her. This is no small matter and is noteworthy for anyone reading this with a similar festering mass of self-doubt or reproach. The smallest fragment of memory can make or break a career in these cases. It can also make or break one's own self-perception over the course of time.

This phantom memory gap is one of three red flags that can cause significant difficulties for officers post incident. Two more will be discussed in the following chapter.

For now however, know that it's critical that memory fragments come together so that you can learn or recall as much of the traumatic incident's events as you can, whether you'd done everything right or not. Rather than bury it, you need to be able to reprocess those memories so that the traumatic aspects can be neutralized. This allows the incident to be redesignated a memory that can be learned from rather than a nightmare of an incident relived over and over again. Accessing such memory fragments allows you to be taught by it or freed by it, or both, so you can finally move on. This translates dramatically into rapid changes and improvements in your life.

OUTCOME OF ROBIN'S FIRST OIS EMDR SESSION

The morning after that EMDR session with Robin, she left a message on my voicemail indicating she was moving back into normal life. Notice below how she refers to the 0–10 scale to measure any pre–post EMDR changes:

Hi Karen, it's Robin. I don't know where to start or what to say! I'm just so happy today; I can't believe it. I still feel this relaxed feeling—I don't ever remember feeling this relaxed. You know, last night when I got home [from the EMDR session] *and was getting ready to go to bed, I thought, 'I don't know how many times in the past I've thought about taking a bath just to relax and I would take a bath and I wouldn't relax, and it just didn't work.' And last night I thought, 'Now I could take a bath and really relax!' I didn't. I just went to bed, but I was relaxed anyway [laughter]!*

Then this morning was really amazing. I've logged a ton of stuff already from last night for you this morning, so I'll go over it with you later, but the main thing was … there was chaos here—you know, what's typical chaos for me. My Mom's here, she's doing her laundry, everyone's taking showers. Jim's home and he was being abrasive. And it's always gotten me to a frustration point that I just can't handle…you know between an 8 to 10 in irritability and all of that.

But this morning everything was going on, but I only felt like a 2 in irritability. And even then, it was just an observation of how he was at that point… it didn't make me feel his stuff.

And I'm just… I just sat at the table this morning and I just cried, because this is just so awesome…Thank you so much!"

ROBIN'S SPECT IMAGES AND PDS SCORES

It's noteworthy to see just how dramatically quiet Robin's brain activity was after she completed all the EMDR sessions in Stage 2 of her treatment plan. While that allowed Robin to become more relaxed and content again in her life, she wasn't sure it was altogether a good thing. As she put it in one session, "I'm far happier and calmer…only I'm 'dumber' now."

Robin is an extremely bright and successful woman and this fact hadn't changed. The feeling of being dumber came about because her brain was no longer functioning on the overdrive stimulant effects of stress hormones that come with PTSD.

Besides the chemical shift that came post PTSD, new information about a prior incident came out on re-assessment: Robin had been involved in a motorcycle accident many years before the OIS incident. It hadn't seemed noteworthy during the intake and mapping of her trauma history in Stage 1, compared to the other critical incidents she'd been involved in. (NOTE TO SELF: *ALWAYS ask very specific questions around history of physical injuries or head trauma*. NOTE TO READER: *ALWAYS give that information during intake*).

As it turned out, the accident hadn't traumatized Robin emotionally, but it had definitely traumatized her brain. That traumatic brain injury (TBI) was then self-medicated for many years by the PTSD-induced production of stress hormones. When the PTSD was resolved, the stress hormone levels dropped and the brain, no longer in chronic Code 3 state, quieted down. That caused the TBI to became more clearly apparent in Robin's brain and her day-to-day functioning. I referred her to an exceptional psychiatrist who also used SPECT imaging clinically. He was able to see the pattern of underactivity and provide the medication Robin needed to help increase her brain activity.

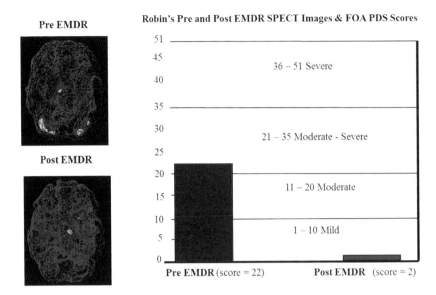

Pre EMDR

Post EMDR

Robin's Pre and Post EMDR SPECT Images & FOA PDS Scores

36 – 51 Severe

21 – 35 Moderate - Severe

11 – 20 Moderate

1 – 10 Mild

Pre EMDR (score = 22)   Post EMDR   (score = 2)

A CRITICAL NEED FOR MORE RESEARCH

With the overwhelming number of traumatic brain injuries and cases of PTSD coming out of the Middle East theatres, it is essential that clinicians, vets and their families and veterans' groups urgently call for funding for progressive and well-designed treatment research. We need to figure out how to help these injured brains heal faster. For now, the medical interventions that target specific areas of the brain that can't maintain adequate activation are helpful. Neuroimaging is extremely useful for this. So are the methods of exercising the brain to improve memory that have come available through the Internet. Of course, physical exercise helps brain function, as well. However, these are not enough.

Researchers and clinicians have moved heaven and earth to get better at treating and curing PTSD. Now, the next vital problem—that of memory and brain function in TBI and PTSD injuries—is where we must aggressively seek improvements.

ON KILLING & GRIEF

Lt. Col. Grossman has pointed out that there is a heavy burden that comes with having to take a life. The grief accounts for a significant amount of that "cost of the kill," as manifested in courtrooms or investigative tribunals when the officer who fired the fatal shot/s testifies. In July 2005, the Jean Charles de Menezes shooting in the UK occurred amid the terrorist attacks in London. The shooting clearly left in its wake an officer who was grieving. He was grieving, having killed an innocent man on that day and he was grieving for the de Menezes family.

An article in *The Guardian* at the time of the trial describes the scene. *"For members of the public, he was merely a voice, hidden behind 10-foot screens to protect his anonymity, and known only as Charlie 12. At 1:46 p.m., two hours into his evidence, he suddenly became human.*

"'I cannot begin to put myself in the position that they [de Menezes' family] are in,' he said. 'I am a family man myself and to lose a son or any member of your family in this situation, I just cannot believe. I offer them my sincere condolences.' But it was only after the hearing that his feelings overwhelmed him, and he broke down."[12]

The existence and significance of post-shooting grief appear to have shown up in the SPECT images of our six OIS clients. At the time of their incidents, all the officers believed that their lives and/or the lives of others were at risk. They knew there were no other options left to them. Not one felt that they'd done the wrong thing, given the situation. Following full investigations, all six shootings, including the suicide-by-cop,[13] were deemed justified.

However, despite that justified belief, their brain images showed activation in three regions that have been connected to grief. This may further confirm the intrinsic nature of humankind. While our species does kill, the human condition is not inclined to do this naturally to its own kind. Lt. Col. Grossman does an excellent job in *On Killing* reviewing the historical proofs of this fact (see "Overcoming the Resistance to Killing: The Problem" pp 250 – 260).[14]

There were, in some cases, a reflection of grief over the very necessity of having to take a life. One of my officers expressed his sheer sadness as we were in the midst of his EMDR session working through the shooting: *"Look at what I've done … Look at what I had to do."*

What surprised us in the analysis of the brain images were the neurological tracers that might indicate that grief was being worked through in the process of EMDR. What we saw was a de-activation in three areas that have been found by researchers to be associated with image-induced grief (triggered by what is seen).[15] There was also deactivation in areas involved in processing motor imagery[16] (what is done).[17] Then there was deactivation in the area that judges emotional moral and non-moral social judgements (what is decided to be right and wrong).[18] Deactivations in these areas post EMDR may be evidence of what research and clinicians have found: EMDR brings relief to trauma-induced grief.[19] [20] [21]

The best way that I can attempt to put words to the grief that the officer I quoted above was struggling with, is to say this: It was grief over a part of himself that he felt had been taken because of having to do the very act of killing. There's a French saying that expresses this beautifully: *Partir c'est mourir un peu.* "To part is to die a little."

Despite the training, the absolute necessity and even the absolute righteousness of a shooting, there are salient elements of the normal human condition that can't be erased. Along with the automatic clicking into training, these must temporarily be put aside. They may or may not require your attention later on. That is to say, the sense of fear, rage, and perhaps even helplessness at being caught up in that deadly situation due to another person's actions are in there and very real. Yet they're often contained as one fights for life. And among those reactions, after the smoke clears, can also be grief.

Even though the officers described above all had been declared justified by the investigations, and even though they each knew that they were right in what they'd done, beneath all of that there were reactions that needed their attention. The trauma-filled horizon had kept things buried (albeit still very much alive, and not in a pleasant way). In all six cases above, significant resolution of that grief came when the fragmented memories of the shootings were able to surface and the officers could process through them.

After the final resolution of the PTSD, all six officers no longer experienced the intense emotional reactivity, the restricted access to sensory input, and the limited access to critical information that had been overshadowed by the traumatic fragments of memory. What came with resolution helped complete the puzzle: clarity about critical information that could override errant and negative beliefs, a more complete context and that all-important adaptive learning for moving into the future better prepared and better trained.

CHAPTER NOTES:

Grief and Neurology (From Lansing, Amen, et al):

"We found deactivation in three areas found by Gundel et al. to be associated with image-induced grief[28]: the left cuneus, which has been suggested to process motor imagery,[29,30] the right lingual gyrus, which has also been implicated in processing motor imagery[30] and in judging emotionally evocative stimuli;[31] and Brodmann's area (BA) 4 of the right precentral gyrus. Deactivations in these areas may be relieving trauma-induced grief." [22]

Memory and Fatigue:

Dr. Lewinski of Force Science Research Center released the findings of exertion and fatigue in FSN Transmission #176 (April 26, 2011). There were significant findings relating to physiological and memory recall and all were surprising.

Outcomes in testing how quickly an officer becomes exhausted physically and cognitively indicated that there's an extremely small window of stamina and effectiveness for officers involved in physical conflict. Depletion of physical resources for the officer study subjects occurred on average within 56 seconds of going all out hitting a boxing bag.

"The officers started out strong, driving hard with penetrating hits that visibly moved the heavy bag," Lewinski reports." But by 30 to 40 seconds, most were significantly weakened. They were not able to breathe properly, their cadence dropped, their strikes scarcely moved the bag, if at all, and they were resorting largely to very weak, slowly paced blows that would have had little impact on a combative assailant."

The more alarming discovery, however, came in the case of highly physically fit and expertly skilled fighters. Those officers rendered more powerful and rapid strikes, expending a higher level of effort. This proved to exhaust their higher levels of reserve in approximately the same short window of time as their fellow officers who were less fit and less skilled.

The TV program, *Daily Planet* (October 18, 2010 – Clip 1) aired footage from the actual research experiments. You can watch it at this link: http://watch.discoverychannel.ca/daily-planet/october-2010/daily-planet---october-18-2010/#clip362857

THE IMPORTANCE OF CROSS-TRAINING WORKOUTS

In response to the FSN exhaustion study, this comment was posted in the May 20, 2011 Transmission #178:

"The short duration of the activity and the massive increases in blood lactate suggest that the primary metabolic pathway utilized by the experimental group was NOT aerobic, but rather, anaerobic. So if the fitness level of a given officer was rated as high employing an aerobic measure, then the fact that an officer fatigued in roughly the same time as a less fit officer means only that the "more fit officer" had indeed no more training in utilizing the anaerobic pathway than did the less fit officer. You cannot train only aerobically and expect that you can derive anaerobic fitness. Training for high intensity, anaerobic engagements should make use of brief, high intensity efforts."

H. Anthony Semone, Ph.D. Member, Police Policy Studies Council Specialist in clinical, health, and exercise psychology Wyndmoor, PA

GRAHAM V. CONNOR ON "REASONABLENESS" INQUIRY

The Fourth Amendment "reasonableness" inquiry is whether the officer's actions are "objectively reasonable" in light of the facts and circumstances confronting them, without regard to their underlying intent or motivation. The "reasonableness" of a particular use of force must be judged from the perspective of a reasonable officer on the scene, and its calculus must embody an allowance for the fact that police officers are often forced to make split-second decisions about the amount of force necessary in a particular situation. Pp. 490 U. S. 396-397

PHOTO CREDITS:

1. Night Combat ©iStockphoto.com/Bluberries
2. Basic Training ©iStockphoto.com/Rockfinder
3. SWAT Officer ©Karen Lansing 2012
4. Broken mirror ©iStockphoto.com/eCal
5. Cracked Ground ©iStock/SergeyZavalnyuk
6. "Robin's" SPECT Images: © Karen Lansing & Daniel Amen

ENDNOTES:

1. D. Grossman. *On Killing: The Psychological Cost of Learning to Kill in War and Society.* Little, Brown and Co., 1996, 237.
2. *Holy Bible.* New Living Translation. Tyndale House Publishers, Inc., Carol Stream, IL: 2007.
3. R. M. Solomon and J. H. Horn. "Post shooting traumatic reactions, A pilot study," *Psychological Services for Law Enforcement Officers,* Ed. James T. Reese and Harvey A. Goldstein, Washington, DC: U.S. Government Printing Office, 1986.
4. R. M. Solomon. "Post shooting trauma," *The Police Chief,* pp. 40-44, October 1988.

5. A. Artwhol and L. W. Christensen. *"Deadly Force Encounters: What Cops Need to Know to Mentally and Physically Survive a Gunfight."* Paladin Press, Boulder CO: 1997.

6. A. Artwhol. "Perceptual and Memory Distortion during Officer-Involved Shootings." IACP Net document No 564080), *FBI Law Enforcement Bulletin,* October 2002, 18.

7. A. L. Hoenig and J. E. Roland. "Shots fired: Officer involved," *Police Chief,* October 1998.

8. D. Klinger. U.S. Department of Justice, National Institute of Justice. *Police Responses to Officer-Involved Shootings.* NCJRS 192285, Washington, DC: October 2001.

9. W. Lewinski. "Why is the suspect shot in the back?" *The Police Marksman,* Nov./Dec. 2000, http://www.forcescience.org/articles/shotinback.pdf.

10. D. Grossman and B. K. Siddle. *Critical Incident Amnesia: The Physiological Basis and the Implications of Memory Loss During Extreme Survival Situations.* Millstadt, IL: PPCT Management Systems, 1998.

11. W. Lewinski, J. William, L. Anderson, L. Hope. "Final findings from the Force Science exhaustion study." *Force Science News,* Transmission #176 Apr., 26, 2011.

12. S. Laville, and V. Dodd. "The officer who killed Jean Charles de Menezes breaks down at inquest." *The Guardian,* Oct. 25, 2008. http://www.guardian.co.uk/uk/2008/oct/25/jean-charles-de-menezes-trial

13. Graham v. Connor, 490 U.S. 386 (1989).

14. Ibid., Grossman and Siddle.

15. H. Gundel, M. F. O'Connor, L. Littrell, et al., "Functional neuroanatomy of grief: an MRI study." *American Journal of Psychiatry,* vol. 160 2003, 1946–53.

16. P. Servos, R. Osu, A. Santi. et al. "The neural substrates of biological motion perception: an MRI study." *Cereb Cortex,* vol. 12, 2002 772–82.

17. F. Malouin, C. L. Richards, et al., "Brain activations during motor imagery of locomotor-related tasks: a PET study." *Human Brain Mapping,* vol. 19 2003, 47–62.

18. J. Moll, R. de Oliveira-Souza; I. E. Bramati, et al. "Functional networks in emotional moral and nonmoral social judgments." *Neuroimage,* vol. 16 2002, 696–703.

19. G. Sprang. "The use of eye movement desensitization and reprocessing (EMDR) in the treatment of traumatic stress and complicated mourning: psychological land behavioural outcomes." *Research on Social Work Practice,* 2003, vol. 11 no. 3, 300–20.

20. F. Shapiro and M. Silk Forrest. *EMDR: The Breakthrough Therapy for Overcoming Anxiety, Stress and Trauma.* Basic Books, NY: 1997.

21. R. Solomon and T. Rando. "Utilization of EMDR in the treatment of grief and mourning," *Journal of EMDR Practice and Research,* 1(2), 2001, 109–117.

22. K. Lansing, D. G. Amen, C. Hanks, L. Rudy. "High resolution brain SPECT imaging and EMDR in officers with PTSD." *Journal of Neuropsychiatry and Clinical Neurosciences,* 17, 526–532 (2005).

Chapter 9 Introduction
"I JUST WANT TO TALK ABOUT IT"

Theodore Knell
From the Corners of a Wounded Mind

Sitting here alone on my cot
Surrounded by my friends in a silence that is deafening
Apart from the one voice that's no longer here
but now booms out around the room

Few are willing to make eye contact
but those that do quickly turn away unwilling to share their feelings
Feelings that are trapped behind their pleading eyes
Eyes dancing with questions searching for answers
Answers to questions
that none of us are willing to ask

We've been back over an hour now
But still we are unwilling to surrender our weapons
Instead we cuddle them like small boys with our favorite teddy bears
It's the only comfort we have left
Providing the false safety we so desperately desire

Eventually, the silence is broken by the oldest and wisest amongst us
A heavy burden for one who's still twenty-three
"Let's get these weapons cleaned
grab some scoff and "shut eye"

But me, I would rather sit here and talk
Speak his name out loud
Search for those elusive answers
Shed some of this guilt

Because it coulda, woulda, shoulda been me[1]

CHAPTER 9
THE DEADLY LITTLE SECRET

In the previous chapter, Robin's case brought up the difficulties that gaps in memory can generate for officers if left undiscovered and unresolved at a conscious level. Reference was also made to the research on OIS perception and memory issues that had been brought to light staring back in the 1980s. Of specific interest as we move into this chapter is the issue brought up in Alexis Artwhol's previous article quote. This concerned the freeze perception issue as it relates to the altered sense of the flow of time during shooting incidents.

In this chapter we will look at another performance concern regarding movement. This relates to actual physical paralyses that are of a profound and concerning nature. This condition of stress-induced paralysis is rarely spoken of and therefore it's removed itself from visibility and into the shadows. This can be deadly for those officers who know that they've got a problem with this condition.

It's important to know that this condition is not common. However, to not discuss it would be irresponsible since I have seen it occur in more than a few cases. I will review both the during and post shooting dynamics that may indicate that this condition is a possible factor needing to be to ruled out. In discussing this, it is not to be inferred that if your case reflects the same or similar characteristics being brought forward, you're destined to have this difficulty. If you do however, it is critical to have a medical evaluation to rule out any physiological cause.

The reason I have come by the number of cases that I have is that officers successfully treated will talk about it. Once I treated the first officer, he told others and they in turn told others. While I still believe that this is a rare condition, I have found it's out there. I refer to this problem as "transitory shooter's apraxia." Transitory—meaning it can come and go; shooter's—who specifically have this difficulty; apraxia—meaning muscle failure where there's no physical causation.

In all of the cases I've worked with, the physical mechanisms have been site specific to shootings. It has never involved movement functions other than the arm, the hand, the thumb or the trigger finger. Officers have also experienced extreme distress over the manifestation of this problem, as you will see in Sean's case.

SEAN'S STORY

One night, a pair of Specialized Crime Team officers were working along the waterfront, where drugs were known to be coming and going. In the early morning hours, they conducted a felony car stop (aka a "hard stop") with suspects inside who were known to carry weapons.

One officer, Rick. exited the unit from the passenger's side. Having drawn down on the vehicle, he began issuing verbal commands to the occupants inside the car. The other officer, Sean, exited from the driver's side and took up position to provide cover for his partner.

It was at the termination of that car stop when Sean made the horrifying discovery that he had never taken his weapon off safety. He was a 16-year, highly seasoned, highly skilled officer. This had never happened to him in all of his years of service...ever.

One piece of information that is relevant to this event is that 18 months earlier, Sean was in a fatal OIS—a suicide by cop. The perpetrator of that shooting had engaged in attention-seeking behaviors, including pulling a gun on some teens in a crosswalk. When Sean and another officer called out to investigate arrived on the scene, the suspect drew down on Sean, who then shot him. The shot proved fatal. Moments later the suspect's weapon was found to be a toy gun.

In the wake of that OIS, Sean had been sent to see a "counselor" for a number of sessions. Sean recounted that this non-professional had "dealt with the shooting by talking with me about it and then about his own days in Vietnam." Sean returned to duty; he had done shooting time on the range; he seemed to be fine... but he wasn't.

At the critical moment during that felony car stop a year and a half later, Sean's body, specifically his right thumb, had failed him. His brain sent the automatic order to draw down, but the command was not received fully enough to complete the action. Sean's arm had worked, his hand had worked, but his thumb hadn't. Sean was keenly aware something was horribly wrong after realizing this had occurred.

That car stop was carried off without gunfire. Even so, when he returned to the station immediately after that event, Sean went directly to his shift supervisor and took himself off duty. The next day he applied for worker's compensation sick leave.

He began therapy again, but this time with a licensed psychotherapist who was able to do excellent assessment and stabilization. They worked together for six months. She established a significant comprehensive treatment plan that included psychotherapy, chiropractic message therapy—due to chronic pain from possible fibromyalgia (see chapter notes)–and a medical assessment for medication.

Eventually it became clear that they were not making further progress, so she acted ethically and in her client's best interest by referring his case to another therapist me. Sean's case was transferred to me. Fortunately, I'd worked with the condition, beginning with my first generation of cops. By the time Sean graced the threshold of my office, my cops and I had worked out a successful protocol. I'd also been adequately trained in the tactical and weapons end of the deadly game and knew how to bring him back in off the DL.

Sadly, there are tragic stories that didn't turn out as well as Sean's. One was recounted to me posthumously by grieving fellow officers during a Hostage Negotiation Training we were taking years ago.

One of their team members had been involved in an OIS. He took a brief administrative leave and then returned to duty. He seemed okay on the surface, but those who knew him well (the officers recounting his story to me) sensed that he wasn't. At some point he confided in one of them that he wasn't sure he'd be able to take the shot the next time, if there ever was a next time. Tragically there was. Another incident occurred one night. He took a call that ended him up in another armed confrontation. He was shot and killed by the perpetrator. The officer had drawn his weapon, but never fired.

The issue of action versus reaction could have been the reason for this tragic murder-in-the-line-of-duty. The FBI LET training on this issue (as well a more recent study by Blair, et. al) underscores the danger an officer is in with any armed suspect, even if the suspect is not yet holding his weapon.[2] An officer with gun drawn, unless behind hard cover, is not in a winning position. There's just no way the officer can out shoot a perpetrator should the latter decide to go for his gun and fire. But that wasn't what the surviving officers believed at the time of our conversation. They were convinced that their friend just lost the ability to pull the trigger. They'd seen how he'd changed.

To deal with this issue, the protocol my officers and I designed was based on the EMDR Peak Performance Protocol,[3] developed by Drs. Sandra Foster (2000[4]) and Jennifer Lendl (1996[5]). I had used this successfully with athletes who had developed performance blocks. We augmented it to work with equal success with the "athletes" in the deadly game.

Even so, there were two big differences to navigate: this was a new game with new rules, and the game could kill its players. It's impossible to know how many officers, in the same situation as Sean, either haven't survived or have decided to quietly leave the job as Jack, whom you'll meet further on, nearly did.

There have been historical references to soldiers on the battlefield having physiological blocks to being able shoot. Lt. Col. Grossman discusses the thousands of cases of soldiers diagnosed with "conversion disorder" in WWII because they lost the ability to fire their weapons.[6] Episode 1 Part 2 of the TV series *The Truth About Killing* [7] describes the physical conditions of soldiers on the front lines witnessed by field doctors. Soldiers in the American Civil War reported paralysis limited to their shooting hands. German soldiers got frostbite only in their trigger fingers. Diagnoses have been given (cowardice, conversion hysteria, conversion disorder, somatic dissociation), but I've found them altogether inappropriate for what I've treated in my client base.

In my clinical construct, I consider site-specific paralysis as one of a number of possible symptoms that can come with lethal-contact trauma. It's important to know that this symptom occurs in a minority of cases and is very treatable, as Sean's case will underscore. In addition, there are preventative measures relating to the nature of the OIS and the nature of the investigation afterwards.

COMPLICATED SHOOTINGS & ANTICIPATORY FEAR

No shootings are simple. Even the most straightforward cases are heavily encumbered with the weight and responsibility that come with taking another's life. That said, some shootings fall outside normal shooting circumstances. I refer to these as "complicated shootings." And they are the second red flag for potential difficulties down the line. They involve particularly counterintuitive situations, such as having to shoot an armed teenage gang member who's around the same age as the officer's own son, or having to shoot a female or a "vulnerable" suspect who is, say, mentally disabled. And, as in Sean's case, having shot a suspect using a toy mistaken to be a viable lethal threat. Add to that, the incidents in which the officer who has shot the suspect then has to give medical assistance after the threat has been stopped. This can be even more difficult if words have been exchanged between the officer and the suspect.

In complicated shootings, the usual emotional hardship and the possibility of the community's reproach of the officer are magnified. The issue is that the weight of taking a life is heightened by the common core values such as not killing kids, mothers, or vulnerable or innocent people. These ideas are so ingrained that officers are trained to cross that mental barrier in their weapons ranges by using paper targets of images such as a young, perky mom holding a baby in one arm and pointing a Glock at you in the other. This is an attempt to sensitize the brain to the fact that females of our species can be as lethal as males. However, it does little to ease the anguish that may follow an actual shooting. There's a vast difference between hitting that paper target with good body-mass groupings and having to shoot to survive when the threat is, for instance, a living, breathing female and mother.

Incidents like the Halloween 2000 shooting in Los Angeles, California, of actor Anthony Dwain Lee after he'd pointed a prop gun at officers[8] and Jean Charles de Menezes's shooting in the UK amid the 2005 terrorist attacks in London can result in torment for officers. The public rarely has a view into the emotional price paid by officers. The surprised reaction from civilians when they find that I specialize in lethal-contact trauma reflects this. Comments such as, "You mean officers or soldiers feel sad when they shoot someone who's trying to kill them?" show the influence that Hollywood has made on the public. The movies make it appear that for a cop, the taking of a life is just another day at the office. This notion is finally being confronted now by solid, evidence-based information. For more on this, see the chapter notes on Lane County Sheriff's Office and District Attorney's video, *Hollywood vs. Reality: Officer-Involved Shootings.*[9]

The potential for trauma after the fact in these cases becomes significant when poor investigative techniques are used. In one OIS case I worked with, the suspect, who'd been shot by the officer in self-defence, spoke directly to that officer just before he died. That proved to be hard enough, but harder still were the antiquated investigative techniques still being used:

In one interview a pointless shock technique that could have come straight from the series "Life on Mars" was used. After some time of rigorous questioning, suddenly several graphic photos of the deceased suspect's body were slammed down on the table in front of my client by the independent investigator. The reaction, of course, was what one would expect: my officer left the room highly distraught and his lawyer terminated the interview. This set back my client's progress and did nothing for the investigation.

After such complicated shootings, there can be untold stories of the deepest levels of emotional pain. Those who have come back in the aftermath of such extreme circumstances are some of the most incredible and resilient individuals I've ever met. That road back is never easy, straight or well marked.

THE LONG SHADOW OF INVESTIGATION

A third potential red flag to consider can come with any on-going OIS investigation. This arises with a hesitation to use deadly force if required, while being investigated for a prior shooting. Investigations can go on for months, and even years in parts of the world that have no statue of limitations on them. Living under that long shadow creates additional pressure on an officer who returns to duty before the investigation is completed. This can translate into a fear piled onto the already existing concerns whenever he must draw his weapon. This is especially true if the investigation has treated the OIS officer as a suspect rather than a survivor.

DE-CODING THE BODY'S POST-TRAUMA MESSAGES

Sean's difficulties after being returned to duty the first time were significant. He was averaging between an hour and a half and two hours of sleep each night. His body was in abject pain around the clock. Whenever he tried to sleep lying in bed, he'd wake up choking, so he had to sleep in a recliner in his living room. This sleep-disordered breathing (SDB) occurs in 40-90% of PTSD cases.[10]

Sean's back and right wrist were chronically strained. He told me that every night, when he did manage to fall to sleep, he'd wake up to find his right hand clenched in a tight fist, his wrist curled around so that it was turned inward on himself and pressed against his collar bone, and his back arched backwards. This is periodic limb movement disorder and occurs in 30-70% with PTSD.[11]

Then there were nightmares and broken molars cracked from nocturnal tooth grinding. Sleep for Sean was a pain racked and injury producing nightly event. By the time he'd gotten in to see me, this had gone on for approximately three years.

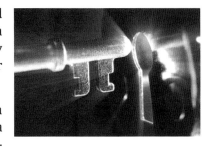

During the day, if Sean had to go into public places in uniform, he suddenly could be hit with severe nausea and/or vertigo. This difficulty grew out of the "rent-a-mob" activists who shouted epithets at him and called him "murderer." (U.S. officers involved in shootings are named in the media, so they have no protection from this kind of activity as their counterparts do in places like the UK).

While this all sounds extreme, Sean's case is very similar to many of the officers I've worked with who are unable to shoot after the OIS. They have commonly manifested the lion's share of their trauma through physical symptoms, as did Sean. Men are exceptionally skilled at doing this.

All of the Stage 1 training in logging and Going to Baseline is about officers being able to "cotton on" to internal reactions that they normally don't notice. Just because the reactions are hidden, doesn't mean they don't exist—the stress reactions have to go somewhere, so they often go into the body. Among the extreme physical manifestations I've seen are:

1. Vertigo
2. Irritable bowel syndrome
3. A return of childhood asthma after decades of no symptoms

4. Severe nocturnal teeth grinding and clenching that causes broken molars
5. Hives that tend to occur or move around (often occur in the groin, torso or legs)
6. Fibromyalgia and increased frequency of urination (4-6 times) during usual sleep time
7. Chronic joint injuries or sprains caused by physical activities during sleep

SEAN'S EMDR TREATMENT

In Stage 2 of Sean's clinical work, we discovered in the EMDR session that he was re-injuring his back and right wrist by sleep-driven movements that caused his body to behave in specific ways. While he described during the EMDR sets what he was witnessing in the OIS, I found him describing exactly the things he was doing in his sleep.

First, the backward arching of his back was a re-enactment of what he'd witnessed the suspect's own body do when he was shot. Second, Sean realized that his right hand and wrist movement in his sleep was an attempt to turn the gun away from shooting the suspect. He didn't want to have to shoot, but he had not had that option at the time. In his sleep, he was acting out that desire, knowing in hindsight what he had not known at the time.

In that first EMDR session, we progressed through the incident, reprocessing all the layers of sensory and muscle memory and the negative belief that had grown out of the incident. Then at the end of the EMDR, with the disturbance and pain dramatically reduced from 9–10 to a 2, we replaced the negative belief with the positive, accurate truth. For Sean it came down to finally being able to believe at a visceral level, what his head knew all along: He wasn't a murderer. He'd only been doing his job to protect the public, while trying to survive at the same time.

The next day's check-in voice message from Sean reported he'd slept a full 13 hours that night!

In the next EMDR session, we incorporated the dispatch tape of the incident. Hearing the radio traffic before and after the shooing helped to bring up more material to work through. Those memory fragments that surfaced in images or new details then were brought down in disturbance levels in that desensitization phase of the EMDR session from 8 and 9 levels of disturbance to 1 to 2. These EMDR outcomes remained constant, so we progressed to what's referred to as clinical cross-checks.

This stage included our going to the location of the OIS and Sean giving me a detailed walk-through of the incident. In this process, I have my clients wear heart monitors so we can identify stress-induced increases in heart rate. That gives information about what work still needs to be done. In that session with Sean, two new fragments of memory were identified by spikes in heart rate. Those we worked through to resolution in another EMDR session at the office.

Finally, we did the Peak Performance EMDR specially augmented for dealing with weapons-performance issues. To treat players in the deadly game, therapists must also know and understand the game themselves. This part of treatment cannot be accomplished solely in the safe, sterile confines of the therapist's office. It requires solid weapons and tactics training, access to a weapons range and the inclusion of an excellent weapons and tactics instructor in the treatment plan.

Sean returned to duty. He eventually trained and became a very skilled Field Training Officer (FTO). He then tested for the SWAT team and made that. He later qualified as an exceptional SWAT sniper.

SEAN'S POST-TREATMENT INCIDENT

About two years after Sean was graduated out of my office, I received the following voice message one morning from his Sergeant. A man of few words, all he said was, "Hey...your boy was golden out there last night! Call me so I can fill you in!"

The previous night an individual broke into the house of a vacationing family in an attempted suicide-by-cop. The neighbor next door, a deputy from the local sheriff's department, had called in to report suspicious activity going on. Sean's sergeant arrived first and he along with the off-duty deputy entered through the open front door. The lights had all been turned on throughout the house. It didn't seem like a robbery; it certainly wasn't being done with any stealth if it was.

Almost immediately, because in fact they'd been expected, the intruder appeared at the top of the stairway and drew a gun on them. Both officers rapidly exited, unharmed. The sergeant called in his team; they arrived and set up a perimeter around the house. Sean was on that team.

This began a stand-off that went through the night and into the early morning hours. During that time, the suspect came out of the house several times and yelled as he pointed his weapon at the team of officers stationed behind hard cover. Sean was given a break and he went to the sergeant and told him that he didn't believe that the suspect's gun was real.

The sergeant later admitted he'd been sceptical and thought that Sean's suspicion might have been a carry-over from his earlier suicide-by-cop OIS. He asked Sean why he thought the gun was fake. Sean described the suspect's initial attention-getting behavior and that after watching this guy for several hours, Sean thought the suspect's gun appeared too light and easy to keep pointed at officers for extended periods of time. The suspect was clearly trying to goad them into defensive engagement...in fact he had from the start. Sean also pointed out that the sergeant and the deputy had not been shot while inside the house, when the suspect had held high ground on them. No shot had even been fired.

Shortly after the conversation between Sean and his sergeant, identifying information came back regarding the suspect, along with some critical background info. The suspect's brother had accomplished a suicide-by-cop by staging a house robbery several months earlier. In that case the now-deceased brother had drawn a gun on the police officer who'd been first to the call, and the suspect had been fatally shot. It was discovered shortly thereafter that he'd used—you guessed it—a toy gun.

The current incident ended with the sergeant getting on the bullhorn and telling the suspect inside that he wasn't going to die that night and that if he wanted to commit suicide-by-cop he'd need to find another town because they weren't going to shoot him in this one. Shortly thereafter they made the arrest.

This is what "stronger" can look like after an OIS and PTSD. I have seen officers come back more tactically sound and rock solid after fighting their way back with hard work and courage every inch of the way. When they're able to process and resolve fragmented memories, the brain is able to make a complete picture out of what seemed like disjointed chaos pre-EMDR. Those who've experienced these traumatic incidents can become extremely skilled trainers.

PTSD cases resulting from complicated shootings, as severe as the symptoms sound, are very treatable. The deadly little secret of an officer's sudden inability to shoot post incident should not be allowed to put them or the public at risk. It should not be allowed to end careers that can go on to success. The key to attending to the problem is to recognize the indicators of potential difficulties that may be awaiting some OIS officers. Early intervention with specialize treatment is essential to officer and public safety in such cases. Sean had made two different attempts at treatment. The results of the first could have cost him and one other officer their lives. The second got him closer to finding his way. Then, more than three years after his OIS, he was still very responsive to appropriate treatment. He got his life back and returned to excel in his career.

CAUGHT BETWEEN THE ROCK & HARD PLACE

Each of the three red flags described in this and the previous chapter indicate hardships and potential double-binds for officers in similar circumstances:

1. Gaps in memory after a highly charged, lethal-contact incident create ambiguity that can disable the brain's capacity to access, process, learn from and finally generalize and apply that learning. This lack of resolution about the best way to react the next time then causes the amygdala to inhibit the movement initiation function. This leads to hesitance and locking up.
2. A complicated shooting OIS creates a double bind because the deep impact can result in a return to the human brain's natural aversion to killing.
3. Long investigations create a double bind because the PD's administration, often with reminders by the press and public, is aware that the officer has been in one shooting already. If another shooting occurs with the same officer, the question arises whether he or she is just "a killer cop." A second shooting may quickly become a political issue as well as a matter of public trust in the community's police department.

All of the problems listed above can contribute to a correlation that's been discovered in animal research around the "freeze" mechanism. This is what I believe connects those three red flags to the physical locking up in the officer's ability to initiate the complete "draw down" response.

THE WORLD OFF ITS AXIS

After a complicated shooting, it often happens that (1) the officer's life, environment and all the training that was "normal and reliable" becomes suddenly *foreign and uncertain terrain*, and (2) a riveting *negative outcome* is attached to the act of attempting to survive and save others from a real or a perceived threat.

The officer's world has made a dramatic *shift off of its axis of normalcy* as a result of several circumstances, including:

1. The officer, a trained observer, can't recall the blow-by-blow details of what he did in one of the most critical events in his life.
2. The officer suddenly feels like a pariah when he's taken off the team and out of the game and then is investigated.
3. The officer's action of shooting, the result of years of high-level training, to extinguish a lethal threat in order to protect others or survive himself, is now investigated as a possible crime.
4. The death of an innocent person is sometimes the result of tragic errors even when following intelligence and training.

This world-off-its axis experience was apparent during the inquest by the special firearms officer (SFO) who had fatally shot Jean Charles de Menezes in the UK. The Met special weapons team had trusted the intelligence that told them that de Menezes was a terrorist suicide bomber. The SFO had used the training he'd received in threat assessment. When the SFO was asked on the stand during inquisition how he'd felt the day after the shooting when he was told he'd killed an innocent man, he answered: "*A sense of disbelief, and shock, sadness, confusion. Everything I have ever trained for, threat assessment, seeing threats, perceiving threats and action on threats proved wrong, and I am responsible for the death of an innocent man. That is something I have got to live with for the rest of my life.*[12]

OF MICE & MEN: DERAILMENT OF PRIMARY DEFENSIVE RESPONSES

In May, 2003 the *Journal of Neuroscience* published an intriguing study of the neurological competition between the *flight* and *freeze* fear responses in mice (Mongeau, et al). Mice are rarely seen to shift into "fight" mode when faced with a predator's threat. Their preferred response in their natural outdoor environment is flight.

The study found[13] that when mice were (1) suddenly put into a *foreign environment*, or (2) given a *negative outcome* such as a shock to their feet, which placed them in a state of fear with a newly learned fear stimulus, their neurological and behavioural response was unexpected.

When first administered the fear stimulus in their familiar environment (their "home cage"), one group of mice responded predominantly by going into their normal flight reaction. However, when another group of mice was administered the same fear stimulus, but after being placed into a new and foreign cage, they predominantly went into a "freeze" response.

A third group of mice was administered a fear stimulus on one day, paired with foot shocks (a negative outcome). On the next day, when exposed to the same fear stimulus, these mice reacted only with a "freeze" response. They never opted for flight.

The authors of the study theorize that the reason for the shift from "flight," the preferred defensive tactic, to "freeze" stems from a higher level of *anticipatory fear* due to high anxiety and stress generated by either (1) being placed in a foreign environment or (2) having the paired negative outcome and fear stimulus.

Those two conditions constructed in the study parallel what officers must often naturally contend with after OIS incidents, especially those of a complicated nature. There can be related conditions, however, generated by other instigating factors involved in an incident that make it more complicated.

JACK'S STORY

Jack's incident involved an ambush at the scene of a domestic violence call. His department came extremely close to losing him. Given the exceptional leader he's become, that would have been a tragedy.

Jack had been in therapy for 10 months by the time of our first session. Despite his commitment to therapy and despite the wonderful therapist he was working with, he wasn't getting better. He was losing hope that he'd ever "be normal again." Jack was only six weeks shy of leaving the job he'd once loved for 14 years.

The OIS had become complicated due to a muscle-memory issue. Jack had started his career using a weapon whose safety was turned on by putting it into the "up" position. He used that weapon for approximately six years. Then there was a departmental change in weapons, and the safety on the second weapon was on when it was in the "down" position. He'd been using this weapon for eight years by the time of the ambush.

The problem occurred under the stress of the incident. Jack had been weapon-ready coming onto the scene, but in the heat of the ambush, his brain went to the old muscle memory of his first gun and turned the safety off instead of on.

The mechanics of the problem were later resolved by his changing over to a Glock. However, Jack had to work through performance issues and trauma around the incident as well. He never spoke to others about his lack of confidence in himself if he were ever in another OIS, but it was filling his horizon. On duty, he'd find himself obsessively checking his weapon's safety, which distracted him mentally. He had quietly started to make plans to leave the job. As shown in his SPECT image and PDS self-reports at the end of Stage 2, in treatment he saw significant improvements and was once again back to trusting himself out on the ground.

It was a beautiful, hot autumn afternoon when we did Jack's first EMDR session and captured a still shot of that process in a SPECT scan. I witnessed him fighting his way through that incident and I saw him step out on the other side stronger and more at peace. That session had enabled a remarkable shift to occur for Jack. There was still more work ahead, but he'd accomplished an incredible amount in that first EMDR session.

It was early evening when we left the Amen Clinic. Heading out the front door, we found ourselves staring across the nearly empty parking lot and into a huge field of tall, wheat-like summer grass. The sun was dropping low in the sky and its light seemed to be shining through and defining every blade. Jack and I stood for just a brief moment taking in the sweet smell of grass and that beautiful scene. Then he turned and smiled, and I could see it. I said to him what we were both thinking… "Welcome back."

Jack chose to remain in the police. He tested for and got a promotion not long after the third and final brain image (post EMDR) was taken. Jack became the type of leader who takes care of those on his team. He's got a level of empathy and insight that he never had before his PTSD.

ANTICIPATORY ANXIETY ON RE-ENTRY

Several years post promotion, Jack had been taken off patrol and assigned to IA (Professional Standards Division) for a very long 36-months. Each time I'd return from a tour-of-duty offshore, I'd ride along with officers from that PD to catch up on what had been happening since I was last in town.

Every time I did this while Jack was in IA/PSD I got extremely good reports on how fairly and how well he was conducting investigations. Even so, he was really glad to be released back out on the streets to be "a real cop again" when the time came.

After he was back out on patrol, we set up for a ride-along one night just after I'd gotten into town. It was a beautiful, sunny and hot summer evening. As we were heading out, he told me we were first going to Emerson Street (the location of the ambush). When I asked why, he replied that he'd been wanting to do another walk-through of the incident with me.

When we got to the apartment unit where the ambush had happened, I lamented that I didn't have a heart monitor with me. I was impressed when it turned out that Jack now had a watch with a heart monitor built in. I had him set it up and then we went over and saw that the place was empty and quiet.

First we checked to see if all of the bullet holes had been filled in and painted over. For years they hadn't been, and for all involved in that OIS, seeing those holes still in the wall had been a trigger for quite some time. On this July evening, the bullet holes were gone. We checked Jack's heart rate (HR) and it was at 86. Then I had Jack walk me through the incident that we both knew so well. Even with the heat of being in a Kevlar vest, in direct sun, walking and pointing and describing everything blow by blow, Jack's HR never got past 113 BPM... excellent.

If he'd spiked at any point up to 140 or higher, it would have indicated a stress point from some unprocessed memory needing some work or a peak performance issue. As it was, he was just fine. This cleared his concerns that something might have been lying beneath the surface that could cause trouble. (I suspect that concern was just normal re-entry anxiety after having been off the streets for three years). What he had done, in fact, was good preventative maintenance. He gave himself a mental refresher training at re-entry after a significant time away from being with his team out on the streets.

Then, just three days later, Jack ended up in the closest call he'd been to for another OIS since that occurrence at that same location.

11 Years Post Treatment (Approx. 3-Days Post Walk-Through)
June 22 2011: Voicemail Message Recorded at 4:38 P.M.

"Hey...it's your favorite police officer checking in. I had an interesting shift last night and since you're in town I thought I'd tell your v.m. about it. I had a near shooting last night and guess where? You got it—on Emerson St. Same complex we were doing that walk through in last Monday evening... No kidding.

I drew down, had good cover and I managed to talk the guy into not leaving that s--t hole in a body bag. Amazingly, he took me up on that option. I knew as this thing was happening that if it had to go the other way, I could do it. There was no doubt in my mind, but it managed to turn out fine.

I'm so glad we did that walk-through when you hit town. Kind of strange, after all these years since that last shooting, that I would decide to take you back over there. What timing...So thanks!

We'll talk later...Bye."

THE TWO DIFFERENT FACES OF PTSD

Seeing Jack's brain with PTSD illustrates how it can present itself in two different ways. Aaron (Chapters 2 and 3) looked anxious and shut down, and his brain images showed no overactivity in his temporal lobes. Jack, on the other hand, just looked angry all the time, and in truth he was.

I've circled in Jack's SPECT image the overactivation in his left temporal lobe (LTL). Remember we're looking at the underside perspective of the brain, that is, from the chin up, so left is right. Compared to Aaron's PTSD SPECT where his LTL was quiet, Jack's overactivation in that region reflected a real difficulty with flashpoint anger (over or under-activity in that region can cause this). He also struggled with dark thoughts, but in fact, we saw that improve with the logging and Going to Baseline. So much so that he never needed to go on antidepressants.

The important thing to realize is that flashpoint anger does actually come from something happening in the brain, not from someone just suddenly becoming a jerk. Once we pulled

Jack out from beneath the rubble of PTSD, he was once again a guy who could maintain a good attitude and control his anger reactions most of the time. In other words without PTSD, he was a very good husband, father, friend, cop and sergeant.

Post-PTSD, Jack went back to his old self and that old self still had some warmth (not the raging heat he'd had with PTSD) in the cingulate gyrus and the left temporal lobe. That slight edge is just the way he's made, but it's not a problem now. He's still happily married to his amazing wife with kids who are growing up healthy and strong. They've got great a dad who's involved and engaged in their lives and their interests—a dad who's not "scary" to them any more.

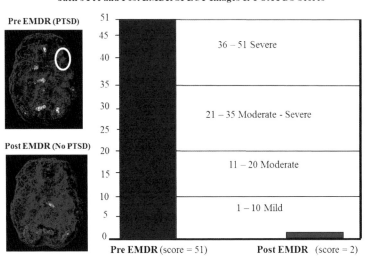

Jack's Pre and Post EMDR SPECT Images & FOA PDS Scores

THE INVISIBLE TRIPWIRES

Even when the physical freeze reaction occurs without any indicator of what the tripwire is connected to, the freeze reaction acts as a warning that the officer may be heading into harm's way.

Tom is a retired special weapons officer who works these days a bit east of Eden for fairly good pay. On one furlough he was home and up on a ladder doing a project on his place, when his "Bat Phone" rang. He answered and the voice on the other end asked him if he'd be willing to come to work two weeks ahead of schedule to do a special assignment that was being scheduled.

Tom asked for the exact date that he'd need to fly out and that was given. Operational specifics are never discussed in such situations, of course, but one detail that was given was that he'd be flying into a certain region to make a connection to the end destination where the job would start. Tom replied that he wanted to fly into another place and head out from there, and that was refused.

Tom's said that he wanted to talk it over with the wife first, but in truth he wanted to think it over for a while on his own. The conversation ended and Tom went back to his project.

The travel plans bothered him, because they showed that this job was being run by someone willing to save money (by allowing an unnecessary increase of the threat level) even before he hit the ground to "punch in." In Tom's line of work, that kind of "bean counting" can get you killed.

Twenty minutes later, Tom reluctantly decided to accept the offer. He punched in the phone number to call the voice at the other end of the line back. But when he went to hit "Send," his thumb went dead and wouldn't work. Try as he might, his thumb wouldn't—in fact, couldn't—move to hit "Send." Being a guy who pays attention to the finer details in life, Tom couldn't help noticing this.

At that point Tom decided he wasn't going to take the job after all. He also decided right then that he was done with this outfit; it was time to find one he could trust. Once he made that decision, his thumb worked just fine. He used it to make the call and let the voice know he was going to stay home for that last two weeks of his furlough. And then, as men do, he blamed it on the wife.

Tom liked the work he was doing about as much as he liked being alive. However, his finely tuned limbic system knew that this choice involved a matter of life and death—his, in fact; and *it* wasn't going to go there, so neither was he.

"I CAN'T DO THIS!"

What happened when Tom's thumb stopped working can manifest in other ways that also stop action in its tracks. In *Deadly Force Encounters*, Alexis Artwhol and Loren Christensen tell a story recounted by a highly trained self-defense and firearms instructor with enough experience and ability to handle himself quite effectively. The incident, which had occurred years before, began when he heard a call go out about a drunken patron at a local bar who was tearing up the place and beating up customers. This was a 220 pound, 6' 2" officer who described himself as a man who "loved a good fight."

This was somewhat similar to Tom's situation, only it involved a radio handset rather than a cell phone, and it was this officer's hand and arm, but rather than a thumb that went off-line. When the police officer went to lift the radio handset to take that call, he couldn't move. What he described perfectly was that internally declared belief, "I CAN'T DO THIS!"

If that phrase sounds familiar, it's because it's been previously mentioned. It results from the cross communication in the limbic system between the amygdala and the basal ganglia. Remember, those sectors can help to cause anxiety or panic attacks.

The officer described his experience: *"I'd been to hundreds of bar fights, but this time I had a weird, powerful feeling that I was going to get hurt, and hurt badly. I just couldn't get past the thought that the guy was going to attack me and beat me, and I would be hurt and embarrassed in front of my buddies."*

As these thoughts occurred, he experienced physical responses as well. *"My heart was racing as if I'd run a mile and my eyes were watering like crazy. I just sat there unable to move; it was like I was completely enveloped in pure, raw fear."*[14]

This incident had occurred years before, but the interview with Dr. Artwhol was the first time this officer had ever spoken of his experience.

Possible Causes:

Although we don't know exactly why this freezing happens at the particular times it does, two possible causes can be considered:

1. Fatigue. In Chapter 3 it was pointed out that the startle response can increase dramatically due to fatigue levels. The brain can pick up and send warnings regarding this dangerously compromising condition on a subliminal level. This awareness can then increase anxiety, stepping that up the scale until the thought "I CAN'T DO THIS!" sets in on a conscious level without necessarily understanding why.

Physical and mental fatigue, from working midnights, too much overtime, too many interrupted sleep cycles, etc., may sap all but a minimal reserve of stamina without your awareness. It's insidious. The brain may not become aware of the fatigue until it becomes extreme, such as falling asleep at the wheel…or after you've come out of that "micro sleep" of 2 -10 seconds, if you're fortunate.

Dr. Bryan Vila, a 17-year police L.A. Sheriffs Department deputy, an ex-Chief of Police and a renowned sleep researcher states: "Human beings are lousy judges of how impaired they are from fatigue…Your cognitive ability can be affected by fatigue, without your realizing it, to the same degree as someone who's drunk. In tests even in elite professionals, people's reports of how tired they are don't relate accurately to how tired they really are. In short, you just can't self-monitor fatigue worth a damn."[15]

That being the case, however, there are deeper, more primal levels of awareness running like a powerful current beneath the seemingly peaceful surface of the water. The limbic system can contribute to the physical freezing by creating a compelling argument that incorporates one's most horrifying fears. Remember, this part of the brain is the origin of our dreams and nightmares.

When the limbic system realizes that there are not enough reserves in the tank to fuel a fighting chance of survival, it will take desperate measures to convince us that getting into that barroom brawl at that moment isn't a good survival strategy.

Signals sent by the body and brain are not the only ones affecting the officer at that moment. Dr. Anthony Pinizzotto and Ed Davis of the FBI Behavioral Science Unit researched subtle "shorthand" messaging that occurs in encounters with suspects. Their study underscores that perps are able to read subtle signs of weakness in officers at the same time officers are attempting to read the perps'. Suspects often make decisions based on what they pick up. If they pick up indicators of weakness, they may opt to attack officers when it's advantageous to their own escape or survival strategy and / or "career development" scheme.[16]

2. Getting out of shape. Chronic sleep deprivation, carb- and sugar-loading diets or late night snacks, are a recipe for low energy levels. This can cause an officer to train less or not at all and to become out of shape. This can generate justifiable concern about his physical response capacity to a threat.

THE CREATIVE BRAIN AT WORK

In view of the accounts in this chapter, it's clear that it's the brain's job to keep the entire human system it is a part of alive. It sees to this task in highly creative and accurate ways. If the conscious mind refuses to take a course toward what the amygdala considers survival, then it will pull the plug on other things, such as movement, vision, hearing, etc. And yet, as the officers featured in this chapter found, that power is not one-sided. The brain will negotiate among its many sectors. To do that, it needs to join critical fragmented memories to increase the base of knowledge and learning. This is what increases the chances of survival.

I see this capacity of the brain as an amazing "factory-installed" survival feature. The worst thing that can happen isn't that an officer one day has to come in to get a problem such as site-specific paralysis resolved. The worst thing would be that he would choose *not* to and then have to pay with his life at a later time.

As Lt. Col. Grossman said, *"We're only as sick as our secrets."*[17]

CHAPTER NOTES:

OFFICER'S ACTION V. REACTION AS IT RELATES TO GRAHAM V. CONNOR

Force Science[18] research has reported on an important research study related to armed confrontations. It addresses the chronic "behind the reaction curve" matrix found consistently in the action vs. reaction scenario rendered to officers in FA trainings (including the FBI's LET courses).

FSN Transmission #178 (May 20, 2011) states: "The reasonableness standard [set forth by Graham] is based on what a well-trained, prudent officer would do in a given situation. Our results show that even well-trained officers with their guns aimed at a suspect cannot reasonably be expected to react faster than a suspect can raise his or her gun and fire."[19]

Other sources include: "Hollywood vs. Reality: Officer—Involved Shootings"

This Lane County Sheriff's Office and District Attorney's video can be viewed at:
http://www.youtube.com/watch?v=MmfTyFAp1eI

PHOTO CREDITS:

1. Military Helmet ©iStockphoto.com / RogiervdE
2. Key & Keyhole with Light ©iStockphoto.com/haveseen
3. Sniper Training © Karen Lansing 2012
4. Rock ©iStockphoto.com / princessdlaf
5. Seek Peek ©iStockphoto.com/CGinspiration
6. Wood Mouse ©iStockphoto.com/Andrew_Howe
7. SWAT Officer © Karen Lansing 2012

8. SWAT Officers © Karen Lansing 2012
9. Wheat in Sun ©iStockphoto.com / freie-kreation
10. SWAT Officer © Karen Lansing 2012
11. "Jack's" SPECT Images: © Karen Lansing & Daniel Amen

ENDNOTES:

1. Theodore Knell. *From the Corners of a Wounded Mind*, Night Publishing, 2011 http://theodoreknell.com
2. P. J. Blair, J. Pollock, D. Montague, T. Nichols, J. Curnutt, D. Burns. "Reasonableness and reaction time," *Police Quarterly, December* 2011, vol. 14, 4: pp. 323-343.
3. S. Foster, J. Lendl, "Eye movement desensitization and reprocessing: Four case studies of a new tool for executive coaching and restoring employee performance after setbacks," *Consulting Psychology Journal: Practice and Research,* Vol. 48, Issue 3, Summer 1996, p. 155-161 (1996).
4. Ibid., 63.
5. S. Foster. *Coaching for Peak Performance*, In J.E. Auerback (Ed.) *Personal and Executive Coaching: The Complete Guide for Mental Health Professionals* (1st ed.) Ventura CA, Executive College Press, 2001, 113-16.
6. D. Grossman. *On Killing: The Psychological Cost of Learning to Kill in War and Society*, Little, Brown and Co., 1996.
7. G. Johnstone, J. Weston, J. Bradshaw. "The Truth About Killing" 2004, Produced by Tigress Productions (Episode I, Part 2).
8. BBC News. *Prop Gun Blamed for Actor's Death Tuesday*, 31 October 2000, http://news.bbc.co.uk/1/hi/entertainment/999720.stm
9. Lane County Sheriff's Office and District Attorney's Office. "Hollywood vs. Reality: Officer Involved Shootings http://www.youtube.com/watch?v=MmfTyFAp1eI
10. T. A. Mellman, R. Kulick-Bell, L. E. Ashlock, B. Nolan. "Sleep events among veterans with combat-related posttraumatic stress disorder." *American Journal of Psychiatry,* 1995; 152:110–115.
11. T. M. Brown, P. A. Boudewyns, "Periodic limb movements of sleep in combat veterans with posttraumatic stress disorder," *J Trauma Stress,* 1996; 9:129 –136.
12. S. Laville, V. Dodd, "The officer who killed Jean Charles de Menezes breaks down at inquest," *The Guardian*, Oct. 25, 2008.
13. R. Mongeau, G. A. Miller, E. Chiang, D. J. Anderson. "Neural correlates of competing fear behaviors evoked by an innately aversive stimulus," *Journal of Neuroscience*, May 1, 2003, 23(9).
14. A. Artwhol, L. W. Christensen. *Deadly Force Encounters*: *What Cops Need to Know to Mentally and Physically Survive a Gunfight,* Paladin Press, Boulder CO, 1997.
15. W. Lewinski. "Anti-fatigue measures could cut cop deaths 15 percent, researcher claims" PoliceOne.com, March 24, 2011
16. A. J. Pinizzotto, E. F. Davis. "Offenders' perceptual shorthand: What messages are law enforcement officers sending to offenders?" *FBI Law Enforcement Bulletin*, June 1999.
17. D. Grossman. *Bullet Proofing the Mind.* Audio, Callibre Press. 1st Ed. 1996.
18. *Police Quarterly,* December 2011, vol. 14, 4
19. FSN website: http://www.forcescience.org/aboutforcesciencenews.html and in *Police Quarterly,* December 2011; vol. 14, 4: pp. 323-343.

CHAPTER 10
DREAMS

"When one of your dreams comes true, you begin to look at the others more carefully."

Anonymous

Dreams are a combination "message in a bottle," form of self-expression, and method of learning and resolving. They often play a significant role in the work of resolving PTSD, because dreaming is one of the ways the brain sends information from deep in the amygdala to the clear light of day. The information then can be reckoned with, warnings be heeded and lessons be learned.

We'll be looking at a wide array of types of dreams that can visit during sleep or even while awake. The first thing I'd like to stress is that just because you may have nightmares during a sleep state or waking state (more on this later), it doesn't mean that there's something wrong or that you're heading into PTSD.

Everyone has nightmares and everyone has worrisome or fearful mental images that can come to them when they're awake. This chapter may surprise some of you in terms of how normal even the seemingly strange dreams are.

A JOINT VENTURE

Dreams weave themselves into EMDR sessions on occasion, especially as REM sleep begins to increase. The first indication that a client's dream holds information pertinent to therapy is that the dream, or a piece of it, will "stick with him." He has heightened interest in it or confusion or distress about it. Inevitably—and appropriately—the dream comes up in session.

Given time with a client and a good understanding of his traumas, the dream code can be easy to crack, giving access to useful information. However, as with all that occurs in the therapy, it takes a good working alliance to make sense of the dream's message.

"COORDINATES" & HISTORICAL DREAMS

Clinical working dreams fall into two categories. The first, which I call "reporting dreams," reveal the coordinates of where the officer is in the therapy process. These dreams mirror the three stages of therapy:

1. **Stage 1:** The officer is highly traumatized and having nightmares:
   "My holster is always empty or I've packed the banana from my lunch in it. No one knows where I am because the radio has gone to s---t. I'm totally exposed and I've got no cover...I'm taking live rounds..."
2. **Stage 2:** The officer is processing and working through the trauma and is starting to find solutions or relief at points in the dreams:
   "I reach down and there's no gun but my radio is now working and they can hear me. I've got a car; I'm hunkered down behind the engine block but I'm worried that I'll have to move soon."
3. **Stage 3:** The officer is done with the trauma and moving beyond the PTSD; in his dreams, things work together and turn out well:
   "I'm in pursuit and then they're boxed in. I gain hard cover in a good position; I've drawn my weapon. I've radioed in, I can hear the Code 3 coming closer so they're coming and they know exactly where I am, so there won't be any blue-on-blue. I'm being fired at and I'm able to return fire. I'm good...I'm solid...I'm in command of their movements. I can lay down fire to keep them pinned where they are if I have to. I'm reacting just as I need to."

Coordinate dreams may be either crystal clear or extremely symbolic. The latter are initially confounding, but once figured out, they typically lead to a sense of wonder and an, "Oh yeah, that *is* where I am right now!" reaction. It's truly amazing how the human brain is able to key into things with detailed accuracy on a subconscious level and represent them symbolically to us.

A second category of dreams that I call "historical dreams" direct us back into a critical incident to allow more aspects of the event to be uncovered for reprocessing and resolution. Quite often these dreams are like pointer dogs in the hunt. It may be that all of the trauma on the tactical and operational fronts have been worked through, but there's still something more to deal with. Historical dreams can tell a Warrior/Rescuer with great accuracy where he has unfinished business with an incident to wrap up. These dreams direct us to where we need to go next in our clinical work.

A WINDOW INTO NORMAL "WARRIOR DREAMS"

This chapter includes illustrations of normal dreams that may come up during clinical work. In my early days, I thought these officer dreams were trauma-induced because the cops telling me about them had PTSD. As time went on, I realized that a vast number of officers have these types of dreams as a matter of course. Given that understanding, I think it will be helpful for you, also, to understand what's typical to Warrior's dreams without the presence of PTSD.

An extremely well-written article on the topic of "cop dreams," by Sgt. Betsy Brantner Smith (Ret), appeared in the May 7, 2011 issue of *PoliceOne.com*, aka P-1.[1] Despite that term "cop dreams," these nighttime aberrations are universal across the Warrior spectrum, regardless of the weapon of choice. I've worked with military who, in their dreams, have had something fail with their beloved tank in the heat of battle, just as a cop's gun may fail in his dreams. The *OSM* with weapons theme is just the nature of the beast and size, make and model have nothing to do with it.

Sgt. Brantner Smith's article describes the nature of the dreams she and other fellow officers have had the courage to share with each other over the years, which is a true sign of health, by the way. At the end of this chapter, I have linked this article to another excellent one on the same topic by *Force Science News* Editor-in-Chief and P-1 Senior Contributor, Chuck Remsburg.[2]

Betsy's article generated an extraordinary number of wonderfully candid responses. She, along with PoliceOne.com, graciously gave me permission to share some of them. I do not include any commenter's names to protect their anonymity. I thank them and P-1 for this brilliant collection of thoughts and insights.

WARRIORS' RECOUNTING OF THEIR DREAMS

Dream #1

This may sound crazy, but I had a "premonitory dream" the other night that came true... Not a good one either. I dreamed that I was getting shot by buckshot and no matter what I did, I could not get to cover and out of the line of fire. This morning, I got the news that one of our officers had been shot by buckshot responding to a man-with-a-gun call. I guess whatever dream you have, pay attention to them—they're telling you that anything can happen to anyone at any time! The officer is out of surgery and recovering at this point.

Dream #2

I have the same reoccurring theme in my cop dreams and the funny thing is I'm not the only one in my office that has it. I get in a firefight and I might shoot a few rounds, but the kill shot (and I always know it's the kill shot) is the heaviest trigger pull I have ever experienced, like 20 pounds. It always goes off and kills the guy but it's pretty much every bit of energy I can muster to pull the trigger, and it doesn't matter if it's a shot from 100 yards or contact to the head. I finally told someone about it only to find out at least 3 other guys in my office have the same dream.

Dream #3

I had a dream when I was first assigned to the Special Reaction Team for the Marines. We were running down a hallway to assist another team. For some reason all I had was my pistol, which was still in my drop holster. I was engaged and despite how hard I tried to draw my weapon, it was stuck in the holster. But yes I've also had the ones with the heavy trigger and where I fire point blank, but the rounds do nothing.

Dream #4

When we transitioned to S&W 40s, from revolvers many years ago, I was having trouble with misfires. I began having dreams of situations in which my gun would not fire. The most disturbing were where my son was with me when I needed to shoot and couldn't. I was able to change out my weapon for a smaller 40 and my misfires stopped and my nightmares did also.

I think our dreams can clue us in to the concerns of our subconscious. We need to listen.

Dream #5
Yeah, I don't know how many times I've been naked in my dreams, but I'd say that my propensity for being unclothed happens about 80% of the time. I've been retired for 21 years as of today, but I still have dreams of being at work both in uniform and plainclothes. Nothing dramatic about them, I'm just at work with fellow officers. Clothed.

Dream #6
I've kept a dream journal off and on since before graduating high school. All your dreams symbolize something in your life. You just have to figure out what it means to you. Water represents life to me, teeth = acceptance and so on. If you are really interested, keep a journal and work through the images on your own or with a friend that "really gets you." Otherwise, just enjoy the show, work through the fears as they come up, and remember that you are not alone, even if no one else will cop to having the same type of dreams.

Dream #7
Whoever said you can't die in a dream is full of crap. I've been killed twice in cop dreams (and it scared the hell out of me each time)—not to mention having some of the other listed ones over the last 30 years. They stopped when I got off the street years ago and started pushing papers.

Dream #8
When I first got my taser 2 years ago, I had a few successful probe deployments, and then I started having a recurring dream where I would tase someone and for whatever reason NMI [neuromuscular incapacitation] *wasn't achieved, so in my dream I would do a drive stun follow-up that worked. After having a few tasings in real life where I had to do a drive stun follow-up that worked, the dream went away.*

Dream #9
I used to have the dream in which I needed to fire my duty weapon and it would not fire. That dream ended after I was in a close-quarters combat (housing project bathroom) gun battle with a gentleman in which he lost. That put an end to that reoccurring nightmare.

DREAM INVENTORY

After reading those dream recollections, the first thing to notice is that dreams 2, 3, 4, 7 and 8 all expressed weapons-concern issues. As you can see with dream 8, the taser was causing worrying dreams just as a gun would. No matter what the weapons are, trust issues will inevitably be attached to them at some point in a weapons-bearing career. Of the 19 comments in response to Betsy's article, 13 had dreams about weapon issues that generated fear or concern.

Because having to deploy—and trust your life to—a weapon (lethal or not) lies at the heart of the dangers involved in policing, it makes perfect sense that this would be the most common type of dream (or nightmare). Related to that is the haunting and unanswered question, *"If the time comes will I be able to do it if I have to?"* Dream 9 is a perfect example of how your ever-so-symbolic brains can fuse your "self" into the image of your gun. Once this officer had passed the undesired but necessary test, his dreams of weapon failure stopped.

The "clothing optional" issues are pretty common around feelings of vulnerability or identity. I see them show up most often in officers during extremely stressful times, such as being under investigation, or in major life transitions such as marriage or retirement. Dream 5 may illustrate a response to such a major life transition. What greater transition in life affects identity than hanging up the uniform for the last time?

The hard-to-pull-trigger-for-the-kill-shot (dreams 2 and 3) is, I think, a very healthy dream. Taking take a life should carry a burden/weight. The fact that warriors have this dream is, at least in my way of seeing things, confirmation that they're normal, healthy human beings versus psychopaths who can kill without any sense of remorse. You can see that this is a shared dream that went across agency lines (i.e. police officers and a Marine); this is a universal issue for the 98%.

Dreams 4 and 8 show what I consider an important connection to the fight–flight–freeze response discussed in Chapter 9. The freeze aspect seemed to be projected onto these officer's respective weapons (the gun and taser didn't "deliver"). The two officers found resolution through changes they enacted either by choice or experience. One changed to a more user friendly weapon. The other gained enough experience in navigating a weapon's "failure" to be able to go to drive stun. With these changes, both of their troubling dreams stopped.

The most exceptional aspect of dream 8 is that it was "giving" the officer the solution to the worrisome lack of NMI. That's an excellent example of training being reinforced and solidified by the brain making connections to constructive information during REM sleep. The connections end up providing positive learning for use in real life.

The resolution of making real-time changes and seeing the nightmares abate for a time or for good were reflected in six out of nine of the online comments about the article. A variety of self-directed interventions were mentioned, including:

- Increased their range time (2 officers)
- Gained clarity about why the dreams were happening at that time (1 officer)
- Changed job to "driving the pine" rather than pushing a patrol car (1 officer)
- Self-interpreted and proactively intervened in the direction of their dreams (2 officers)

Of all the descriptions of dreams, note especially dream 1. This dream had a "foretelling" nature. I appreciated the officer who chose to share this dream, even though he may have been concerned that others would think it was crazy. Such dreams give the dreamer no way of knowing *if* it's really going to occur until it has. We don't really understand why such dreams occur. It could be coincidence, or it could be that the limbic system in the brain has picked up some subtle clues. For example, there might be subtle indicators of potential escalation of violence on the streets. If that's the case, the conclusion of the commenting officer is wise. The best way to respond to this kind of dream is to become more careful and situationally aware and to just go on with life.

Below I quote one last online comment about dreams. I couldn't agree more with the officer's attitude regarding taking an active interest in one's dreams.

> *I've kept a dream journal off and on since before graduating high school. All your dreams symbolize something in your life. You just have to figure out what it means to you. Water represents life to me, teeth =acceptance and so on. If you are really interested keep a journal and work through the images on your own or with a friend that "really gets you." Otherwise just enjoy the show, work through the fears as they come up, and remember that you are not alone even if no one else will cop to having the same type of dreams.*

This officer's comment explains why I can so freely state that you are the experts when it comes to your own dreams. You may not have the motivation or the ability to wake up and make notes of your dreams, which for most people is the best way to recall them later. However, if you pay attention and know yourself or, as this officer said, if you have someone else who "really gets you," figuring out your dreams is not rocket science.

It's amazing what the brain will do to communicate to us. It can tell us we need to put in some time on the range, when it's time to start working out again, that it's time to get in to see the dentist or doctor. Dreams are the best way for our brains to talk back to us. It can pay to listen every so often. In fact, sometimes it can be life changing or even life saving. So, dream on...

THOSE THINGS THAT HAUNT US

Since our brain has no keyboards or cellular system to transmit messages to us, it uses symbolic imagery and even color to convey things as effectively as it can. It never ceases to amaze me just how powerful a simple image can be.

Just this picture with the interplay of darkness and light can evoke a sense of foreboding and fear about what's behind the door. In a similar way, "working dreams" can attempt to communicate with us inside and outside of treatment.

Through the years, I've learned who's ultimately in control of the timing and navigation of what occurs in the work my clients and I do: Their brains call the shots...hands down. The brain knows exactly where it needs to go from waypoint-to-waypoint in order to get back home. There's a remarkable order and sensibility to the course we navigate. My officer's brains have never failed us—ever. Their timing is incredible and as accurate as a Swiss watch.

Your brain, then, has a mind of its own, and sometimes it's best to work with rather than fight it. Remember what I told you: your brain with PTSD is *not* out to get you, despite how it might feel at times. Understanding how dreams look at the beginning, the middle and the end of a "tour of duty" in my office may help you appreciate the fact that you're not alone inside of that head of yours.

The brain is created to both survive and to heal. Sometimes dreams are the only means by which it can reach you to tell you where you are, where you need to go, or even, in those wondrous closing days in treatment, that you've finally come home. Then there is the type of "dream" that may occur that isn't even a dream at all, because it occurs while we're awake. Despite that, it has the qualities of a nightmare.

THE "WAKING-STATE NIGHTMARE"

Owen was one of those officers you could trust with your life quite easily. He was experienced, calm, clear thinking and huge. I'd witnessed him put potentially explosive incidents into "chill mode" many times over out on the streets.

When he came in for his session after having been off for ten days, I was shocked by his appearance. His shoulders were hunched, his head bowed, his eyes cast down. This was not the Owen I knew. It was clear that he wanted desperately to tell me something but was fighting a huge battle inside. After a few attempts to encourage him, I finally asked him what his worst fear was if he told me what clearly was haunting him?

His reply was, "I'm afraid that if I tell you what's been going on in my head, you'll think I'm a murderous son-of-a-bitch and that I can't do this job anymore."

Knowing the answer, I slowly asked, "Have you murdered anyone, Big O?"

This 6' 8" gentle giant started to shake and then broke into sobs. With his face in his big hands, unable to speak, he shook his head to indicate that he hadn't.

"Well that's...that's good. So far we're okay then."

The tears continued unabated. So I asked another question that I felt pretty sure I also knew the answer to..."Okay now, do you have plans to murder anyone?"

Again, Owen shook his head "no"...this time more adamantly.

This was one of those times when having had a rocking case of PTSD in my own past helped me to be a good enough therapist to Owen.

So I asked him to look at me, because I wanted to be sure that he'd hear what I was about to say to him next. He finally lifted his head, but his eyes were still closed. I then asked him to open his eyes and just trust me...and he did.

I said, "I'm going to take a guess here, Sport, and you can just let me know if I'm getting warm. I'm going to tell you what it was like some nights when I'd come home when I had PTSD, and all you have to do is tell me if this sounds familiar...okay?"

"Okay.... "

"So, I'd come up the driveway at 10:30 at night. My husband and son would be in bed already and the whole house would be dark. I'd get to the door and when I put the key in the lock, I'd have this terrifying feeling like...like when I'd go inside I'd find they were dead... murdered while I was away. Does that sound familiar to you?"

With that Owen's eyes got big and a combined expression of disbelief and relief washed over his face. He said, "It's worse than that, Karen. I see the scene...it's too terrible to describe! I feel

157

like I've failed them by being away protecting other people! I'm afraid this is really going to happen. I'm going to get them killed because of my job."

This is what I term the waking-state nightmare. These things are horrifying and terrifying on several different fronts. They are not uncommon for anyone who is living under threat, being stalked, or suddenly hurled into the public eye. They can come on because of "the job," especially undercover work in the U.S. or serving in a war zone or terrorist areas.

The reality is that any first responders (including firefighters, paramedics, lifeguards, search and rescue, dispatchers, ER doctors and nurses) have a tendency to have these forebodings due to the chronic exposure to the horrible things that can happen "out there." It comes with the paycheck, I'm afraid.

However, keep in mind that Owen had PTSD and when you have PTSD, this tendency can go *absolutely viral.*

The most common reactions to the mental images are horror and terror, often followed by the thought, *"What kind of a sick SOB would ever envision such hellish things happening to his family? I've got to be twisted, nuts, evil...."* In other words, the thought of having the very thought of such things is horrifying. The good news is that you're not alone in this and you're not going round the bend.

So why does this happen?

That list of sensory distortions given in *Deadly Force Encounters* gives some clues. During OIS incidents, 19% of the 72 officers interviewed *experienced* something during the shootings that they later found out had never happened at all.

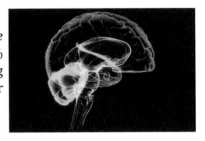

A classic example recounted there illustrates this:

"As I shot the suspect I could see blood spurting out of my partner as the suspect shot him. After the suspect had been neutralized, I ran over to help my partner, praying that he would survive his gunshot wound. As it turns out, he had also shot the suspect, but the suspect had never got off a round. My partner was not only fine but a little annoyed by my overly zealous concern for his welfare. (p. 44)[3]

In the kill zone, the brain, in some cases, presents us with the image of the worst-case scenario to get us to fight harder or run faster. And when PTSD is present, the brain believes it's in the kill zone 24/365. The brain wants you to survive, and knowing what matters to you most—typically our loved ones—it paints a horrifying picture to say, *"You need to be ready to keep this from happening...this is how bad it could get if you're not prepared!"*

With PTSD and that constant war inside, your body is producing a chronic over-supply of stress hormones. Add sleep problems, mental over-practicing of how to react due to intrusive images, nightmares and flashbacks of the incident and the issues can take on a life of their own. These waking-state nightmares don't mean you're sick, murderous or unworthy of wearing the uniform. They do mean you need to get in and get the PTSD sorted out.

Back in my office with Owen, things calmed way down once the basics around why he was having the horrifying images were explained.

Next, I did with Owen what you may want to try yourself, if you're suffering from these types of waking state nightmares. I reminded Owen that "shit happens" and that the horrific images are just his brain reminding him of that fact, on steroids. Remind yourself of that, and remember that all you can do is your very best to keep safe yourself when out on the job. And then just go on with your day. If you are in treatment for PTSD, be sure to share these waking-state nightmares with the therapist. No need to suffer alone.

It's important to point out that none of my waking-state nightmares, nor any that my officers shared with me, have ever come true. Other, unrelated calamities may have occurred, but not those.

During the course of work to resolve PTSD, you're likely to have a variety of nighttime dreams.

Familiarity with them can pave the way for using them to your advantage whenever possible.

A STAGE 1, PRE-EMDR, DREAM: CRACKING THE CODE

The ambush occurred one night to a special crimes team that had been sent into a bad part of town to check out a complaint. Kurt, their lieutenant, was behind in his paperwork and needed some time to get caught up so he sat this one out. As his team was enroute, they called in to recheck the coordinates of the location. Kurt was listening to the radio traffic.

Then suddenly, Kurt heard the sound of the radio handset being dropped and shots ringing out as his team came under fire. At the end of that night, one of his team members lay dying in a hospital bed, too unstable to be flown out. This lieutenant remained there with his man until he was ordered out by the medical staff. He left to attend to the rest of his team. The wounded team member died during the early morning hours.

Kurt had "been there" in that incident as he heard what was unfolding and yet was helpless to do anything to help his team. This can be far more traumatic for Warriors, and especially for commanders, than being on scene when the hammer comes down. He had the "weight of the bars" issues of having sent his team into harm's way and not having been out there with them. Most of all, what haunted him was the loss of his team member and friend.

Just as we were about to transition from Stage 1 into Stage 2, Kurt made mention of a "strange dream" that was waking him up at night in a panic. *"It's the strangest thing. There's no storyline, there's no danger going on, but I've never been so upset by a dream in my life."*

When I asked him to describe the dream, he began by explaining: *"So in this dream I'm standing at some kind of a table, and there are others there with me. I'm the commander and I've got a stick with a flat end. I'm using it to push around small soldiers made out of glass on this table. That's it...that's the dream. It's not a terrifying scene but every time I've had it I've woken up with a start ... something's really upsetting about it, but I can't figure out what it is."*

I took notes of the few most critical elements in his description of the short dream.

1. Table
2. Commander
3. Stick
4. Glass soldiers

I told him I was going to recite back to him one-by-one each of those words and asked him to free associate, just giving me the first thing that came into his mind.

Me:	Kurt:
1. Table	*Exposed–open place*
2. Commander	*Lieutenant*
3. Stick	*Pushing them out*
4. Glass soldiers	*Fragile–broken*

I then read his associations back to him so he could notice what came up and rate the reaction 0-10: *"Exposed – open place, lieutenant, pushing them out, fragile– broken."*

My lieutenant's reaction came @ 10. The dream was telling us that he was still stuck in that high trauma point in the critical incident that he heard his men going through in real time. For him, it was linked directly to feelings of responsibility for this murder-in-the-line because he'd sent his team out.

The dream didn't offer anything we weren't already keenly aware of, but remember, reporting dreams will tell us where things are at that point in one's therapy and life. One benefit of this dream was that it allowed a dam to break, to let a lot of reactions find their way up to the surface and to do that in a safe place. The dream certainly did get us into the deep end of the pool, where the work was waiting. Right on time, in fact.

Telling this dream also showed that our trust alliance was such that we could work effectively as a team now. There had to be enough trust in me within Kurt's limbic brain for this kind of an exchange to happen. And when it did, the sky hadn't fallen in, and he hadn't turned into a "girly man." Instead, on that day, we crossed over into the work to get him back from what could have become a career-ending traumatic incident.

Again, what we do with dreams in my office isn't rocket science. That simple exercise works most of the time. This illustrates once again how our brains creatively articulate things through highly symbolic images. Kurt's single-frame dream carried with it a powerful message about what he was struggling with and where we had to go.

A MID-STAGE-2 HISTORICAL DREAM

Scott had completed his first EMDR session a couple of weeks prior to the session when he reported this nightmare to me. His brain was beginning to push material up to the surface for us to start to deal with in the next round of EMDR.

He began the layout of this nightmare:

"I'm with about two or three other officers. I don't know them, but we're in an old building— it's made of really old bricks and it's crumbling in places. We're the only ones in there, but there are mobs of people outside trying to get in at us. I'm blocking the door and trying to keep it closed and the others are at the windows where the mobs are breaking through. Their arms are reaching through the holes in the walls and windows and we're trying to beat them back and away from grabbing at us with their hands."

The salient elements to this dream that I repeated back to him and Scott's free associations of them were the following:

Me:	Scott:
1. Old building	*Isolated*
2. Officers	*Strangers*
3. Mobs	*Crazy*
4. Windows	*Breaking*
5. Arms	*Striking*
6. Hands	*Reaching*

When I read these words to Scott–*isolated, strangers, crazy, breaking, striking, reaching*–all I got was a blank stare...nothing registered.

Then I offered this thought: "You know what image comes to my mind? It reminds me of being in a riot and of being segmented away from the pack of other officers in the line. Scott, have you ever had that happen?"

Then the light immediately went on, and he knew exactly where this dream was coming from.

"It was when I was still in the military and stationed in a place where riots could happen spontaneously at any time. We'd gone into a riot situation caused by a strike, in order to back up the local police. The riot was happening in a really bad area. Once we were deployed in there, the mobs all scattered. They'd run either into houses, where we couldn't follow, or up the network of alleys that tied the maze of streets together. When we were chasing those who'd headed up the alleyways, we broke formation. I got separated from my team and mixed in with some of the police. They were all strangers to me. We got spread too thin and then the mobs surrounded us in our smaller groups of two's and three's. We lost our cohesion and strength. Things went crazy and we just got clobbered."

His nightmare was telling us what the next EMDR session would be on the "dance card." It was recounting a historical incident that had happened years before. This one had been lying dormant until another incident hit the tripwire and brought it to the surface. This can also happen after the first and most pressing incident has been resolved with EMDR. That then makes room "on deck" for the next trauma to be worked on and if any others need resolution, they start to line up.

A HISTORICAL DREAM – THE INJURED ABILITY TO TRUST

Ryan was a survivor of an incident that had nearly cost he and his team their lives. Tragically, the leadership calling the shots on that night failed them miserably in the heat of battle and because of this, many were injured.

Ryan's nightmare had him waking up drenched in sweat and so distraught that he'd be unable to return to sleep. Sometimes his wife would wake him up because he was sobbing uncontrollably. Every time, it was this tenacious dream that brought him to that desolate place.

Ryan said that the highly charged nightmare had first appeared just after the critical incident. Eventually, it had become a nightly visitor. He'd had the dream at least a dozen times by the time he'd decided to bring it into session. (To understand the dream, it helps to know that at the top of Ryan's list of "safe people" was his brother.)

"I'm walking with my brother down a sidewalk. We're laughing and joking as we usually do when suddenly, a huge mountain lion appears. It's coming right toward us on the sidewalk and when it sees us, it locks onto me. I yell, "Run!" and my brother heads to the other side of the street while I climb up a wall alongside the sidewalk. It's not that tall. I'm just barely out of reach of the mountain lion, but he's trying to scale up after me.

I scream as he's clawing at my feet. I'm being slashed badly. I look for my brother. He's standing a safe distance away, laughing. He's doing nothing to help me. I call to him to throw something, to get help...that I'm going to die here! He just keeps laughing and doing nothing at all."

The following was how Ryan free-associated to the salient elements in his nightmare:

Me:	Ryan:
Mountain Lion	*Death*
Wall	*In the balance*
Slashed badly	*Desperate*
Brother	*Thought I could trust him with my life*
Laughter	*Loneliness. I'm alone with no one to help me*

Death, in the balance, desperate, thought I could trust him with my life, loneliness, I'm alone with no one to help me.

It wasn't difficult to realize that Ryan's brother, his most trusted friend, symbolized his LE agency's commanders. We already knew that Ryan and all of the other officers who'd been sacrificed that day had lost all trust in the commander's leadership. All of the officers involved in that incident developed significant relational trust-aversion defenses that impacted their lives.

POST OIS AND DURING THERAPY DREAMS

As mentioned at the start of this chapter, dreams tend to change with the progression of treatment from Stage 1 all the way through Stage 3. These serve as tracking devices to clinical progress. If ever there is a jump over the middle-stage type dreams to the end-stage type dreams, it may be that there is a "flight to health" being enacted. This is where an officer wants to get back to work without going through the trauma work and cross-check/re-training segments and things are suppressed. The process will come to a dead stop at that point.

In truth, I've had very few experiences of this but when I have, the situation involved a younger officer extremely motivated to get back to duty. This would be in order to prove that he's not a weak link to the team. Extremely good clinical cross-checks need to be done in all cases and these types of rapid recoveries are no exception. Heart monitors and, ideally, the use of video scenario range time and a specifically trained FA instructor to work along with the trauma specialist are critical to these cross-checks.

DREAMS AFTER A POST-TREATMENT INCIDENT

Chapter 9 gave a post PTSD treatment follow-up account by Sean's sergeant regarding his exceptional tactical insights into an attempt of another suicide-by-cop incident.

Below are descriptions by Sean of two dreams that he had following that incident. These dreams were very different from the types of dreams he had had years earlier, when we were working through his original OIS. These new dreams were a bit baffling, extremely vivid and very memorable to Sean. That said, they were not upsetting to him, because he was in the dreams experiencing the incidents that played out. After we identified the purpose of the dreams—to report that he was in a good place—they stopped.

Dream #1

Sean responds to a call for a man with a gun. It turns out to be a guy he knew back in high school. He's waving the gun around. Sean, from behind good cover, with his gun drawn, tells the subject that it doesn't have to end this way, that he can help. He keeps talking to the gunman until finally he relinquishes the weapon. The dream ends peacefully, with Sean telling the subject that he did the right thing.

Logged response after the dream:

"First, it felt like it had actually happened, @ 10 for realistic. Second, I felt relieved and very good, @ 10 that it had ended without having to shoot him."

This reflected what had come out of an EMDR session years previously concerning his past OIS, when he concluded, *"I'm not a murderous cop. If there's any way to resolve a deadly situation, I will do my best to try that first."*

Dream #2

Sean responds to a call out on the streets. There's a man acting in a menacing manner. He gets there and the man pulls a gun and starts firing at other officers who also responded to the call. Sean fires at him and kills him.

Logged Response after the dream:

Again it felt like it really happened, @ 10 for realistic, but then I was resigned that I had to shoot in order to protect the lives of others and myself.

This too reflected what had come out of an EMDR session years previously following his past OIS when he concluded: *"If I have to use lethal force to protect my life or the lives of others, I will do it and I will shoot as I'm required to do and as I've been trained to do."*

Summary of Both Dreams:

These were reporting dreams that gave us Sean's coordinates in the wake of that attempted suicide by cop. In both cases the dreams reflected that he was on very solid ground with a balanced view of tactical decision-making and a clear willingness to pursue options based on what an unfolding event may present.

We can see from these two dreams that the EMDR resolutions described above had held solidly. They were "reactivated" following a potential OIS situation. However, the reactivation did not bring up traumatic material. It brought up the outcomes of the tactical psych work Sean had done in a very site-specific mode of treatment and how he had worked and trained during and beyond that to be ready.

Sean's REM sleep cycle was working to reinforce his balanced view of less lethal and lethal options. In other words, his brain was doing its job during his sleep so it could help him do his job with exceptional skill while awake.

DREAM TRAITS TO LOOK FOR

To gather information from your dreams, you can ask yourself questions about them. The answers can make it easier to understand and make good use of the dreams.

1. *Is there a consistent theme?* This can show up as being overwhelmed by, for instance, a force of nature, such as being hit by a wave and taken out to sea. The characteristic elements may change (the wave becomes a landslide or a fire), but the theme that you're out of control and overwhelmed remains consistent.
2. *Does a perceived instigating event in your life trigger the appearance of the dream?*
3. *Is there a sense of, "Oh...I've been here before," or "Oh no...not again!"*
4. Is anything recycling through your life in terms of lessons that need to be learned that might change the course you're charting for yourself?
5. *How are your dreams changing?* For instance, is the nature of the terrifying or chaotic nightmare at the start of therapy changing to improved levels of functioning and safety as time goes on and the brain is healing and learning?

YOU CAN CHANGE YOUR DREAMS

You can learn to identify when you are dreaming. With that skill, you then can learn to do self-directed interactions in the dream to change its outcome. One of the comments in response to the P-1 article offers a good example of this:

"As I've aged, I kind of trained my mind to realize they are just dreams and know when I have a firearm failure, in my dream I go straight to hands-on and usually work over the bad guy pretty good. It helps that my bad guys never shoot or not well.

"I have a new recurring dream where I suddenly go back to work at my old agency. Like really suddenly. I show up in roll call in uniform and no one, including me, had any idea I was coming back. Glad to know we're all in the same crazy boat!"

NOT SO CRAZY AFTER ALL

Betsy's article resulted in officers sharing their "crazy boat" dreams that really aren't so crazy after all. A number of officers had come to realize that nightmares were their brain's way of telling them there was something that they needed to work on, in the same way that the officers I've worked with have gained direction from their dreams.

In truth, there's not much difference between nightmares or worrying dreams that come with PTSD and those that show up in normal life. In fact, both are doing the very same thing.

Just as the day-to-day dreams/nightmares are tapping one on the shoulder to point out something that needs to be focused and worked on, PTSD dreams and nightmares are doing same. They are directing you back to your trauma that needs to be worked through and resolved.

As your brain heals, you can often see that process reflected in the nighttime journeys you take in your dreams. And, as you heal, nightmares tend to fade away and be replaced with dreams of more warm and welcoming places. The same transformation can happen in your life, over time. Thank goodness…

PHOTO CREDITS:

1. Door to Sky: ©iStock/Palto
2. The Door: ©iStock/ToddSm66
3. The Tanks Are Home: © Karen Lansing 2012
4. Tank Crossing: © Karen Lansing 2012
5. Warm & Inviting: ©iStock/pixhook

ENDNOTES:

1. B. Brantner Smith. "What do our cop 'dreams' tell us? *PoliceOne.com* April 29, 2011 (distributed on-line May 7th, 2011) http://www.policeone.com/health-fitness/articles/3502401-What-do-our-cop-dreams-tell-us/
2. C. Remsburg. "Dream haunted: A young cop's close call clarifies instructor's startling statement: How 'when I dream, I dream of killing' began to make sense," *PoliceOne.com* June 16, 2010. http://www.policeone.com/patrol-issues/articles/2075604-Dream-haunted-A-young-cops-closecall-clarifies-an-instructors-startling-statement/
3. A. Artwhol, L. W. Christensen. "*Deadly Force Encounters: What Cops Need to Know to Mentally and Physically Survive a Gunfight,*" Paladin Press, Boulder CO, 1997.

CHAPTER 11
EMDR

EMDR ON A UCO'S WORST NIGHTMARE

The light shimmered through the blue curtains in my second-floor office window. They moved softly with the gentle warm breeze of the summer afternoon. Despite this tranquil setting, my undercover officer (UCO), Matt, sitting across from me, was hard at work in a very different scene. One we'd revisit several times in this two-hour session.

In each hand Matt held a wireless EMDR mechanism that vibrated in one hand and then the other. This gave his brain the bi-lateral stimulation needed to bring memories up while allowing him to go through the scene with his eyes closed.

Matt: *We're in shopping for a dresser for our son. I had our little 20-month-old with me, and my wife was up one of the home-furnishing aisles. We're just leaving her in peace. My head was nowhere near anything to do with work. Me and my "buddy" were just having some fun together. I was pretending to drop him...he loves that game. I was looking into his face as he was laughing uncontrollably...we're both laughing.*

And that's when I see them...on the other side of the checkout. They're picking up hotdogs and turning to find a table. They're right over there, maybe 40 feet away, just when I look past my son's face...and then they see me. There's no question that it's them, and they've clearly just recognized me. What are they doing in my town!? What are they doing here!?

It's hard to breath. It's that band-like thing at 8–9 now inside my chest. It's really tight...at 8.5.

KL: Okay Matt, just notice it and go on...

Matt: [Nods]... I turn and head in the opposite direction and then make a couple of more turns up aisles they can't see down. I'm making for the loading docks that I know are at the back of the building.

I rush past the loading-dock guys, who tell me I'm supposed to DRIVE in for pick-ups...I wave at them and smile like I'm fat, dumb and happy, pointing to my son as if to say, "Hey guys... this is a kiddie emergency; what can I do?"

It works and I head out and turn around the corner. I'm hearing my kid laughing...the entire time he's thinking that we're playing a hide-and-seek game with Mommy...huh! I had totally forgotten about that. To him this was just another game we were playing.

So I find my way back to the car and move it to where I'm harder to be seen but can watch for my wife. Then I call her on her cell. I give her descriptions of these guys. I tell her to look around to be sure they're nowhere near her. Once I know she's "clean"–not being followed–I tell her to leave. I tell her to got out through the loading docks to keep her away from the checkout and food area. She takes the same way out I did. I tell her which way to head once outside and that I'll find her.

I then hang up and call in to report that I've seen them and they've seen me...they've seen my son and maybe even my wife...F---! They've seen my family!

KL: Okay Matt, just notice and go on…

Matt: Okay...My son was in his car seat, singing to himself. And it hits me–I've taken away his innocence by exposing him to that s---t. I've ruined his simple little world. I've brought the fight to him. I've failed as his father.

God...what have I done?!

KL: Just notice that and go on…

Matt: Why couldn't I have been prepared for something like this? Why didn't I shield him?

KL: And what's your job as his father?

Matt: To keep him safe...to protect him.

KL: Good...go with that.

Matt: I...I've brought that on him...I put him right there...right for them to see! I should have tried to hide his face. They were looking right at me...they couldn't have missed him!

They know him now...they know how he looks...they know he exists! They know...

KL: And what's your job as his father, again?

Matt: To protect him.

KL: Good. And so you left him there, did you?

Matt: No. I... I... (even with his eyes closed there's a sudden slight turn of his head to the right, like he's just seen something). *No...I kept him with me.*

KL: And so you had no exit strategy then…?

Silence as things are processing...

Matt: *Oh...ha!* (laughing) *Ha! No...I kept him WITH me! I got him out of there! I knew exactly where to go...I kept him with me.*

KL: Good. Now go with that.

Silent processing...

Matt: *That feeling in my chest has just changed. It's not tight inside any more, but there's pressure now across the outside, along the front. Just not as strong but something's there.*

KL: Okay...good.

Silent processing and then a sudden lifting of his head, eyes still closed but a look of surprise ...

Matt: *Oh ...YEAH! I forgot about this! When I turned to get out of there, I repositioned my son as I was turning around so he wouldn't be facing them over my shoulder. I completely forgot that! I swung him around and then carried him in front of my chest. I'm actually feeling that pressure from him right now...pressure ON my chest, not IN it...it's changed!*

KL: Good...Good. Go with that.

Matt: *All they've seen are his shoes and before then they were looking straight at me...he was looking over my shoulder away from them. They hadn't spotted me until then. He never turned around. They never saw his face! All they'd have seen was the back of his head!*

KL: Good. Good...

Matt: *I purposefully didn't go back to my wife. I went up another aisle...to keep her out of the picture. We'd been playing out in the main thoroughfare where people were lined up to check out...she was up a side aisle...I went the opposite direction, heading for the rear of the store... out to the loading docks.*

Silence...processing things...

Matt: *When I call her on the cell she's all... "Hi! Where are you two...have I lost you?" Not upset, just wondering.*

KL: Okay...go with that...

Matt: *They never connected my wife to us... I was protecting my son and my wife! I didn't contaminate them... They never got a clear look at him...I got him out of there! I got him away. I did what I had to do to keep us all safe.* Smiling and nodding he takes in a deep breath. *I'm so proud of my wife. She was just so solid. She took this all with such ... I can't find the word.*

Silently processing briefly...

It's not one word...it's two. She did this all with intelligence and grace. Even after. She never got angry at me. She never got angry at 'the job.'

KL: Good...go with that then.

Matt: Yea...my little guy is still innocent. I kept that stuff from reaching him...Ha! You know that pressure on my chest? It's totally gone, just like that band of tightness (smiling and shaking his head). I swear, Karen, it's at a 0...my chest feels light now!

This story offers a snapshot of what an EMDR session is able to accomplish in a relatively short amount of time. The UCO had lived with this "worst nightmare" for nearly two years following the incident, all the time feeling like a failure as a father and a husband. Finally, he decided he just couldn't stand the effect it was having on him and his family anymore.

The preparation for this trauma work will be explained further on. First let's go in chronological order and review how things can be put into place for this kind of rapid and complete success.

STAGING FOR EMDR: STARTING WITH THE BASICS

There's a paperback novel sitting in a prominent place on my office shelf. It's a genre that I typically don't read (cop novels), but this one I did. It's because it was a gift and it came with the following inscription on the inside front cover...

> *"Karen ~*
>
> *Thanks again. As Harry Bosch would say...'You're the only one I can trust in China Town.' Read on..."*
>
> *"O"*

Trust is the lifeblood of every model and treatment plan of psychotherapy. That said, it can take a bit longer to set that cornerstone into place for Warriors and Rescuers. In Matt's case, we had to spend a respectful amount of time in Stage 1. This is because UCOs come in with a well-established inability to trust (unless they knew me prior to going undercover; then it's not an issue).

At the end of our work, Matt said to me, "I couldn't understand why it was taking so long for you to get me into EMDR, but you were working the whole time! I saw that after the EMDR session. You knew exactly when I was ready to go in. Any sooner and I don't think it would have worked. Any longer and I'd have given up and dropped out. Your sense of timing was right on the mark."

Your therapist needs to know you well enough to see your points of readiness. In return, you need to have trust in your therapist. You need to know that this person is safe (fully within the constraints of the law). She has got to pass the tests you put out there. And let's be honest, you're testing a lot–especially in the beginning, and rightly so.

You need to be convinced that the therapist knows what she is doing with "sheepdogs." EMDR can fail even at the hands of highly trained EMDR therapists because they went in too soon. Warriors are not like civilians and any clinician thinking that they can move into EMDR sessions without having established a solid trust has made a clinically fatal mistake right out the gate.

WHERE THINGS ALL TIE TOGETHER

At this point, I have brought you through a huge amount of informational terrain. You walked through a general overview on how key sectors of the limbic system and prefrontal cortex work with no PTSD present and then how they behave with that injury in-play. We've looked at how the brain following EMDR sessions is able to return to a non-trauma-sustaining level of normal functioning.

We've looked at the important function of containment techniques, including logging and specific life patterns, for increased control over symptoms and moods. You've been through discussion around the crucial issue of sleep and possible options for improvement. You've gotten confirmation regarding the absolute need for exercise and for a strong, supportive herd in your life.

In previous chapters, you have seen cases in which First Responders have come back from PTSD to accomplish some amazing things. You've seen how the brain looks when it's able to go from Code 3 (high threat/emergency status) back down to Code 4 (all is well).

In other words, you've seen that for all of these remarkable things to come to pass, it takes more than just moving your eyes back and forth. You've learned that a lot of pre-emptive staging is needed, and that once things move, they move rapidly and in the right direction.

The middle part of Matt's EMDR session above shows how all of these things tie together. It's important to know that Matt went through all of the preemptive education on PTSD and the brain. He went through all of the training and the daily use of the containment techniques—all of the logging and rating things on the 0-10 scale. He and I carefully formed that "herd of two" within his greater herd. Only then could we enter into the place of fear and torment to bring him out of it for good.

There are UCO's I've served with in another part of the world who would say about their *tradecraft* and mine that "It's a good game, played slow." And so it must be. For the clinician in this "good game," trust is a privilege that must be earned. It's earned by the integrity of the working alliance, by the integrity of clinical skill.

On the officer's end, he must be courageous enough to stand in his fear of the therapeutic process and not run. He must move purposefully toward that goal of healing after he's been properly trained—properly prepared for success. In the end, this good game played slow is a team sport.

BUILDING CONNECTIONS

Dr. Abram Kardiner was about a half-century ahead of his time in his ability to identify the cognitive lockdown that comes with the narrowing of a PTSD soldier's attention field. The most important thing he figured out was that the healthy ability to take in and process information was being impaired by the condition.[1] In that, he was able to highlight two of the foundational aspects of this trauma-induced injury to the brain. The difficulty is in processing information from both the past trauma and from the current daily life. Both of those feed into one's future.[2]

Matt was unable to access aspects of the original incident for all of those many months following that day. Those memories included everything he'd done in order to protect his son and wife in that situation at the warehouse store. Even though he knew he'd done those things, what didn't carry across was that he had, in fact, been reliable and was protecting his family through it all.

In his day-to-day life, he wasn't able to believe that he was still a reliable and protective father and husband, even though he knew that he was. The negative belief he came out of that close call with was just the opposite. This became a huge divide between Matt's brain and "heart."

This post-trauma reaction creates an obstacle that stops the ability to both know and believe a positive and true belief in the wake of something terrible occurring. This divide needs to be bridged in order to recover and take in more useful (adaptive) information and to be able to learn from it. Then one can assimilate that, move beyond a traumatic event and return back to the land of the living once again with new wisdom.

In Matt's session, you can see the ease with which he observed and took on-board important input. He reported seamlessly on physical changes in his body as they came up. He was so good at it that the observations didn't distract him from other important awarenesses coming to the surface. By the time of that EMDR session, he was such a skilled internal observer he could discern between the tightness inside his chest and the pressure on the outside of his chest.

In the pre-EMDR preparation, Matt was able to identify the inside tightness at 8 on the 0-10 scale and the reaction attached to fear his son had been seen.

The outside pressure that Matt felt on his chest came up moments later. It was a body memory that surfaced. He had held his son tightly against his chest as he moved to get them both out of the line of sight and then out of the building. That physical memory began to build a bridge to fragmented, previously inaccessible information.

You can see in that brief section of the session just how little I actually had to do. It was Matt and his brain that took the controls and steered things in the right direction. Only at one point did I need to become slightly more active, when he became stuck and couldn't pull out of a tangle of negative thoughts and reactions. That's called "looping."[3] His brain's neurological networks (neurons and synapses) were continuing to feed off the negative reactions and beliefs attached to the trauma-based memory. The networks had been neurologically pumping iron for a long time, so in this EMDR session, the same looping had already occurred several times. It was time to step up the game.

The intervention that helped Matt get untangled and back on track is called a *cognitive interweave.*[4] All that was needed to make him the new sheriff in town was to ask three questions: First, I asked Matt what his job was as a father. He answered that it was to protect his son. That laid the footing for the soon-to-be-built bridge. Second, I asked if he had left his son behind. He knew he hadn't. With the sudden movement of his head, it was clear that something had just clicked and had caught his attention. That slight movement let me know that once-blocked neuro networks had just started to connect with that cognitive interweave and he was taking in newly accessible information. The third question asked about his exit strategy. Both Matt and I knew he'd executed one immediately.

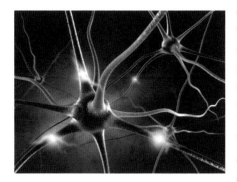

Those cognitive interweaves helped to form the bridge between neurons and synapse so that the true and accurate (once fragmented) memory and information could connect up. The bridge was connecting things and allowing a whole untapped source of positive information to flow across freely. Now that the trauma was neutralized, Matt's mental tunnel vision was able to open up to more clarity.

That's when Matt was able to gain the high-ground vantage point over the once limited perspective and gain access to the positive truths about that event. He was also able to access other positive things. For one thing, he realized how he felt about his wife—the pride in her solid, unshakable, fair way of dealing with the incident. He also had a sense of celebration in knowing that his little son hadn't been contaminated by the sudden intersect of his dad's job and his own innocent world. In other words, he was accessing the deep love he held for his family.

THE EMDR SESSION PREPARATION:

There's an old familiar saying that states, "If you fail to prepare, prepare to fail." One of the reasons Warriors and Rescuers take so well to EMDR is that it has a linear structure. There are no hidden chutes or ladders in the process. We formulate an operational plan and once that's in place, we go into the scene prepared.

As my officers are transitioning into Stage 2, we're gearing up for the first EMDR session. The week before our planned EMDR session, I go over with them what they can expect in the upcoming session; I give instructions on what they'll need to do and introduce them to the hand-held EMDR gadget that provides the bi-lateral stimulation. I explain how an EMDR session plays out and answer any questions they may have.

Prior to starting the EMDR, we go through the procedural outline—a standard form we fill out at the start of every EMDR session. Then we're good to go. I briefly review with them again the instructions and then we go to work. Below is a typical form, similar to the one Matt and I completed.

Presenting problem: What scene are you wanting to work on today?
The incident at the store.

Image: What picture represents the worst moment or worst part of that incident?
When I realized they were looking at my son and saw his face.

Negative Cognition: What words best go with that picture to express your belief about yourself now (express this in the present tense)?
I'm unreliable as a father and as a husband.

Positive Cognition: When you bring up the picture of that incident now, what would you like to believe about yourself now (express this in the present tense)?
I'm a good father and a good husband…I take care of and protect my family.

Volition of Positive Cognition: When you think of that picture now, how true does that positive belief feel on a scale of 1 - 7, where 1 = untrue, and 7 = totally true?
It's at a 2.

Emotions/Feelings: When you bring up that incident and the words, "I'm unreliable as a father and husband," what do you feel now?
I'm angry…. [after giving it some thought] … and afraid. I'm afraid for my son right then.

Subjective Unit of Disturbance: On the scale of 0 – 10 how strong is the anger?
It's at a 9.

Where do you feel that anger right now?
In my hands…it's like a tingling almost. It's at a 7 right now.

How strong is the fear?
It's at a 10.

Where do you feel that right now?
In my chest…it's tight inside. It's up there too…@ 8.

Desensitization: Okay, I want you now to bring up that picture and those negative words, "I'm unreliable as a father and a husband," and just notice what you feel physically in your body.

At this point the bi-lateral stimulation is started and it continues until the officer decides to take a break (more on this to follow). Desensitization refers to the reduction or complete elimination of fear brought on by a traumatic incident. Accomplishing this leads to the reduction of other symptoms connected to that fear, such as increased startle response, avoidance of things that might remind you of the incident, flash-point anger, etc.[5]

The Positive Installation: The desensitization process of going over the incident with the bi-lateral brain activation allows the disturbance related to the incident to be brought down. This is due to all of the adaptive information processing and memory reformatting (from present tense to past tense) that's able to occur. Once the disturbance level is at 2 or lower on the 0-10 scale, the positive cognition is reviewed for accuracy. Then using bi-lateral stimulation again while holding the thought of that positive belief and the mental picture of the incident, that new positive belief is fused to the now no-longer-traumatizing scene.

This is what is meant by the "Positive Installation." This is a process that helps to strengthen the bridging of previously inaccessible neuro networks that hold highly useful information or affect reactions/emotions. A good example of this happening in Matt's case was the sudden access he had to the extremely positive feelings he held for his wife in the midst of that close-call event. Pride, admiration and appreciation for his wife were suddenly accessed in relation to what had been a highly distressing event previously.

We measure, on a scale of 1-7, the volition of cognition, i.e., the strength of the truth of that cognition. We continue briefly several times to join that positive, accurate true belief to the no-longer-disturbing image of the scene. Each time this is done, it further strengthens the positive affect that has taken the place of the negative one/s. At the end of the session, the client is reminded about logging and what to do if any strong reactions surface between sessions.

While the pre-EMDR preparation form may seem like boring paper work, in fact it's all very important information that will be useful and needed in the session. We'll be measuring the levels of disturbance further along as the desensitization process works the intensity of disturbances down from highly traumatizing to "only a memory" status.

The key to successful treatment lies in staying with the EMDR protocol while making it adaptable enough to be highly effective for the client. That's the art of this tradecraft of therapy.

LEARNING FROM OUR CLIENTS

"Every person I worked with gave me new insight into the clinical application and helped me refine it further. I simply kept altering the procedure through trial and error to improve the results."

Dr. Francine Shapiro, Creator of EMDR, on her innovative process[6]

I was trained in and doing EMDR with civilians for approximately two years during my marriage and family therapy (MFT) internship. I did the EMDR protocol for Levels 1 and 2 just as I was trained. This meant that I used eye movement as the form of bi-lateral simulation; we'd start at the worst part of the scene and I'd stop after brief sets of eye movements to have the client report on any reactions or body sensations that were coming up. Then we'd proceed to the next set. At the end, we'd do the installation of the positive cognition and call it a day. Typically, these sessions took around an hour and a half to two hours.

The very first EMDR session I ever did with an officer occurred in the late summer of 2005. In this model of therapy, we don't go into any of the traumatic events at any depth in Stage 1 of treatment. We do identify what incident is the most upsetting and intrusive one on the "dance card" and that's the one we target for the first EMDR session. All of that Stage 1 time leading up to that point is spent in building resiliency and getting prepared to go operational in Stage 2.

My client, Robert, was a bit anxious about his first EMDR session, which is normal. But he was prepared and ready to go. We'd done all of the preemptive work described above and had started in on the desensitization phase. After around 10 passes of my hand back and forth in his field of vision, he suddenly grabbed my wrist in mid-pass and told me he couldn't do the work with my hand going past his face like that.

I told him I could slow it down and he agreed to try that. That didn't work either, and neither did changing the angles of the hand movements. Eventually he stopped my hand again and told me to "knock it off!" Sounding defeated, he said that the EMDR wasn't going to work for him.

I asked him if he was having stuff come up and he said, *"Yeah, I'm getting pissed off at you! I can't concentrate on the f---ing scene with your hand going back and forth and you keep interrupting my train of thought. You keep asking me what I've got and I'm right in the middle of something in my head. You keep throwing me off, Karen! It's like I've got no control here!"*

Now that was a lot for me to process: an officer with control issues...go figure. Rob was giving me a crash course on what he needed for EMDR to succeed for him. Control, of course, was a biggie. So I asked him what he would suggest that would help. His answer nearly floored me: "I need to do this with my eyes closed and I need you to let me do this without getting in my way."

A cop willing to sit in a room with a therapist and keep his eye closed?! Not only that threw me off, but I'd never done EMDR without the eye movement. The only thing I could figure out right then was to use the kinesthetic bi-lateral method. I'd learned from Dr. Shapiro's training for EMDR that there were different options for bi-lateral stimulation of the two hemispheres of the brain, among them auditory stimulation, with sound alternating in each ear and the hand-tapping technique (kinesthetic).

We agreed to try the hand tapping, and just like that, Rob was off and running. I immediately noticed that he was talking me into the critical incident. At one point, I asked him to take a break when he was ready (to keep the control with him versus me). When he did, I suggested he do the work silently and not talk so much, explaining that things would process faster for him if he did. (I was also afraid that the talking was distracting him). He said he'd try, but after a short time he said that he needed to "talk it through," because it helped him to focus and he was able to pick up on things better.

This meant that Rob was able to access his reactions and feelings better when he talked. This was turning my EMDR world upside down, but since it appeared to be working, I strapped in, not knowing if it would be a success or if we would crash and burn. As it turned out, Rob's EMDR session was very successful. He couldn't believe what had hit him.

Quite frankly, neither could I. I felt that I had broken all the rules of EMDR, but it had work wonderfully well. I assumed that Rob was just one of those unique clients who marched to a different drummer, and accepted that this was how we were going to work our way through EMDR in his treatment.

Rob told his friends on the force that he'd gone into therapy to deal with some of the incidents that they had been involved in. When they saw how much better off he was, they came in, too. They all needed to do trauma work and they all wanted this EMDR thing that Rob had told them about. As it turned out, every time I tried to use the standard EMDR protocol with eye movements, short sets, and silence during desensitization sets, they each without fail insisted on doing it with the same elements Rob had—eyes closed, kinesthetic bi-lateral hand tapping–and all went on through the incident from start to finish without any stops in between. Not only that, but these guys were all "talkers." EMDR and silence just didn't work for them.

Within six months, I was seeing only officer clients. This same group of issues around the EMDR session practices held consistently. When I realized that I had to accommodate for these needs, I decided I had to study what I was doing. The question was whether I was still doing EMDR with the alterations or if I was doing something else, like hypnosis or what's called "exposure therapy."

The hypnosis was easy enough to test out. During EMDR I'd test for suggestibility with my officers. Their extreme lack of suggestibility and their agitation when I tried to bend things even a tiny bit confirmed what I knew already: cops are not good candidates for hypnosis. Their control issues won't let them drop their guard.

The exposure issue was a bit more challenging to test. The reason EMDR is designed with short sets and breaks is to maintain what's called "dual awareness." This means that as the client is going back into that traumatic scene, she's still keenly aware that she's in the therapist's office and in a safe place. This provides an ability to stay grounded so that the information and memories being processed don't become overwhelming. My belief at the time was also that having clients keep their eyes open during the bi-lateral stimulation reinforced that dual awareness.

Instead, what I came to realize was that my officers' need to talk as they went through their self-modulated sets gave them that dual awareness. My responding to them, even briefly, i.e. "good…just notice it and go on…" during those sets let them know they were still in the office with their therapist. One of the more traumatizing things that can happen to officers is the loss of radio contact when they're heading into something that may go sideways on them. If they lose their radio, the danger and intensity rises dramatically.

In the typical EMDR session in my office, we're heading into events that have really gone sideways; the last thing the officers need is to feel like they're out there solo without anyone to communicate to. The good thing about EMDR is that my clients are not sent out to contend with whatever comes up in isolation. While they do the work, they're given the control. I'm just there to render aid if things get stuck. Once back on track, I get out of the way so they can do their work in that scene.

As the trauma drops in intensity through the session, they tend not to need to talk as much, if at all, as they go through the sets. The sets also become shorter. The incident changes from the initial pass through, where it seems like a video. Then, as things are processing from "now" to "back then," the sets become more like a slide show. The gaps between "slides" are parts of the incident that are no longer important and not the object of focus.

Eventually, at the end of the EMDR process, we end up with what seems like the psychological equivalent to a black-and-white photo of a very old, historic event. That's when we check the 0-10 Subjective Unit of Disturbance levels to be sure that's at 2 or lower. If that's the case, we then take that "old photo" image that's left of the incident and use it for the Positive Installation.

We had to figure out all of these things in those early days, with the result that now we're using what works naturally for my highly specialized clients without going off course with the EMDR model.

In 2009, I discovered that similar adaptations had been made to the protocol by a number of highly skilled EMDR therapists in places such as the Middle East. These adaptations, like mine, included allowing clients to have their eyes closed and to talk during sets without interruptions. (However, those therapists maintained control over the sets.) The adaptations have also been used in intense settings, such as places where heavy bombing is occurring or terrorist activities are traumatizing civilian populations. What we've all found is that these changes have better served our clients clinically.[7]

Still another modification of the approach had to be worked out, which involved my ability to do cognitive interweaves. The officers could start looping and get stuck within a memory, just as Matt did when he spiralled into self-blame for what he believed to be endangering his family.

In more tactically oriented traumas, if I didn't know how to put a clear, accurate interweave into the process, things could spin out of control pretty quickly. It became obvious to my first generation of officers that I needed to be trained in weapons and tactics. And so the tactical and weapons training began and it will continue for as long as I'm a therapist for players in this deadly game.

Officers first got me out on the weapons range and on patrol on a regular basis. I was later brought into specialist teams and allowed to be along for more specialized operations. There I could put officers on heart monitors with "memories" to study heart rates at pre-briefings, in transit, in-the-stack and on through the dynamic entries. This helped me to identify the stress points throughout the process. I could then train the officers in how to make good use of tactical psych methods to help attain peak performance when it's needed the most.

There have been public-order trainings (I caught on fire a lot!), close protection trainings (as a "principal" to protect), specialist weapons teams (stuffed into trunks of fast cars or closets to be hostage-rescued), and intelligence and source-handling trainings (if I told you I'd have to kill you). All these and more have taught me skills I integrate into the clinical work and the tactical psych trainings I offer the teams. From the boots-on-the-ground to the Gold, Silver and Bronze Commanders making operational decisions, this cross-training has brought about a hybrid of tactical sports psychology that is highly effective.

There's a symmetry to this unique approach that has served to improve treatment, officer and command performance under extreme stress, and most important, help prevent duty-induced PTSD over the years. The key ultimately rests in how wise and teachable the leadership can be and how much they care (or, sadly, don't) for those under their command.

SO HOW DOES EMDR WORK?

Memory is stored in different formats within the brain. There are visual, auditory, kinaesthetic, olfactory, muscle/movement and emotional memories. All of these are connected but also separate in nature. It's as if these different sensory memories are written in their own documents but share the same file, which is labelled "NOW."

So when EMDR is used to neutralize a traumatic incident, it works through that file related to the incident. It metaphorically takes out all of the "NOW" documents and reassigns them to the file labelled "BACK THEN." This means that the memory, sensory aspects and all, is no longer set up to convince the brain that the incident is still occurring in the present. Often, for my officers, the visual memory is the first, most dominant one to surface. When the images start to become less disturbing, other sensory aspects come into play. Sounds, movements, smells that had been unavailable can then find their way to the surface without being blocked.

As mentioned before, smells are the fastest way to bring up memories (pleasant or traumatic). For example, the scent of lilacs on a hot summer afternoon may take you back to the yard of the house you grew up in as a child. You see it in your mind's eye. You remember the lawn, the sprinkler being on, the sunlight shimmering in the droplets of water flying through the air.

Then you recall running through the water with your brother and your best buddy, laughing and feeling the cold splash of water and being so happy to be cooling down on a sunny 90º day. All of that can get ushered to the surface with the simple smell of lilacs. The same things could have been brought to mind by sight. It could be seeing a sprinkler going, with the sun at just the right angle so that it's shining though the droplets. That could take you right back there too.

One of the more recent findings in neurological research explains why different sensory formats of memory (sight, sound, movement, et al.) come up to be integrated into the memory. It was found that REM sleep "recruits" multiple sensory activations during sleep. These different sensory information bits weave together to render a more cohesive (3-D) perception picture with sights, sounds, movement, etc. The study also found evidence that the brain is able to do this while both awake and dreaming.[8]

The theory that EMDR is somehow similar to the function of REM sleep and that PTSD has some kind of connection or impact on REM sleep is becoming more widespread with the progress of research. Brain imaging studies have shown that both REM sleep and PTSD share the same pathways in the brain.[9] In other words, the same regions of the brain activated during REM sleep are activated when the brain has PTSD and is triggered (Rauch et al., 1996[10] & Shine et al, 1997[11]). In these studies, the research subject's triggering was caused by listening to a written recounting of the traumatic events while the brain was being imaged. This is called "*script driven imagery.*"

This research supports the current understanding that traumatic memories are reprocessed during REM sleep and that PTSD disrupts the normal functioning of the brain's ability to have REM sleep. That disables the brain's ability resolve the trauma, to learn from it and then to adapt that new "training" into one's future. In other words, it blocks the ability to heal, learn and move on.

This may explain why EMDR is able to desensitize and reprocess memory as it integrates learning gained as the trauma-based memory is worked through. As more research on the brain is being done, we're finding more indications that EMDR and REM sleep imitate each other's functions. EMDR is indeed doing extremely similar to what REM sleep should be doing but can't when PTSD interrupts its function.

WHAT EMDR IS NOT

EMDR Is Not Hypnosis: One of the first questions that typically comes up as I'm educating my clients on EMDR and what to expect is, "This isn't hypnosis, is it?" That's a fair question coming from a population that is not comfortable with going into a trance state under the control of another.

Research has shown that EMDR has nothing in common with hypnosis.[12] No trance is involved.[13] In fact, it's critical to have a client fully awake and engaged actively in the process.[14] This is because clients are not just along for the ride. They're actually steering that train as it's going down the track. The therapist is just on board to clear away any debris might anything show up on the tracks and interrupt the train's progress to its intended destination.

Several characteristics disqualify EMDR as a form of hypnosis. First is the aforementioned lack of suggestibility during the process that I discovered when I was checking to insure that I was still doing EMDR in the wake of the changes we had made in the procedure. Dr. Francine Shapiro points out that the distinguishing difference between EMDR and hypnosis comes down to the type of brain waves that occur during EMDR versus hypnosis.[15] EEG studies have shown normal waking brain-wave patterns during EMDR, whereas hypnosis generates brain-wave activity similar to what occurs during sleep.[16] An additional difference is the lack of suggestibility of clients when doing EMDR in session.[17]

There is another treatment modality that EMDR is often mistaken for called "exposure therapy." Some types of exposure therapy require that the client spend time between sessions focusing on the traumatic memory to the point of becoming activated (disturbed) by it. They are to do this on a regular, scheduled basis to bring the disturbance down by desensitization through either direct (for example, going to the place of the trauma) or indirect (by writing about the trauma) exposure. This can be a slow process and the client has to do these homework assignments in isolation. The dropout rates of such treatments can be significant, perhaps due to that aspect of the treatment plan. In all the years I've worked with officers with EMDR, only one client has dropped out of treatment, and that was a case of malingering.

EMDR Is Not a Lonely Place: With EMDR the trauma work occurs in session and in a "team" structure. Early on in my work with officers, I discovered how isolated they can feel even if

they were involved in a critical incident with others. Shootings were the first incidents in which this dynamic became apparent to me. In one incident, several officers had fired their weapons. All ended up coming to me to work through the incident.

In every case, each had a reason they were segmented away from the other officers involved. Things that could create this sense of being on the "outside" could be due a number of situations:

Rank:
"I was the sergeant and the rest were officers, so they had each other...I was alone because I was the one with rank."

Position in the incident:
"I was the only one in that position around the corner and everyone else was in the parking lot together."

Length of time on the team:
"The rest of the guys have been working together for a long time; I'm relatively new to the team and so things were different for me."

There are, of course, many incidents in which officers were out there having to go-it-alone, as well.

By it's very nature, EMDR is able to attend to that sense of isolation when an officer is going back in to reprocess that critical incident. This factors into the power of the herd.

EMDR is able to resolve PTSD in a shorter period of time than exposure therapy and without increasing the aspect of isolation. This is especially helpful for men who, as already mentioned, tend to withdraw from others when contending with PTSD.

There are, of course, no guarantees that EMDR will work for you, but I have found that to be extremely rare. Some officer clients were unsuccessful with EMDR therapists who used the traditional protocol. In each of those cases that subsequently came to me, I explained that I work differently and asked that they give EMDR another try. It turned out that all those officers had been unprepared and untrained in the techniques that I set up in Stage 1. For every one of these cases, EMDR worked perfectly. The critical piece of the matrix was Stage 1. If it is short changed, the officer will end up losing.

Stage 1, the beginning of EMDR really matters. It determines what happens in the all-important middle stage. So then, if you succeed in preparing, prepare to succeed.

PHOTO CREDITS:

1. Warehouse Corridor and Handcraft ©iStock.com/DigitalZombie
2. Adorable Family Moment Between Father &Son ©IStockphoto.com/PhotoEuphoria
3. Puzzle Bridge©iStockphoto.com/mstay
4. Folders & Files copying ©iStockphotos.com/-hakusan-
5. Child Running Through Sprinklers ©iStockphoto.com/grandriver
6. Clock in Motion–Hypnotism ©iStock/Andresr
7. Tumbleweed ©iStock.com/archives

ENDNOTES:

1. A. Kardiner. *The Traumatic Neuroses of War*. New York, Hoeber 1941.
2. F. Shapiro. *Eye Movement and Reprocessing: Basic Principles, Protocols and Procedures*. Gilford Press, New York: 2001, 18-20.
3. Ibid., Shapiro, 7.
4. Ibid., Shapiro, 249-52
5. C. R. Figley, "C.R. Editorial Note," *Traumatology*, Vol. 12, No. 1 3/2006
6. E. Shapiro and B. Laub. "A summary, a theoretical model, and the recent traumatic episode protocol (R-TEP)." *Journal of EMDR Practice and Research*, Volume 2, Number 2, 2008, 79-96
7. F. Shapiro. *Eye Movement and Reprocessing: Basic Principles, Protocols and Procedures*. Guilford Press, NYC, 2001 pp 18-20
8. C. Chong-Hwa Hong, J. C., Harris, et al. "MRI evidence for multisensory recruitment associated with rapid eye movements during sleep," *Human Brain Mapping* Volume: 30, Issue: 5, Publisher: American Chemical Society, Pages: 1705-1722, 2009.
9. J. A. Hobson, R. Stickgold, and E. F. Pace-Schott. "The neuropsychology of REM sleep dreaming, *NeuroReport*, 1998.
10. S. L. Rauch and B. A. van der Kolk, et al. "A symptom provocation study of posttraumatic stress disorder using positron emission tomography and script-driven imagery," *Archives of General Psychiatry*, 56, 380–387 (1996).
11. L. M. Shin, S.M., Kosslyn, et al. "Visual imagery and perception in posttraumatic stress disorder—A positron emission tomographic investigation," *Archives of General Psychiatry*, 54:233–241
12. E. J. Frischoltz, J. A. Kowall, D. C. Hammond. "Introduction to the special section: Hypnosis and EMDR," *American Journal of Clinical Hypnosis*, 43, Washington, D. C., 2001 179–182.
13. C. G. Fine, S. A. Berkowitz. "The wreathing protocol: The imbrication of hypnosis and EMDR in the treatment of dissociative identity disorder and other maladaptive dissociation responses." *American Journal of Clinical Hypnosis*, 43, 2001, 275–290.
14. M. Phillips. "Potential contributions of hypnosis to ego–strengthening procedures in EMDR," *American Journal of Clinical Hypnosis*, 43, 2001, 275–290.
15. F. Shapiro. *Eye Movement and Reprocessing: Basic Principles, Protocols and Procedures*. Gilford Press, New York, 2001, 326.
16. G. Nicosia. "Brief note, EMDR is no hypnosis: EEG evidence," *Dissociation*, 3, 1995, 65.
17. M. G. Sabourin, S. D. Cutcomb, H. Crawford, K. Pribram. "EEG correlates of hypnotic susceptibility and hypnotic trance: Spiral analysis and coherence." *International Journal of Psychophysiology*, 10, 1990, 125–142.

CHAPTER 12
THE HOMECOMING

Not that the pines were darker there, nor mid-May dogwood brighter there,
nor swifts more swift in summer air; it was my own country,

yet being mine; its face, its speech, its hills bent low within my reach,
Its river birch and upland beech were mine, of my own country.

Now the dark waters at the bow fold back, like earth upon the plow;
Foam brightens like the dogwood now, at home, in my own country.

From: "The Long Voyage" *Blue Juniata: A Life*,
by Malcolm Cowley[1]

As this book rounds the final corner, you may now be out beyond the far borders of PTSD and finally coming down the last hill toward home. For others of you, it may be that you're just beginning to find your pace in this journey. It may be that you've got some distance yet to cover before you can finally put PTSD behind you once and for all. If that's the case, it's my hope that you are working toward that time with more clarity of vision and determination in your steps. I hope you've found renewed strength in the wake of all you have discovered in the pages of this book. I hope, as well, that you are being strongly supported by the traveling mercies[2] of others in your life–of those in your herd.

No matter where you are in the journey, in the back of your mind you may be asking, what will home be like after all this time? The reality of any journey is that, given enough time away, the place we return to is changed, as surely as we are. And this is equally true of PTSD—it changes everyone it comes in contact with. But then, so does the passage of time. The next question naturally is, yes, but changed *how*? By now you know that change is not always for the worse.

I began this book in the predawn hours of a morning looking out at the harbor and watching the early assaults of an approaching storm. I have since written chapters in hotel rooms while doing work in the Middle East and in planes flying into and out of two post-conflict countries that have emerged out of communism in this generation's time.

I'm still taken aback by how much alike war and PTSD truly are. Neither are conditions that sensible folks ever want revisiting their home soil again, once finally over. When the Warriors from U.S. and EU allied forces from NATO and the UN have left, what citizens want most of all is to never, ever go back into war again. More than anything else, those who live in those noisy places on this planet want desperately to be normal. They long to lead normal lives, have normal jobs and be unafraid for their children and themselves in their day-to-day dealings. This is also true for those struggling through every day with PTSD. They long for normality to return to life.

Once beyond war, there are three ways to defend against its return: First, *foresight*, second, *maintaining* the peace, and third, the *ability to leave* the war behind while remembering its lessons but no longer residing within it.

There are only a few thoughts still to pass on to you now, and as it happens, they fall in line under those three banners.

FORESIGHT: CAN YOU SMELL THE RAIN?

It's important to realize that, indeed, lightening can strike twice in the same place, and so can trauma.

While resiliency can come from weathering and then overcoming the storm, it is bought with a price.

It requires good maintenance that makes use of well-honed observation skills and the courage to seek assistance when it becomes apparent you have need of it.

In the final part of Stage 3 in treatment, as my officers are preparing to graduate out, we debrief. We talk freely about what worked in treatment, what didn't work, what could improve, and finally, what signs they might have missed early on. In other words, I ask them what the indications were that the storm was coming and whether it was going to be a massive and destructive force to contend with in their lives. Outcomes from those discussions are critical for formulating future strategies.

EARLY WARNING SIGNS:

In the answers to the question regarding early warning signs they missed before PTSD actually hit lies the wisdom gained by those Warriors and Rescuers. The signs that they didn't recognize before they now can clearly identify. The answers commonly include signals such as:

- The vertigo started
- I was always angry
- My body constantly ached
- I broke teeth grinding them in my sleep
- I just wanted to be left alone all the time
- I had to have alcohol in order to fall asleep
- I ate a lot of junk and gained 25 pounds in 7 months
- I stopped working out/I started working out obsessively

What tends to happen is that your bodies, and at times even your dreams, try to get your attention well before the storm bells toll. The problem is that you don't know yet what you don't know. After PTSD, that should never be the case. If you re-experience any of those early warning symptoms, it probably won't indicate that you've got PTSD again. What it commonly means is that stress is hitting and you're having reactions to it, just as anyone does. The best course of action, whether you've ever had PTSD or not, is to get to the cause of it. The sooner the better.

MAINTAINING THE PEACE INTENTIONALLY

Having had PTSD won't make you immune to ever being injured by it again. What it can do, however, is make you far more savvy about how to chart a course so lightning *doesn't* strike a second time. Still, if through foresight, you start to notice early warning symptoms, getting in for a tune-up is wise and proactive maintenance.

In all of the years I have worked with Warriors and Rescuers, none who have graduated out of treatment has ever had to come in for a second full-course of treatment for PTSD. If they need a tune up, it's short-term and highly effective. Some officers call to schedule a tune-up if they've had a really close or hard call. They know how to read the skies and respond proactively. That's what good maintenance looks like.

SPEAKING ALOUD THE UN-SAYABLE

With the exception of discussing in general terms trauma after-the-fact in Chapter 6, I have not written about any unspeakable acts that have been inflicted upon officers I've worked with. This doesn't mean such things haven't happened. Wrongs have occurred in theatres of war and through all ranks of LE organizations that have devastated good men and women. I've seen only a small fragment of the carnage that is out there as I've attended to those who've witnessed or fallen prey to it.

I can state that the torment suffered by those who have seen or been victims of horrifying acts done by their own peers or commanders does extensive damage. It significantly impacts their sense of self, sense of the world, sense of mission, sense of right and wrong and sense of trust and honor. The effects on their lives can be of global proportions. Coming out of such trauma is an arduous endeavor. The most difficult step is the act of speaking the unsayable aloud to another human being. The courage this requires is magnified significantly if you took part in such acts yourself (see Chapter Notes). The power of this speaking aloud is as great as the courage it takes. Healing comes closer with speaking.

CHOOSING A NEW WAY

In the process of working through all that causes PTSD, any number of things need to be set aside. As life and priorities begin to be re-established, it is wise to take stock of areas of your life that now need your care and attention.

I told you earlier in the book that in the midst of PTSD, marriage or relational therapy often is not likely to be productive. However, once beyond PTSD, it may be necessary and can be very effective.

The beauty of being in a couple relationship is that when one person is struggling, the other will rally. This is beneficial in the final end of PTSD and beyond, because often as the one with PTSD regains better footing, the one without PTSD needs shoring up. It's totally normal. This ebb and flow in intimate relationships is a known phenomenon called "homeostasis," which means balance.

TAKING BACK GOOD GROUND

If a relationship was good and solid before PTSD entered the picture, often problems that have developed due to the injury can self-right over time. That said, even in healthy relationships, any number of issues may need to be addressed. It might be time to focus on regaining more healthy patterns within the relationship or it may be time for relational CPR.

Over the course of living with PTSD, an atmosphere of criticism may have become a problem. It may be that conflicts begin, out of habit, at higher levels of agitation or volume due to the disproportionate anger that PTSD can cause. Conflict avoidance may be the other side of that coin. As life becomes normalized over time, such issues may need to be discussed and jointly worked through, either on your own as a couple or by making good use of professional help.

Your children may need attention as well. It's not uncommon for youngsters to develop anxiety and/or vicarious PTSD when a parent is struggling with the condition. This is especially possible if they've witnessed flash-point anger at home. On the other side of this, I have witnessed families in which the children have happily come to discover, some for the first time, who their no-longer PTSD parent truly is. It's never too late to take back good ground and reconstruct your marriage and family.

It may take time for everyone to trust that the changes after PTSD are not just temporary. Despite this, recovery from PTSD can be a wonderful second chance to build new and healthier relationships.

THE ULTIMATE HEALING

The final phase of healing from PTSD takes time for everyone, although it may take longer to navigate if you had to deal with the unspeakable. Still, no matter what circumstances caused this injury to the hardware of the soul, the final healing comes through your ability to forgive. What forgiveness means here is that you're making a conscious choice to take another course, to live your life *not caught in irons* by wrongs that have been done.

This final aspect of healing can't occur until the traumatic memories are neutralized and no longer active in the present tense. Until then, forgiveness can only be theoretical. (Unresolved trauma will block your ability to extend forgiveness to others or to take in and accept forgiveness yourself).

Forgiveness doesn't mean being unjustified in seeking restitution when appropriate under the law, nor does it mean that you are accepting or condoning the wrongs done. It means that you are choosing to let go of hatred and resentment so you can focus on expanding the meaning and quality of your life. With forgiveness, you're leaving a prison behind and walking out a door unencumbered by those burdens. This takes time; it's not an easy thing to do. But it is a critical and final step.

THE RETURNS OF THE DAY

Today, I'm finishing this book in the same place it began, looking out the same window. This morning the summer sailboats were brought out from winter storage. Soon there will be children learning how to sail in the shelter of this harbor. The air will be filled with their excitement and laughter.

Then, eventually, they'll be taken out of the harbor to hone their skills in the loch.

Peace has returned to these waters since I was last here. It's hard to recall the violence of that cold November storm.

This same feeling can come over officers once they've fully recovered from their PTSD. Every now and then, a wife or a child will recount some act that he did back in those hard times when the war had come inside. A new door wouldn't install properly, so it was smashed to bits with a sledgehammer on the backyard patio. A highchair's tray wouldn't slide back into place, so the empty highchair was witnessed sailing out the open door only to shatter into pieces in the driveway.

These stories are now told with laughter, because the laughter has returned to these homes. Now and then the star of those tales can't believe that he'd once behaved that way. On one of those stories-by-the-fire occasions when the tale was told, the officer asked his wife if he'd actually thrown the highchair out the kitchen door. His truly remarkable wife nodded and gently replied, "It was a really dark time."

In the beginning of the book, I told you that there was reason for good hope. This is why. Angry waters do become still, houses again are filled with laughter. Humans are designed to heal...and when given time and the means to mend, we do.

I close now, leaving you with these parting words:

Don't give up on yourself. Don't give up on your life. Some days, hope is all you will have to hold you above the waterline. And some days that hope is just enough. In the midst of those days, recall what I have told you before:

PTSD will leave you stronger or weaker but never the same. So choose strength ...

Choose strength.

CHAPTER NOTES:

Whenever a new potential client enters into an initial consultation with a psychotherapist, a written policy giving full disclosure about confidentiality, payment, cancellations and other details should be provided to read and discuss.

This document should clarify the legal mandate that the therapist is accountable to uphold regarding confidentiality. Often these documents are signed by the prospective client to indicate that its contents are fully understood and agreed upon.

The laws regarding this are different from country to country, so when disclosing information within the client/therapist alliance, you need to be very clear on what confidentiality includes and doesn't include in your specific location.

PHOTO CREDITS:

1. The Homecoming: © Karen Lansing 2012
2. Can You Smell the Rain: © Karen Lansing 2012
3. Tip of the Iceberg ©iStock/hidesy
4. Changed Priorities Ahead: © Karen Lansing 2012
5. Held Captive: © Karen Lansing 2012
6. Getting a Life Beyond the Border: © Karen Lansing 2012
7. The Boats of Summer: © Karen Lansing 2012
8. A Life Redeemed: © Karen Lansing 2012

ENDNOTES:

1. M. Cowley. *Blue Juniata: A Life,* Penguin, New York, 1985.
2. A. Lamott. *Traveling Mercies: Some Thoughts on Faith*, Pantheon Books, New York: 1999.

BIBLIOGRAPHY

Adler, C.M., McDonough-Ryan, P., Sax, K.W., Holland, S. K., Amdt, S., Strakowki, S.M. "FMRI of neuronal activation and symptoms provocation in undedicated patients with obsessive compulsive disorder," *Journal of Psychiatric Research,* Vol. 34, Issues 4-5, July 2000.

Amen, Daniel, M. D. *Healing the Hardware of the Soul: How Making the Brain–Soul Connection Can Maximize Your Life.* The Free Press, New York. 2002.

Amen, Daniel, M.D. Amen Clinic Website, Summaries of brain functioning in key sectors that are impacted by PTSD:
http://www.amenclinics.com/brain-science/cool-brain-science/a-crash-course-in-neuroscience/cingulate-gyrus/
http://www.amenclinics.com/brain-science/cool-brain-science/a-crash-course-in-neuroscience/basal-ganglia-system/
http://www.amenclinics.com/brain-science/cool-brain-science/a-crash-course-in-neuroscience/limbic-system/
http://www.amenclinics.com/clinics/professionals/how-we-can-help/brain-science/cerebellum-cb/
http://www.amenclinics.com/brain-science/cool-brain-science/a-crash-course-in-neuroscience/prefrontal-cortex/

Artwhol, A., and Christensen, L., "*Deadly Force Encounters*: *What Cops Need to Know to Mentally and Physically Survive a Gunfight,*" Paladin Press, Boulder CO, 1997.

Artwhol, A. "Perceptual and Memory Distortion during Officer-Involved Shootings," IACP Net document No 564080), *FBI Law Enforcement Bulletin* October 2002, 18.

BBC News: *Prop Gun Blamed for Actor's Death Tuesday*, 31 October 2000, http://news.bbc.co.uk/1/hi/entertainment/999720.stm

Blair, P.J., Pollock, J., Montague, D., Nichols, T., Curnutt, J., and Burns D.,

"Reasonableness and reaction time," *Police Quarterly,* December 2011; Vol. 14, 4.

Blum, L.. *Force Under Pressure: How Cops Live and Why They Die.* Lantern Books, New York. 2000.

Braltenberg, V., Heck, D., Sultan, F. "The detection and generation of sequences as a key to cerebellar function: Experiments and theory," *Behavioral Brain Science*, Vol.2, June 1997.

Brantner Smith, B. "What Do Our Cop 'Dreams' Tell Us?" *PoliceOne.com* April 29, 2011 (distributed on-line May 7, 2011)
http://www.policeone.com/health-fitness/articles/3502401-What-do-our-cop-dreams-tell-us/

Brier, J. N. and Scott, C. *Principals of Trauma Therapy: A Guide to Symptoms, Evaluation, and Treatment,* Sage Publications, 2006.

Brown, T. M., and Boudewyns, P.A. "Periodic limb movements of sleep in combat veterans with posttraumatic stress disorder." *Journal of Traumatic Stress* 1996.

Campbell, J. H.. "A Comparative Analysis of the Effects of Post shooting Trauma on the Special Agents of the Federal Bureau of Investigation," unpublished Ph.D. dissertation, Department of Educational Administration, Michigan State University, East Lansing, MI, 1992.

Carver, R.. "This Morning," *Ultramarine*, New York, 1987.

Chong-Hwa Hong, C., Harris, J. C., Pearlson, G. D., Kim, Jin-Suh, Calhoun, D., Fallon, J. H., Golay, X., Gillen, J. S., Simmonds, D.J., Van Zijl, P. C. M., Zee, D. S., Pekar, J. J. "MRI evidence for multisensory recruitment associated with rapid eye movements during sleep," *Human Brain Mapping,* Vol. 30, Issue: 5, American Chemical Society, 2009.

Cleckley, H. *The Mask of Sanity.* (5th ed.). St. Louis, MO: Mosby, 1976.

Conners, C.K., "The Conners' Continuous Performance Test II," *MHS* (Multi-Health Systems), 2000.

Cowley, M. *Blue Juniata: A Life*, New York, Penguin, 1985.

Curtis, B., and Eldredge, J. *The Sacred Romance: Drawing Closer to the Heart of God*, Thomas Nelson, Inc. Nashville, TN, 1997.

Davis, J. "Parents of marine found dead seek PTSD awareness," *Sarasota herald-Tribune*, March 12, 2008.

Duman, R.S., Malbers, J., Nakagawa, S, Shin, D'Sa, C. "Neuronal plasticity and survival in mood disorders," *Biological Psychiatry,* 2000.

Debiec J., and LeDoux J. E. "Noradrenergic signaling in the amygdala contributes to the reconsolidation of fear memory: Treatment implications for PTSD," *New York Academy of Science Annual,* Vol.1071, 2006.

DePascalis, V. and Penna, P.M. "40 hz EED activity during hypnotic induction and hypnotic testing," *International Journal of Clinical and Experimental Hypnosis*, 38.

The Diagnostic and Statistical Manual of Mental Disorders, 4th ed. (*DSM-IV-TR).* American Psychiatric Association, Washington, D.C. 2000. http://www.psych.org/MainMenu/Research/DSMIV/DSMIVTR/DSMIVvsDSMIVTR/SummaryofTextChangesInDSMIVTR.aspx.

Eldredge, J. *The Journey of Desire: Searching for the Life We Only Dreamed Of*, Thomas Nelson, Inc. Nashville, TN, 2000.

Fine, C. G., and Berkowitz, S. A. "The wreathing protocol: The imbrication of hypnosis and EMDR in the treatment of dissociative identity disorder and other maladaptive dissociation responses," *American Journal of Clinical Hypnosis*, 43, 2001, 275–290.

Foa, E. B. *Posttraumatic Stress Diagnostic Scale Manual.* National Computer Systems, 1995.

Foster, S., and Lendl, J. "Eye movement desensitization and reprocessing: Four case studies of a new tool for executive coaching and restoring employee performance after setbacks," *Consulting Psychology Journal: Practice and Research,* Vol. 48, Issue 3, Summer, 1996.

Friedman, M.A. "Post-Traumatic stress disorder," *American Journal of Psychiatry*, Vol. 155, no. 5; p. 8 http://wwwacnp.org/g4GNr01000111/CH109.html © 2006

Frischoltz, E. J., Kowall J. A. and Hammond, D.C. "Introduction to the special section: Hypnosis and EMDR," *American Journal of Clinical Hypnosis*, 43, Washington, D.C., 2001.

Figley, C R. Editorial Note*, Traumatology,* Vol. 12, No. 13/2006.

Foster, S., and Lendl, J. "Eye Movement Desensitization and Reprocessing: Four case studies of a new tool for executive coaching and restoring employee performance after setbacks," *Consulting Psychology Journal: Practice and Research,* Vol. 48, Issue 3, Summer 1996.

Foster, S. *Coaching for Peak Performance*, In J.E. Auerback (Ed.) *Personal and Executive Coaching: The Complete Guide for Mental Health Professionals* (1st ed.) Ventura CA, Executive College Press, 2001.

Friedlander, L., and , Desrocher, M. "Neuroimaging studies of obsessive-compulsive disorder in adults and children," *Clinical Psychology Review.* Vol. 26, Issue 2, January 2006.

Foulkes, D., *Dreaming: A Cognitive-Psychological Analysis*, Hillsdale, NJ.: Erlbaum, 1985.

Germain A., Buysse D.J., Shear M.K., Fayyad R., Austin C. "Clinical correlates of poor sleep quality in posttraumatic stress disorder*," Journal of Traumatic Stress,* Vol. 17, 2004.

Gottesmann, C. "Noradrenaline involvement in basic and higher integrated REM sleep processes*," Program of Neurobiology*, Vol. 85, 2008.

Grossman, D. *On Killing: The Psychological Cost of Learning to Kill in War and Society*, Little, Brown and Co., 1996.

Grossman, D., and Christensen L., W. *On Combat: The Psychology and Physiology of Deadly Conflict in War and in Peace,* PPCT Research Publications, 2004.

Grossman, D. and Siddle, B.K. *Critical Incident Amnesia: The Physiological Basis and the Implications of Memory Loss During Extreme Survival Situations.* Millstadt, IL: PPCT Management Systems, 1998.

Grossman, D.. *Bullet Proofing the Mind.* Audio, Callibre Press. 1st Ed. 1996.

Gundel H., O'Connor, M.F., Littrell L., et al. "Functional neuroanatomy of grief: an MRI study." *American Journal of Psychiatry,* Vol. 160 2003.

Hartmann, T. "*Attention Deficit Disorder: A Different Perspective,*" Underwood Books, Grass Valley CA, 1993 & 1997.

Hartmann, E. "Making connections in a safe place: Is dreaming psychotherapy?" *Dreaming,* Vol. 5(4), Dec. 1995.

Hekman, H., Groth, S., and Rogers, D. "Pain ameliorating effect of eye movement desensitization*," Journal of Behavior Therapy and Experimental Psychiatry*, 25, 1994.

Hicks, B. M., and Patrick C. J. "Psychopathy and negative emotionality: Analyses of suppressor effects reveal distinct relations with emotional distress, fearfulness and anger-hostility," *Journal of Abnormal Psychology*, Vol. 115(2), May 2006.

Hobson, J.A., Stickgold, R., Pace-Schott, E.F., "The neuropsychology of REM sleep dreaming," *NeuroReport*, 1998.

Hoenig, A. L. and Roland, J. E. "Shots fired: Officer involved," *Police Chief*, October 1998.

Hope, L., Lewinski, W., Dixon, J., Blocksige, D., "Witness in action: The effect of physical exertion on recall and recognition," *Psychological Science* 23(4), March 7, 2012.

Husain, A. M., Miller, P. P., Carwile, S. T. "REM sleep behavior disorder: Potential relationship to posttraumatic stress disorder," *Journal of Clinical Neurophysiology,* Vol. 18 (2) March 2001, 148-57.

The ICD-10 Classification of Mental and Behavioural Disorders. World Health Organization. 1992.

Ivry, R. B., Spencer, R., Zelaznik, H. N., Diedrichsen, J. "The cerebellum and event timing," *Annals of New York Academy of Sciences,* Vol. 978, Dec. 2002.

Johnstone, G. , Weston, J., Bradshaw, J. 2004 "The Truth about Killing," Produced by Tigress Productions (Episode I, Part 2).

Jouvet, M. and Delorme, F. *"Locus coeruleus et sommeil paradoxal," CR Soc. Biol* 159, 1965, 895-99.

Kardiner, A. *The Traumatic Neuroses of War*. New York, Hoeber 1941.

Klinger, D. "Police responses to officer-Involved Shootings," Final Report submitted to NIJ, Police Responses to Officer-Involved Shootings (grant number 97-1C-CX-0029), *NIJ Journal* No. 253, January 2006.

Klinger, D. U.S. Department of Justice, National Institute of Justice, *Police Responses to Officer-Involved Shootings*, NCJRS 192285, Washington, DC, October 2001.

Knell, T. *From the Corners of a Wounded Mind*, Night Publishing, 2011. http://theodoreknell.com.

Kolb, L.C. "Neurophysiological hypothesis explaining posttraumatic stress disorder," *American Journal of Psychiatry* , Vol. 144, 1987.

Lamott, A. *Traveling Mercies: Some Thoughts on Faith*, Pantheon Books, New York, 1999.

LeDoux, J. "Emotions circuits in the brain," *Annual Review of Neuroscience*, Vol. 23: 155-184, 2000.

Lane County Sheriff's Office and District Attorney's Office, "Hollywood vs. Reality: Officer Involved Shootings" http://www.youtube.com/watch?v=MmfTyFAp1eI

Lanius, R. A., Williamson, P.C., Densmore, M., Gupta, J., Neufeld, R. W. J., Gati, J. S., Menon, R. "Brain activation during script-driven imagery induced dissociative responses in PTSD: A functional magnetic resonance imaging investigation," *Biological Psychiatry,* Vol. 52, Issue 4, Aug., 2002.

Lansing K., Amen D. G., Hanks C., Rudy L, "High resolution brain SPECT imaging and EMDR in officers with PTSD," *Journal of Neuropsychiatry and Clinical Neurosciences, 17,* 2005.

Laville, S. and Dodd, V. "The officer who killed Jean Charles de Menezes breaks down at inquest," *The Guardian*, Oct. 25, 2008. http://www.guardian.co.uk/uk/2008/oct/25/jean-charles-de-menezes-trial

Leeds, A. M. "Positive Affect Tolerance and Integration protocol," EMDR training, June 17, 2006.

Leon, W. C.; Bruno, M. A., Allard, S., Nader, K., Cuello A. C. "Engagement of the PFC in consolidation and recall of recent spatial memory," *Learning Memory,* Vol., 17, Cold Spring Harbor Laboratory Press, 2010.

Lewinski, W., Blocksidge, D., Dixon, J., Anderson, J., Hope, L. "Final findings from force science exhaustion study," *Force Science News,* Apr. 25, 2011. (Force Science Research Institute) http://www.forcescience.org/

Lewinski, W. "Anti-fatigue measures could cut cop deaths 15 percent, researcher claims" PoliceOne.com, March 24, 2011.

Lewinski, W. "Why is the suspect shot in the back?" *The Police Marksman,* Nov./Dec. 2000, http://www.forcescience.org/articles/shotinback.pdf.

Lewinski, W., Anderson, J., Hope, L. "Final findings from the Force Science exhaustion study," *Force Science News*, Transmission #176 Apr., 26, 2011.

Lydiard, B. R., Hamner, M. H., "Clinical importance of sleep disturbance as a treatment target for PTSD," *FOCUS: The Journal of Lifelong Learning in Psychiatry*, Vol. VII, No. 2, Spring 2009, 176-83.

Malouin F., Richards C. L., Jackson P. L., et al. "Brain activations during motor imagery of locomotor-related tasks: A PET study," *Human Brain Mapping*, Vol. 19, 2003.

Mather, M., Lighthall, N. R., Lin, N., Gorlick, M. A. "Sex differences in how stress affects brain activity during face viewing," *NeuroReport*, 2010; 21 (14).

Meares, A. *A System of Medical Hypnosis,* Julian Press, New York, 1960.

Mellman, T. A, Kulick-Bell R., Ashlock, L.E, Nolan B. "Sleep events among veterans with combat-related posttraumatic stress disorder," *American Journal of Psychiatry* 1995.

Mellman T. A., Kumar A, Kulick-Bell R., Kumar M., Nolan B., "Nocturnal/ Daytime urine noradrenergic measures and sleep in combat-related PTSD," *Biological Psychiatry*, Vol. 38, 1995.

Moll J., de Oliveira-Souza R., Bramati, I. E., et al. "Functional networks in emotional moral and nonmoral social judgments," *Neuroimage,* Vol. 16, 2002.

Mongeau, R., Miller, G.A., Chiang, E., Anderson D. J. "Neural Correlates of Competing Fear Behaviors Evoked by an Innately Aversive Stimulus," *Journal of Neuroscience*, May 1, 2003 23(9)

Moulton, E.A., Elman, I., Pendse, G., Schmahmann, J., Becerra, L., Borsook, D., "Aversion Related circuitry in the cerebellum: responses to noxious heat and unpleasant images," *The Journal of Neuroscience,* Vol. 10 Mar. 2011.

Myers, D. "The Four-phase Construct of 'Protect, Direct, Connect, Select' " (unpublished manuscript).

Nicosia, G. "Brief note: EMDR is no hypnosis; EEG evidence," *Dissociation*, 3, 1995.

Nielson, E., "Salt Lake City Police Department Deadly Force Policy Shooting and Post shooting Reactions," unpublished paper, Salt Lake City, UT: Salt Lake City Police Department, 1981.

Nishida, M., Pearsall, J., Buckner, R.L., Walker, M.P. "REM sleep, prefrontal theta, and the consolidation of human emotion," *Cerebral Cortex,* Vol. 19 (5), May 2009, 1158-66.

O'Hara A. F., Violanti J. M. "Police suicide–A web surveillance of national data," *Journal of Emergency Mental Health,* Vol., 11:1, 2009.

Otani, S. (Ed) *Prefrontal Cortex: From Synaptic Plasticity to Cognition.* Kluwer Academic Publishers Group, The Netherlands. 2004.

Pagel, J. F. "Nightmares and disorders of dreaming," *American Family Physician*, Apr., 4, 2001.

Phillips, M. "Potential contributions of hypnosis to ego–strengthening procedures in EMDR," *American Journal of Clinical Hypnosis*, 43, 2001.

Pinizzotto, A. J., Davis, E. F., *Miller, C. E.* "Officers' perceptual shorthand: What messages are offenders sending to law enforcement officers?" *FBI Law Enforcement Bulletin,* June, 1999.

Pinizzotto, A. J., Davis, E. F. "Offenders' perceptual shorthand: What messages are officers sending to offenders?" *FBI Law Enforcement Bulletin,* July, 2000.

Radlick, M.S. *The processing demands of television: Neurological correlates of Television Viewing.* Unpublished doctoral dissertation, Rensselaer Polytechnic Institute, Troy, NY, 1980.

Rando, T. *Treatment of Complicated Mourning*. Research Press, Champagne, IL, 1993.

Rauch, S. L., Whalen, P. J., Shin, L. M., McInerney, S. C., Lacklin, M. L., Lasko, N. B., Orr, S. P., Pitman, R. K. "Exaggerated amygdala response to masked facial stimuli in posttraumatic stress disorder: A functional MRI study," *Biological Psychiatry*, Vol. 47, 2000.

Rauch, S.L., van der Kolk, B.A., Fisler, R.E., Alpert, N.M., Orr, S.P., Savage, C.R., Fischman, A.J., Jenike, M.A., Pitman, R.K. "A symptom provocation study of posttraumatic stress disorder using positron emission tomography and script-driven imagery," *Archives of General Psychiatry*, 56, 1996.

Remsburg, C. "Dream haunted: A Young Cop's Close Call Clarifies Instructor's Startling Statement," *PoliceOne.com,* June 16, 2010.
http://www.policeone.com/patrol-issues/articles/2075604-Dream-haunted-A-young-cops-closecall-clarifies-an-instructors-startling-statement/

Ritchey, M., Dolcos, F., Cabeza, R. "Role of amygdala connectivity in the persistence of emotional memories over time: An event-related FMRI investigation," *Cerebral Cortex,* Vol. 9 (11) 2494 – 2504, March 2008.

Robbins, S. "Seeking better sleep," *Stars and Stripes*, Feb. 5, 2011.

Ross R.J., Ball, W.A., Sullivan K.A., Caroff, S.N. *"Sleep disturbance as the hallmark of posttraumatic stress disorder,"* American Journal of Psychiatry, Vol.146, 1989.

Rothschild, B. "Post-traumatic stress disorder: Identification and diagnosis," (Reprinted for Soziale Arbeit Schweiz), *The Swiss Journal of Social Work,* Feb., 1998.

Sabourin, M.G., Cutcomb, S. D., Crawford, H., Pribram, K. "EEG correlates of hypnotic susceptibility and hypnotic trance: Spiral analysis and coherence," *International Journal of Psychophysiology*, 10, 1990.

Sanford, L. D., Morrison, A. R., Mann, Graziella, Harris, J. S., Yoo, L., Ross, R. J. "Sleep Patterning and Behaviour in Cats with Pontine Lesions Creating REM Without Atonia," *Journal of Sleep Research*, Vol. 3, {4}, Jan., 20, 2009.

Seides, R. *"Should the current DSM-IV-R definition for PTSD be expanded to include serial and multiple microtraumas as aetiologies?"* Journal of Psychiatric and Mental Health Nursing, Vol. 17, Issue 8, 725-731, Oct., 2010.

Servos P., Osu R., Santi A., et al. "The neural substrates of biological motion perception: an MRI study. *Cerebral Cortex*, Vol. 12 2002 772—82.

Shapiro, F. *Eye Movement and Reprocessing: Basic Principles, Protocols and Procedures*, Guilford Press, New York, 2001.

Shapiro, F. and Silk Forrest, M. *EMDR: The Breakthrough Therapy for Overcoming Anxiety, Stress and Trauma,* Basic Books, NY, 1997.

Shapiro, Elan., and Laub, B. *"A summary, a theoretical model, and the recent traumatic episode protocol (R-TEP),"* Journal of EMDR Practice and Research, Vol. 2, Number 2, 2008.

Shin, L. M., Kossllyn, A. M., McNally, S. M., Alpert, R. J., Thompson, N. M., Rauch, S. L. "The role of the anterior cingulate in posttraumatic stress disorder and panic disorder," *Archives of General Psychiatry,* Vol. 54 (3).

Shin, L. M., Kosslyn, S. M., McNally, R. J., Alptert, N. M., Thompson, W. L., Rauch S. L., Macklin, M. L., Pitman, R. K. "Visual imagery and perception in posttraumatic stress disorder—a positron emission tomographic investigation," *Archives of General Psychiatry,* Vol. 54.

Sides, H., "The Man Who Saw Too Much," Outside.com. http://Outsideonline.com/adventure/travel-ga-201101-michael-ferrara-sidwcmdev_153564.html

Solomon, R. M., and Horn, J. H. "Post shooting traumatic reactions: A pilot study," *Psychological Services for Law Enforcement Officers,* ed. James T. Reese and Harvey A. Goldstein, Washington, D.C.: U.S. Government Printing Office, 1986.

Solomon, R. and Rando, T. "Utilization of EMDR in the treatment of grief and mourning," *Journal of EMDR Practice and Research*, 1(2), 2001.

Spiegel, K., Knutson, K., Leproult, R., Tasali, E., Van Cauter, E. "Sleep loss: A novel risk factor for insulin resistance and Type 2 diabetes," *Journal of Applied Physiology*, Vol. 99(5) Nov., 2005.

Sprang, G. "The use of eye movement desensitization and reprocessing (EMDR) in the treatment of traumatic stress and complicated mourning: psychological land behavioral outcomes," *Research on Social Work Practice*, 2003, Vol. 11, no. 3, 300-320.

Stratton, J. G., Parker, D. and Snibbe, J. R. "Post-traumatic stress: Study of police officers involved in shootings," *Psychological Reports,* Vol. 55, Issue 1, August, 1984.

Stickgold, R. and Wamsley, E. *Sleep, Memory and Dreams: Fitting the Pieces Together,* Lecture presented by Dr. R. Stickgold, http://www.youtube.com/watch?v=WmRGNunPj3c , June10, 2010.

Strawn J. R., Geracioti, T. D. Jr. "Noradrenergic dysfunction and the psycho- pharmacology of posttraumatic stress disorder," *Depression and Anxiety,* Vol. 25, 2008.

Thach, W. T. "A role of the cerebellum in learning movement coordination," *Neurobiology of Learning and Memory,* 70, 1998.

Timmann, D., Musso, C., Kolb, F. P., Rijntjes, M., Jüptner, M., Müller, S.P.,

Diener, C., Weiller, C. "Involvement of the human cerebellum during habituation of the acoustic startle response: A PET Study," *Journal of Neurology, Neurosurgery and Psychiatry*, Vol. 65, 1998.

Todd, R.M., Anderson, A.K. "Six degrees of separation: the amygdala regulates social behavior and perception," *Nature Neuroscience*, No. 10: Oct. 10, 2009.

Ursu, S., Stenger, A.V., Shear, K. M., Jones, M. R., Carter, C. S. "Overactive action monitoring in obsessive-compulsive disorder: Evidence from functional MRI," *Psychological Science,* Vol. 14, 4, July, 2003.

van der Kolk, B. A. "The body keeps the score: Memory and the evolving psychobiology of post-traumatic stress," *Harvard Psychiatric Review*, Vol., 1, (5), 1994.

Warner, T.D., Schrader, R., Koss, M., Hollifield, M., Tandberg, D., Melendrez, D., Johnson, L. "The relationship of sleep quality and posttraumatic stress to potential sleep disorders in sexual assault survivors and nightmares, insomnia and PTSD," *Journal of Traumatic Stress*, Vol. 14(4), Oct., 2001.

Worden, J.W. *Grief Counseling and Grief Therapy: A Handbook for the Mental Health Practitioner*, Springer Publishing, NY, 2009.

20100035R00111

Made in the USA
Lexington, KY
20 January 2013